创优导航

英语导学基础模块
（第3册）

主　编　周正清
副主编　李昌海
编　委　彭　敏　黄建舜　赵　建　胡　敏
　　　　郭青红　欧中红　文依霞　何淑芳
　　　　苏　谊　贺　琼

北京理工大学出版社
BEIJING INSTITUTE OF TECHNOLOGY PRESS

版权专有　侵权必究

图书在版编目（CIP）数据

英语导学基础模块. 第3册 / 周正清主编. —北京：北京理工大学出版社，2022.9重印
ISBN 978-7-5682-4151-9

Ⅰ. ①英… Ⅱ. ①周… Ⅲ. ①英语－中等专业学校－教学参考资料 Ⅳ. ①H319.39

中国版本图书馆CIP数据核字（2017）第133185号

出版发行 / 北京理工大学出版社有限责任公司
社　　址 / 北京市海淀区中关村南大街5号
邮　　编 / 100081
电　　话 / (010) 68914775（总编室）
　　　　　 (010) 82562903（教材售后服务热线）
　　　　　 (010) 68944723（其他图书服务热线）
网　　址 / http://www.bitpress.com.cn
经　　销 / 全国各地新华书店
印　　刷 / 定州市新华印刷有限公司
开　　本 / 787毫米×1092毫米　1/16
印　　张 / 14.5　　　　　　　　　　　　　　　　责任编辑 / 武丽娟
字　　数 / 332千字　　　　　　　　　　　　　　　文案编辑 / 龙　微
版　　次 / 2022年9月第1版第3次印刷　　　　　　 责任校对 / 周瑞红
定　　价 / 34.00元　　　　　　　　　　　　　　　责任印制 / 边心超

图书出现印装质量问题，请拨打售后服务热线，本社负责调换

前言 PREFACE

茫茫学海，广袤知原，若失方向，徘徊不定。亲爱的同学们，是否希冀快速走出迷茫？我相信你们的回答一定是肯定的！那么，本书就是专门为你们量身定制的学海导航器！迷路导向牌！黑夜照明灯！

《英语导学基础模块》系列丛书帮助中职学生学习英语、学好英语、开拓思维、提高能力及圆满完成规定学习内容所精心打造的精品学辅。它主要依据现行教学课本——中等职业教育课程改革国家规划新教材《基础模块》1～3册、《拓展模块》全1册，广开思路、潜心研究、多方探讨，更多地凝结着编者多年来积累的编撰经验与智慧，内容更加紧扣最新教学大纲，试题几乎全部原创，编撰思路与时俱进。读后会发现，它是同学们学习英语时解惑的及时雨、顺心风；同时也帮助参加对口升学的考生在复习迎考时科学、高效地进行复习，全面夯实基础，提升解题能力，切实提高复习效率，收到理想的功效！

本书编写亮点：

整合优势，对相关教材所涉及的相关知识点(语言、语法、写作等)精讲、精析、精练。内容上简洁化，形式上多样化，各单元编排夺目耀眼：

目标攻略 主要列出本单元要突破的重点难点等项目及相关技巧。

知识解析 对本单元中知识热点等进行详尽的解析并适当举例论证。

解题引领 由编者牵引怎样解题以突出能力的培养与拓展。

语法点睛 摘要探析与框定语法热点考点。

写作指导 对单元中出现过的写作知识进行针对性的指导。

同步训练 对本单元的重点难点部分设置相关练习以巩固所学。

同时，本书配有创优导航卷一、二；单元检测试卷和期中、期末考试试卷。其中，导航卷和期中、期末试卷属于模拟试卷，难度有所增加。

为了方便师生使用，除参考答案外，书后还附有常见的不规则动词表和各单元词汇表。

各位同学，本教程是由多年奋战在教学一线的中学高级英语教师和教研人员应大家的需求、多方研讨并结合自己多年教学经验及研究成果，根据高等教育出版社出版的中等职业教育课程改革国家规划新教材《英语（基础模块）》《英语（拓展模块）》《英语（职业模块）》而编写的，注重科学性与实用性的统一，信度高，效果好。

全书具有较高的实用价值和指导作用，是考生不可多得的参考用书。

编　者

目录 CONTENTS

Unit 1 He decided to have a big Christmas party. ············· 1
Unit 2 How to open a savings account? ············· 11
Unit 3 What courses do you offer? ············· 17
Unit 4 I'll have to have my watch replaced. ············· 26
Unit 5 We are going to work as packagers on the assembly line. ············· 37
Unit 6 Would you mind saying something about your work experience? ············· 43
Unit 7 The convenience store is over there. ············· 53
Unit 8 That's how most accidents happen. ············· 59
Unit 9 Is your company going to the fashion fair in Shanghai? ············· 65
Unit 10 That's what has been my dream work. ············· 74
英语创优导航试卷一 ············· 81
英语创优导航试卷二 ············· 91
Unit 1 单元检测卷 ············· 101
Unit 2 单元检测卷 ············· 110
Unit 3 单元检测卷 ············· 118
Unit 4 单元检测卷 ············· 126
Unit 5 单元检测卷 ············· 134
Unit 6 单元检测卷 ············· 143
Unit 7 单元检测卷 ············· 152
Unit 8 单元检测卷 ············· 163

Unit 9　单元检测卷························173
Unit 10　单元检测卷························182
期中考试试卷····························191
期末考试试卷····························199
参考答案·······························208
附录　单元词汇表··························222

Unit 1　He decided to have a big Christmas party.

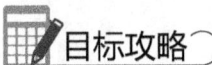

1. 培养良好的交际能力：如何发出邀请及应答；
2. 认知本单元所有词汇；能正确运用重点词汇，如 celebrate, hunt for, dress up, prefer to do, be covered with 等；
3. 背诵"Everyday English"；
4. 掌握非谓语动词中动词不定式的用法等；
5. 以时间为线索写游记。

知识解析

Ⅰ．词汇

(1) be covered with 覆盖……(此词组属于系表结构)。

(2) not...until 直到……才。如：
The boy didn't go to bed until his father came home.
这个男孩直到他爸爸回家才睡觉。

(3) besides 除……外，加之；except 除……外(除去人或物不加在一起)。

(4) break up 打碎，拆散，分解。类似的短语有：
break out 突然爆发，爆发　　　　break off 断开，打断，中止
break away 离开，摆脱　　　　　break down 打破，毁掉，压倒，拆除
break in 破门而入，闯入；打断，插嘴　break into 闯入，破门而入
break through 突围，突破，冲破

(5) prefer to do/doing something 更喜欢做某事。

(6) share in the work 分担工作；share a room with somebody 同某人分享一个房间。

(7) must-have 必须有的东西；must-see 必须看的东西。

Ⅱ．句式

(1) He decided to have a big Christmas party. 他决定举行一个盛大的圣诞聚会。

（2）You can imagine how I felt when I saw that everyone had dressed up except me.
你能想象当我看到除我外大家都盛装打扮后我的感觉是怎样的。

（3）It was covered with thick ice. 它覆盖了厚厚的一层冰。

（4）After that, he invited all his important friends to the party.
此后，他邀请了他所有重要的朋友参加聚会。

（5）She prefers drawing to singing. 同唱歌相比，她更喜欢画画。

（6）We'll share in the work. 我们愿意分担这份工作。

（7）Thanksgiving is a traditional festival that started in 1621.
感恩节是一个传统节日，起源于1621年。

（8）Three "F"s highlight the important parts of Thanksgiving.
三个"F"是感恩节的重要内容。

解题引领

1. He decided _____ a big Christmas party on Sunday.
 A. having B. holding
 C. to hold D. to be held

答案为C。点拨：decide，refuse，hope，want，agree，choose，manage，learn，pretend 等一些动词后跟动词不定式作宾语。而选项D中 to be held 为不定式被动式，与句意不符。

2. Our headteacher prefers football _____ basketball.
 A. to playing B. rather than
 C. at playing D. playing

答案为B。点拨：句型 prefer...rather than...意为"喜欢……而不喜欢……"。A、C、D 分别错在非对称结构和搭配方面。

3. Lily and Rose prefer dancing _____ singing.
 A. with B. on
 C. to D. rather

答案为C。点拨：prefer...to...是一个句型，意为"喜欢……而不喜欢……"或"喜欢……胜过……"。

语法点睛

非谓语动词——动词不定式

动词不定式属于非谓语动词中的一种。关于非谓语动词，简述如下：

一、概述

非谓语动词是指在句中不能独立作谓语，而只能作其他成分的动词。非谓语动词有三种形式：动词不定式、动名词和分词（现在分词和过去分词）。其中，现在分词和动名词又称为-ing 分词。非谓语动词的否定式是在其前面直接加 not，它没有人称和数的变化，仍然保持动词的一般特征，可以接宾语或状语。

二、非谓语动词的时态与语态变化(以 do 为例):

形式	时态	主动式	被动式
动词不定式	一般式	to do	to be done
	进行式	to be doing	
	完成式	to have done	to have been done
	完成进行式	to have been doing	
动名词	一般式	doing	being done
	完成式	having done	having been done
现在分词	一般式	doing	being done
	完成式	having done	having been done
过去分词		done	done

动词不定式概述

动词不定式由"to + 原形动词"构成(有些情况下,to 可以省略),在句中起名词、形容词和副词的作用,在句中可作主语、宾语、表语、宾语补足语、定语、状语、同位语和独立成分。

一、时态

1. 一般式:表示与谓语动词同时或之后的行为动作。如:
She wants to watch TV. (同时)
I hope to see her immediately. (之后)

2. 完成式:表示在谓语动词之前的行为动作。如:
He forgets to have taken his ID card with him. 他忘了带身份证。(之前)
She remembered to have consulted him. 她记得已经咨询过他了。(之前)

3. 进行式:与谓语动词同时的行为动作。如:
She seems to be finding out who did it. 她似乎在查找谁干的此事。(同时)

4. 完成进行时:在谓语动作之前发生且一直进行着的动作。如:
White knew him to have been serving in the hotel as a waiter for 10 years.
怀特知道他在这家旅馆服务已有 10 年了。

二、功能

1. 作主语(常采用形式主语,真正主语后置)。如:
To learn a foreign language isn't easy. →It isn't easy to learn a foreign language.
学门外语不易。
To find a job is difficult these days. → It is difficult to find a job these days.
如今找工作很难。
此句还可转换成:A job is difficult to find. 带宾语的不定式作主语时,可按此模式转换。

2. 作宾语。如:
I want to learn Japanese. 我想学日语。
She decided to go abroad. 她决定出国。

Portia pretended to be a lawyer. 鲍西亚扮成一名律师。

注1：并非所有动词都能接不定式作宾语，能接不定式的只有下列常见单词：agree 同意/arrange 安排/ask 要求/afford 抽得出时间做/care 关心/choose 选择/dare 敢于/decide 决定/determine 决心/demand 要求/fail 未能/fear 害怕/hate 讨厌/intend 打算/manage 设法/mean 打算/offer 想做/plan 计划/promise 许诺/prefer 更喜欢/prepare 准备做/pretend 假装/refuse 拒绝/like 喜欢/seek 试图/want 想要/wish 想要/love 喜爱/long 渴望/hope 希望/expect 期望。

注2：不定式一般不作介词宾语，但下列3个介词除外，它们是 but/except/save（除……外）。如：

He has no choice but to wait. 他除了等待别无选择。

搭配句型为：can but + 原形动词，意为"只能、只得"

can't(help/choose)but 意为"……不能不……"。

There is nothing to do but + 原形动词，意为"……只有做……"。如：

It was too late, I could but walk home. 太晚了，我只好走回家。

He can't choose but tell the truth. 他没办法只好讲真话。

3. 作表语。如：

The first thing is to look for the water source. 首要的事情是寻找水源。

My job is to teach English. 我的工作是教英语。

注1：不定式作表语要注意两点：一是主语由不定式充当，二是主语由抽象名词充当。如：

To see is to believe. 眼见为实。

Our task is to look after the children well. 我们的任务是好好照顾这些孩子。

注2：如果在主语中含有 do 行为动词形式，作表语的动词不定式省略 to。如：

What I want do best is go to Hong Kong. 我最想做的就是去香港。

4. 作宾语补足语。如：

He asked me to go with him. 他请我和他同去。

I told her not to go out alone at night. 我告诉她晚上不要单独外出。

能作宾语补足语的动词还有：

advise 建议/ask 请/beg 乞求/cause 引起/command 命令/dare 挑战/drive 迫使/expect 期望/forbid 禁止/force 迫使/get 使，让/invite 邀请/intend 打算/know 知道/lead 引导/like 喜欢/love 心里希望/mean 打算/need 需要/oblige 强迫/order 命令/permit 允许/prefer 宁可/require 要求/teach 教/tell 吩咐，叫/train 训练/trust 信任/understand 认为/urge 激励/want 要/warn 警告/remind 提醒/request 要求/trouble 麻烦。如：

I want you to accompany(陪伴)me for a few days. 我要你陪伴我几天。

注1：动词不定式作补语时，有些动词在主动语态中要省略 to，这些动词是：①3个使役动词 let/have/make；②所有由人的感觉器官发出动作的感官动词：see/hear/watch/notice/observe/look at/listen to/feel(感觉)等。如：

We saw her play chess with Lily. 我们看见她与莉莉下过棋。

I often hear him sing English songs. 我经常听到他唱英文歌。

当这些句子变被动语态时，动词不定式符号不能省略。have/notice/watch 无被动语态。如：

He is often heard to sing English songs (by me).

注2:let 只作"出租"解时,才有被动语态。如:

The house was let last week. 这房子上周出租了。

作其他意思解且必须使用被动语态时,要用 allow 代替。如:

Mother didn't let him go swimming. 母亲不允许他去游泳。

→He was not allowed to go swimming. (母亲)不允许他去游泳。

拓展:

(1)有些表心理状态的动词带 to be 作宾补。这些动词是:believe 相信,认为/consider 考虑/find 发现/feel 感到/guess 猜测/imagine 想象,认为/judge 判断/know 知道/prove 证明/suppose 认为/think 认为/understand 了解。其中,在下列几个动词后,可省略 to be 的是:consider/find/prove/think/imagine。如:

I believe him (to be) honest. 我相信他很诚实。

(2)动词 hope/demand/suggest 后不可接不定式作补语的复合宾词,应使用宾语从句。如:

We hope that they will have a glorious future. 我们希望他们未来光辉灿烂。

(3)There be 句型的动词不定式复合结构中,there 位于宾语的位置时,be 要用不定式形式。如:

Let there be more hope in becoming winners. 满怀获胜希望。

He doesn't want them to be any misunderstanding among them.
他不想他们之间有任何误解。

5. 动词不定式作定语(须后置)。如:

He has nothing to do. 他无事可做。

There's no time to think about it. 没有时间考虑此事。

注1:不定式作定语与所修饰的词之间存在着逻辑上的主谓/动宾/偏正关系。如:

He is the last man to leave. 他是最后一个离开的人。(主谓关系)

She said she had a lot of work to do. 她说她有许多工作要做。(动宾关系)

注2:不定式作定语,若逻辑上是动宾关系且不定式是不及物动词时,后应跟相应介词,但被修饰词是 place/time/way 时除外。如:

We must rent a house to live in. 我们必须租房居住。

People think the best way to kill time is to bet. 人们认为消磨时光的最佳办法是赌博。

That is a very good place to live. 那是一个很好的居住地。

6. 动词不定式作状语。动词不定式作状语时,主要表示目的、原因、结果、条件。如:

She went to see a doctor. 她去看医生了。(目的)

He is mad to hear the news. 他听到这消息疯了。(原因)

The boy is not old enough to go to school. 这男孩还不到上学年龄。(结果)

To study hard, you'll make good progress. 努力学习,就会取得好成绩。(条件)

拓展:

(1)不定式表目的,可用其强调式 in order to/so as to 表示,其否定式为 in order not to/so as not to。如:

She hurried to the station in order to see him off. 她匆匆赶往车站,为他送行。

(2)不定式表条件,置于句首,其中谓语应含 will/shall/should/would/can/must。如:
To do such things he can't be stupid. 他能做出这样的事,就不可能是傻瓜。

(3)不定式作状语,其逻辑主语是句子的主语,不可弄混。如:
To learn English well, I need a good dictionary. 为了学好英语,我需要一本好词典。

(4)不定式与疑问词搭配,构成不定式短语,相当于一个名词,与 why 搭配时省略 to。如:
Why not go there? 为什么不去那里? (省略 to)
The question is where to find it. 问题是哪里能找到它。
How to learn English well is very important. 怎样学好英语很重要。

(5)不定式的复合结构:for + 名词/代词 + to do 或 of + 名词/代词 + to do。如:
For the students to learn a foreign language is necessary. 学生学一门外语是必要的。
There will be a lot of difficulties for us to overcome. 将有许多困难要我们去克服。

(6)不定式作独立成分,常在句首,也可在句中或句末(但少见)。如:
To be honest, I really hate troubling him. 老实说,我真的不想去麻烦他。

(7)动词不定式被动语态。不定式的逻辑主语是该动词不定式的动作承受者,一般要用被动式,其形式有一般式、完成式(无进行式)。如:
The new building to be finished is our lab. 将要竣工的新大楼是我们的实验室。
The book written by him was said to have been published. 他所写的这本书据说已出版了。
The photo is thought to have been taken by an 8-year-old boy.
据称,此照片由一名 8 岁男孩所拍。

写作指导

写游记

以时间为线索写一篇游记。

_____
_____
_____
_____

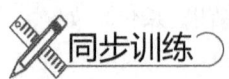

A. 基础层次

Ⅰ. 按要求做题

1. 用对应的英语填空。

_____庆祝   _____美味的

_____穿   _____节日

_____ 结冰	_____ 鬼;幽灵
_____ 更喜欢	_____ 分享
_____ 覆盖	_____ 打扮,穿上盛装
_____ 寻找	_____ 火鸡
_____ 强光照射;着重于,使突出	

2. 思考与问答。

(1) Did he decide to have a big Christmas party? _____.
(2) When is "Dragon Boat Festival?" _____.
(3) What made Mr. Hall want to hold a Christmas party on the ice? _____.
(4) Did Mr. Hall celebrate this Christmas with his friends? _____.
(5) What happened the next day? _____.

Ⅱ. 按要求完成下列各题

1.
Dear Mr. Zhang,

How are you doing? I spent Christmas Day with my foreign friends in America. There were a lot of people in the streets to buy Christmas goods that day.

_____
_____
_____

（根据上下文,用3～5句将横线处补充完整）

It was really fun, wasn't it? I really hoped that you had joined us.

Looking forward to your reply.

Yours ever,
Lily

2. I enjoy _____ (read) English stories.（用括号里的词填空）
3. We decided _____ (celebrate) the Mid-autumn Festival together.（用括号里的词填空）
4. What do you expect to have on the holiday?（回答）→_____.
5. What does "the Lantern Festival" mean in Chinese?（回答）→_____.

Ⅲ. 课堂效应检测:用英语在下面指定处小结你学本单元的收获体会

B. 拓展层次

Ⅰ. 单项选择题

1. _____ from the top of the mountain, the village looks more beautiful.
   A. Looking at　　　B. Seeing　　　C. Looked at　　　D. See
2. He decided _____ a big birthday party and invite all his friends to spend a happy night.
   A. to have　　　B. having　　　C. have　　　D. had
3. _____ the picture, the old man couldn't help _____ him of his childhood.
   A. Seeing; reminding　　　B. Seen; reminding
   C. Seeing; to remind　　　D. To see; to remind
4. What a pity! All the classmates went to see the wonderful performance _____ you.
   A. except　　　B. besides　　　C. beside　　　D. instead of
5. That year the river was _____ thick ice and this gave him an idea to hold a party on the ice.
   A. covering with　　　B. covered with　　　C. covered in　　　D. covering in
6. The ice _____ and carried all his living-room furniture and carpets out to the sea with it.
   A. broken up　　　B. broke out　　　C. broke into　　　D. broke down
7. When it was getting dark, we went outside to watch the moon and imagined _____ with the beauty.
   A. to dance　　　B. dance　　　C. danced　　　D. dancing
8. Please _____ the little boy and then wash him to have breakfast, Mary.
   A. wear　　　B. put on　　　C. have on　　　D. dress
9. People say that she prefers singing _____ dancing in her spare time.
   A. than　　　B. to　　　C. for　　　D. instead of
10. He says that he _____ to live in the countryside because the air is very fresh.
    A. preferred　　　B. enjoys　　　C. prefers　　　D. enjoyed
11. They agreed to share _____ the cost and pay much more than you.
    A. in　　　B. with　　　C. out　　　D. for
12. She had never shared the secret _____ anybody before.
    A. with　　　B. in　　　C. for　　　D. to
13. If you go there, it is a _____ .
    A. must see　　　B. must-see　　　C. must seeing　　　D. must-sees
14. Thanksgiving is a traditional festival that _____ 1621.
    A. starts in　　　B. started in the US in
    C. started　　　D. began at the US in
15. —What _____ three _____ ?
    —Food, family and football.
    A. are; "F"s　　　B. is; "F"s　　　C. was; "F"s　　　D. are; F

II. 交际用语:选择题

1. —Would you like to join us in the party?
   —_____.
   A. With pleasured
   B. I'd like to, but I'm busy
   C. Thanks for your invitation
   D. Good idea

2. —We are all going to take part in the contest.
   —_____.
   A. Well done   B. Good luck   C. Congratulations   D. Enjoy yourself

3. —We had a good time at your party.
   —_____.
   A. I'm glad that you enjoyed it
   B. Thank you
   C. Good party
   D. Well done

4. —How beautiful it is!
   —_____.
   A. You are right   B. Me, too   C. I agree with you   D. A or C

5. —You look so unhappy! Why?
   —_____.
   A. I lost some money
   B. No, I don't
   C. No doubt that I'm happy
   D. You, too

III. 阅读理解:选择题

Hawaii, the 50th state of the United States, is out in the Pacific Ocean, 3,700 kilometers away from Los Angeles. It is made up of eight main islands with a land area of only 16,700 square kilometers and covers over 2,500 kilometers of ocean. Hawaii became a state in 1959 and is smaller than 46 of the other states.

The first Hawaiians arrived from other Pacific islands sometime about 100 A. D. Later, more and more people moved here. Hawaii became an island with traditions of several countries. People celebrate traditional Chinese, Japanese and Filipino holidays as well as the holidays from the United States.

Hawaii has some special traditions. Hawaiians are very friendly and always welcome visitors. They give visitors leis(花环). A lei is a long necklace made from beautiful fresh flowers from the Hawaiian islands. Men wear bright flowered shirts, and women often wear long flowered dresses. Hawaii is known as the Aloha State. Aloha means both "hello" and "good-bye" in Hawaiian. It also means "I love you."

Hawaii has beautiful sceneries. It is famous for beaches. People from different parts of the world like to relax themselves here. So Hawaiians make most of their money from the tourists. The families of the first people who came from the U. S. own most of the important banks and companies. Of course, many people from other countries are also buying and starting businesses in Hawaii.

Sometimes when people from many different countries, races and traditions live together, there are some problems. But in Hawaii, there is very few serious problems, because the people in Hawaii have learned to live together on these beautiful islands in peace.

1. Hawaii has a land area of _____ square kilometers.
   A. 3,700　　　　　B. 2,500　　　　　C. 16,700　　　　　D. 1,820
2. Aloha means _____ .
   A. hello　　　　　B. good-bye　　　　C. I love you　　　D. A, B and C
3. People like traveling to Hawaii because it has _____ .
   A. eight islands　　　　　　　　　　B. beautiful sceneries
   C. many banks and companies　　　 D. beautiful flowers
4. If you get to Hawaii, Hawaiians will give you _____ .
   A. a flower necklace　　　　　　　　B. a flowered skirt
   C. a flowered dress　　　　　　　　 D. a flower hat
5. Which sentence is **NOT** true?
   A. Hawaii is larger than most of the other states.
   B. Hawaiians celebrate different festivals.
   C. Hawaii attracts a large number of tourists from the world.
   D. Hawaiians are friendly enough to live together with different people.

Ⅳ. 根据括号里的中文填空

1. He decided _____(举办) a big Christmas party at once.
2. You can imagine how I felt when I saw everyone had dressed up _____(除我在外).
3. The ice had _____(破裂) and had carried everything out to the sea with it.
4. It sounds interesting but I _____(更喜欢待在) at home.
5. We are partners and we should _____(分担) all the work and all the cost.

Ⅴ. 写作

Write a composition about your favorite festival.

_____
_____
_____
_____
_____

Unit 2　How to open a savings account?

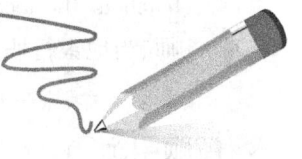

目标攻略

1. 培养良好的交际能力:怎样开户、存取款等;
2. 认知本单元所有词汇;能正确运用重点词汇,如 account,check,invest,savings account, fill in,transfer 等;
3. 背诵"Everyday English";
4. 掌握不定式作宾语补语等;
5. 学习写阅读总结。

知识解析

Ⅰ.词汇

(1) cell phone banking 手机银行;Internet banking 网上银行。
(2) keep account 记账;open/close an account 开/销账户;cast account 算账。
(3) ATM 自动取款机,是"Automated Teller Machine"的缩写。
(4) exchange rate 汇率;account number 账号;savings account 储蓄账户。
(5) deposit at least 10 yuan 至少存 10 元;draw some money 取一些钱。
(6) 1 US dollar to 6.8 RMB 1 美元兑 6.8 元人民币(其中 to 也可以用 for 代替)。
(7) fill in/up/out a form 填表。

Ⅱ.句式

(1) How to open a savings account? 怎样开储蓄账户?
(2) What's the exchange rate today? 今天的汇率是多少?
(3) We'll invest some money in the factory. 我们将把钱投资在工厂。
(4) You need to fill in a form and deposit at least 10 yuan.
    您需填写一张表格并且至少存 10 元。
(5) Please sign your name here. 请在这里签名。
(6) Our real-time Internet banking service is a convenient way to manage your Standard Bank

accounts. 实时网上银行服务是一种经管你的标准银行账户的便利方式。

(7) Sorry for having kept you waiting. 对不起让您久等了。

(8) Can you show me how to use the ATM? 你能告诉我如何使用自动取款机吗？

(9) They raised more than $20,000 by selling 500 dollar shares in the bank to parents, teachers, the local bank clerks and customers. 他们通过将500美元股份卖给父母、老师、当地银行职员和顾客筹集了2万美元的资金。

解题引领

1. How to open _____ account?
   A. a saving   B. saving   C. a savings   D. savings

答案为 C。点拨：a savings account 是"一个储蓄账户"之意。

2. My boss asked me _____ a check, but I don't know how to do it.
   A. cashing   B. cash   C. to cash   D. cashes

答案为 C。点拨：ask, watch, hear, tell, advise 等动词后面要跟动词不定式作补语，即：ask/watch/hear/tell/advise somebody to do something。

3. They _____ more than $2,000 by selling 50 dollar shares in the bank to parents.
   A. kept   B. raised   C. borrowed   D. rented

答案为 B。点拨：raise 在此是"筹集"之意。其他选项意义不对。

语法点睛

动词不定式作宾语补足语

参见上面一单元的阐述。

写阅读总结

用英语写一份阅读总结，100词左右。

A. 基础层次

Ⅰ. 按要求做题

1. 用对应的英语填空。

_____	账户	_____	余额,结存
_____	分行,分支	_____	支票
_____	存款	_____	提取
_____	兑换,交换	_____	指尖
_____	插入	_____	投资
_____	透支	_____	率
_____	签字	_____	(信息和数据)来源
_____	转账	_____	账号
_____	汇率	_____	填写
_____	储蓄账户		

2. 思考与问答。

(1) Do you know how to open a savings account? _____.

(2) Do you need to fill in a form and deposit some money? _____.

(3) What does "Internet banking" mean in Chinese? _____.

(4) Can you speak English fluently? _____.

(5) Is Internet banking service convenient? _____.

Ⅱ. 按要求完成下列各题

1. Why do people say personal banking is convenient?（回答）→ _____.

2. Sorry for having kept you _____ (wait)（用动词的正确形式填空）.

3. keep account & close an account（翻译）→ _____

4. raise more than ＄2,000（翻译）→ _____

5. If you are going to the Halloween, need you dress up?（回答）→ _____.

Ⅲ. 课堂效应检测:用英语在下面指定处小结你学习本单元的收获体会

_____
_____
_____
_____
_____
_____

B. 拓展层次

Ⅰ. 单项选择题

1. Can you tell me how I can open a _____ at a bank?
   A. saving account　　　　　　B. savings account
   C. savings accounts　　　　　D. saving accounts

2. You open an account? You need _____ a form and deposit at least 10 yuan.
   A. to fill up　　B. filling out　　C. filling in　　D. to fill for

3. —What's the exchange rate today?
   —One US dollar _____ 6.8 RMB.
   A. for　　B. on　　C. with　　D. in

4. Excuse me. Can you give me _____?
   A. a head　　B. a foot　　C. a hand　　D. an ear

5. I'd like to _____ some money to buy something, madam. Here's my bankbook.
   A. want　　B. deposit　　C. draw　　D. borrow

6. May I _____ 6,000,000 dollars in your bank, madam? Here's my cash.
   A. borrow　　B. draw　　C. deposit　　D. have

7. I am going to _____ most of my money in that company to run a factory.
   A. invest　　B. transfer　　C. hunt for　　D. raise

8. I'll have to _____ some money to my friends, but I am too busy to go to the bank to do so.
   A. invest　　B. borrow　　C. transfer　　D. give

9. He wants to apply for _____ because he's short of cash now.
   A. exchange rate　　B. goods　　C. overdrafts　　D. account

10. It's a real bank that _____ money for savings and _____ loans.
    A. accepts; makes　　　　　　B. receives; on
    C. makes; receives　　　　　D. borrows; makes

11. They _____ more than 20,000 by selling 50 dollar shares in the bank to parents.
    A. raised　　B. borrowed　　C. invested　　D. drew

12. Public servants (公务员) must be responsible _____ their jobs and _____ the people.
    A. to; for　　B. for; to　　C. for; for　　D. to; to

13. The Olympic Games, _____ in 776 B.C did not include women players until 1912.
    A. first playing　　　　　　B. to be first played
    C. first played　　　　　　D. to be first playing

14. The patient was warned _____ oily food after the operation.
    A. to eat not　　B. eating not　　C. not eating　　D. not to eat

15. A cook will be immediately fired if he is found _____ in the kitchen.
    A. smoke　　B. smoked　　C. to smoke　　D. smoking

Ⅱ. 交际用语:选择题

1. —Will you be free tomorrow?
   —_____.
   A. I think this
   B. All right, I think so
   C. OK, I'll be free then
   D. Yes, I think so

2. —Would you like some more vegetables?
   —_____.
   A. Thank you. I've had enough
   B. Yes, please
   C. They are delicious
   D. Do please

3. —I'm sorry I can't follow you. Would you please speak more slowly?
   —_____.
   A. Why say so   B. Really   C. OK. I will   D. It's impossible

4. —No smoking, please.
   —_____.
   A. Tell me the reasons
   B. Why so
   C. OK, we won't
   D. It's impolite

5. —Thank you all the same.
   —_____.
   A. OK   B. Sorry   C. It's nothing   D. Really

Ⅲ. 阅读理解:选择题

Along the river banks of the Amazon and the Orinoco there lives a bird that swims before it can fly. It flies like a fat chicken, eats green leaves, has the stomach of a cow and has claws(爪) on its wings when it is young. It builds its home about 4.6 meters above the river, and that's an important feature(特征) for the safety of the young. It is called hoatzin(麝雉).

In appearance, the bird of both sexes looks very much alike with brown on the back and cream and red on the underside. The head is small, with a large set of feathers on the top, bright red eyes, and blue skin. Its nearest relatives are the common birds, cuckoos(杜鹃/布谷鸟). Its most striking feature, though, is only found in the young.

Baby hoatzins have a claw on the leading edge of each wing and another at the end of each wing tip. Using these four claws, together with the beak(喙), they can climb about in the bushes, looking very much like primitive(原始的) birds that must have done. When the young hoatzins have learned to fly, they lose their claws.

During the drier months between December and March, hoatzins fly about the forest in groups of 20 to 30 birds. But in April, when the rainy season begins, they collect together in smaller living units of 2 to 7 birds for producing purposes.

1. What is the text mainly about?
   A. Hoatzins in dry and rainy seasons.
   B. The relatives and enemies of hoatzins.

C. Primitive birds and hoatzins of the Amazon.

D. The appearance and living habits of hoatzins.

2. Young hoatzins are different from their parents in that _____ .

   A. they look like young cuckoos
   B. they have claws on the wings
   C. they eat a lot like a cow
   D. they live on river banks

3. What can we infer about primitive birds from the text?

   A. They had claws to help them climb.
   B. They could fly long distances.
   C. They had four wings like hoatzins.
   D. They had a head with long feathers on the top.

4. When do hoatzins fly about the forest in groups of 20 to 30 birds?

   A. Only in December.
   B. In the drier season.
   C. Between October and March.
   D. In the rainy season.

5. Why do hoatzins collect together in smaller groups when the rainy season comes?

   A. To find more food.
   B. To protect themselves better.
   C. To keep themselves warm.
   D. To produce their young.

Ⅳ．根据括号里的中文填空

1. Thanksgiving is a traditional festival that _____(起源于)1621.
2. Could you tell me how I can open a _____(储蓄账户)?
3. You need to fill in a form and _____(至少存)10 yuan in it.
4. What's the _____(汇率)of 1 US dollar to RMB today?
5. They _____(已筹集)over ﹩80,000 and invested it in the company.

Ⅴ．写作

Complete the following diary according to the Chinese information.

May 21, Sunday   __1__(多云)

This morning I went __2__(购物). After I got off the bus, I saw two foreigners __3__(四周张望) with a map in their hands. So I went up to ask if I could help them in English. They said they wanted to go to the bank. I told them I __4__(碰巧) pass by there and it was not far. So we went there together, __5__(交谈着) on the way. When we got to the bank, we found the bank clerk didn't understand English...

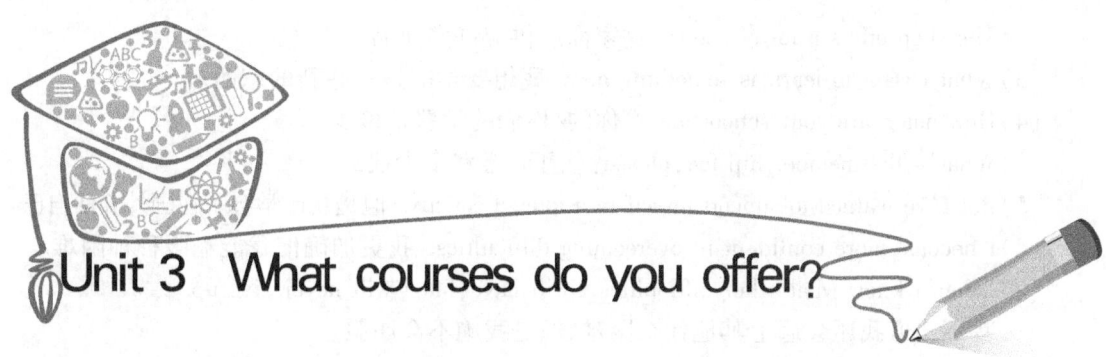

Unit 3 What courses do you offer?

目标攻略

1. 培养询问相关信息的交际能力：如何询问或介绍课程等；
2. 认知本单元所有词汇；能正确运用重点词汇，如 certificate, course, inspire, overcome, support, tuition 等；弄清 fee/fare；How to sign up；be confident of 的用法等；
3. 背诵"Everyday English"；
4. 掌握名词从句：主语从句；
5. 描绘工作经历或制作网页。

知识解析

I．词汇

（1）offer 除意为"提供"外，还有其他用法：offer to do something"愿意做某事"，offer 还可意为"出（价），开（价）；向……出售"。如：

He often offers to help the weak. 他经常帮助弱者。

He offered me 9,000 dollars for my car. 他出价 9 000 美元买我的小车。

（2）sign up 签约参加工作，签约，报名参加。

（3）such as being a Chinese tutor 例如当中文私人教师。

（4）support oneself 养活自己。

（5）inspire somebody with courage 鼓起某人的勇气。

（6）homecoming 回到家乡，校友返校节。

（7）be regarded as 被当作……/被看作……。

（8）register online 网上注册。

II．句式

（1）What courses do you offer? 你们开设哪些课程？

（2）Please offer the guest a cup of tea. 请给客人端上一杯茶。

They offered the boss 30,000 dollars for the machine.

他们向老板出价 30 000 美元买了这台机器。

The shop offers a lot of goods. 这家商店供应许多商品。

(3) What I want to learn is something new. 我想要学的是一些新的东西。

(4) How much are your school fees? 你的/你们的学费是多少？

What's the membership fee, please? 请问，会费多少钱？

(5) But I've learned to support myself in a foreign country. 但是我已学会了在国外养活自己。

(6) I become more confident in overcoming difficulties. 我更加确信我能克服种种困难。

(7) I don't know what other difficulties I will have, but I will never give up.

我不知道我还会遇上其他什么困难，但是我绝不会屈服。

(8) It is good news to me that I can register online. 能网上注册对我是个好消息。

(9) Homecoming is celebrated each fall. 毕业生返校庆祝活动在秋天举行。

解题引领

1. Can you tell me what courses _____?

  A. does it offer   B. is it offering   C. it offers   D. offers it

答案为 C。点拨：what courses 引出一个宾语从句，从句都要用陈述句语序，即：主谓(vi.)/主谓(vt.)宾排列顺序。

2. It impressed me that many Australian students earn their _____ through part-time jobs.

  A. fee   B. tuition fares   C. tuition fees   D. fares

答案为 C。点拨：fee 指：服务费、手续费、会费、赏金等；fare 指：车、船和飞机等费。选项 A 错在没用复数；选项 B、D 指车、船、飞机等费。

3. I don't know _____ difficulties I will have, but I will never give up.

  A. what else   B. what other   C. who else   D. who other

答案为 B。点拨：A 项 what else 后面不可跟名词；B 项 what other 后面要跟名词；C、D 项意思不对。

语法点睛

名词性从句

一、概述

由引导词引导一个句子，在主句中相当于名词功能的句子，能作主语、宾语、表语及同位语。名词性从句包含主语从句、宾语从句、表语从句和同位语从句。

二、用法

1. 主语从句：引导主语从句的引导词有：连词 that，whether；连接代词 who，whom，whose，what，which；连接副词 how，when，where，why。

(1) that 引导主语从句(that 一般不省)。如：

That he will go abroad is true. That she has become a player made us happy. That we'll go hiking is certain.

注 1：that 引导主语从句，多用 it 作形式主语，而把真正主语置后。如：

It is true that he will go abroad.

It made us happy that she has become a player.

It is certain that we'll go hiking.

注2:如果that从句作主语是问句,只能用it作形式主语。如:

Is it true that he will go abroad?

Did it make us happy that she has become a player?

注3:特殊句型:

A. It is + 形容词 + that 从句。如:

It's necessary that she go to see a doctor at once.

此句为虚拟句,she go = she should go,在表建议、命令、要求等意义的it作形式主语的结构中,that从句的谓语动词常用"should + 原形动词",should可省略。如:

It's important that we(should)learn one or two foreign languages.

我们学好一两门外语是重要的。

B. It's + 名词(词组) + that从句(其名词表惋惜)。如:

It's a pity that he should have missed such a chance. 真遗憾,他错过这样的机会。

C. It is + 过去分词 + that从句。如:

It is said that she is a famous speaker.

It is thought that it will snow tomorrow.

此句型中,过去分词表建议、要求、命令等时,that从句中谓语动词用should + 动词原形,should可省略。如:

It's suggested that the sports meeting(should)be put off. 运动会建议延期。

It's demanded that we(should)set out at once. 要求我们立刻出发。

D. It seems/happens等不及物动词 + that 从句。如:

It seems that she is very angry.

(2)whether引导主语从句,意为"是否"。如:

Whether they will come is unknown. 他们是不是会来还不知道。

Whether we will win or not is not clear. 我们是否能赢还不清楚。

需要注意的是,该从句置于句首时,只能用whether引出;置于句末时,有时可用if代替。如:

It is unknown whether/if they will come. 他们是否会来还不知道。

(3)连接代词或副词引出主语从句。如:

What he said is true. 他说的是真的。

Who will become our team leader hasn't been decided yet. 谁将成为我们的队长还没决定。

Why she did so is not clear. 她为什么这样做还不清楚。

When they will come back is a riddle. 他们什么时候回来还是个谜。

Which is the least is not important. 哪一个最少不重要。

注:连接代词或副词引导的主语从句,也常用it作形式主语。如:

It is not clear why she did so. 她为什么这样做还不清楚。

It's a riddle when they will come back. 他们什么时候回来还是个谜。

(4)whatever/whoever/whenever/wherever也可引出主语从句。如:

Whoever breaks the law must be punished. 犯法的人必受处罚。
Whatever you have done is fine for me. 你干了什么我无所谓。
Whenever she visits us makes us happy. 无论什么时候来拜访我总使得我快乐不已。

2. 宾语从句(在复合句中作宾语)，和主语从句一样，只把主语从句放置在宾语位置就可以了。如：

What he said is not true. 将 what he said 置于一个及物动词后或介词后就可以了。
I don't know what he said. 我不知道他说了什么。
That we'll go hiking is true. 将 That we'll go hiking 置于宾语位置就可以了。He says that we'll go hiking.

其他以此类推。

注1：that 引导主语从句时一般不省略，但引导宾语从句带补语时要用 it 作形式宾语，真正宾语后置。如：

We thought it a pity that she should have missed such a chance.
我们认为她失去如此一个机会，实为一大遗憾。

注2：宾语从句中有一条"时态一致"原则，但从句中所叙述的是客观事实或一般真理时，从句要用一般现在时。如：

The teacher told us that light travels much faster than sound. 老师告诉我们光比声传播快。

3. 表语从句(复合句中作表语)，同主语从句和宾语从句一样，将其置于表语位置就成了表语从句。如：

The truth is that she is lying. 真相就是她在撒谎。
This is what I said. 这是我说的。
It is uncertain whether they would give up smoking. 他们是否戒烟还不肯定。
The boy is where he was. 这男孩仍在原处。
The question is when we'll go back. 问题是我们什么时候能回来。

注：as if/as though 也可引导表语从句。如：

She looks as if she has lost something. 她好像丢了什么东西。

4. 同位语从句(复合句中作同位语)

that 引导一些抽象名词，如 fact/idea/news/truth/answer/belief/doubt/hope/plan 等后接 that 引导的同位语从句。如：

The news that our team has won is unbelievable. 我们队获胜的消息不可信。
I had no idea that you moved here. 我不知道你搬到这里了。

注1：that 引导同位语从句与引导定语从句的区别：that 引导同位语从句时为连词，无词义，后面从句是个完整句子，而 that 引导定语从句(后面阐述)是代词，必须在从句中充当一个成分，充当从句宾语时可省略。如：

The news that she is ill is true. (同位语从句) 她病了的消息是真的。
The news that you told me is true. (定语从句) 你告诉我的消息是真的。
在 that you told me 中 that 作 told 的直接宾语，即 you told me that(that 指代 news)。

注2：少数情况下也可用连接副词 how, when, where 等及连接代词 what 等引导同位语从句。如：

I have no idea when he will be back. 我不知道,他什么时候会回来。

Scientists have found answers to the question how life began on earth.

科学家已经找到了生命是如何在地球上起源这一问题的答案。

注3:what 与 whatever 都可引导名词性从句,不过 what 引导的是特指,whatever 引导的是泛指。如:

What you said is right. 你说得是对的。

what = the words which/that(you said)(特指这些短语)

Her husband does whatever she asks him to do. 她丈夫做她要求的任何事。

whatever = anything that(泛指任何一件事)

注4:who 与 whoever 的用法。

who"谁",含疑问意义;whoever "……的人",不含疑问意义。如:

Who breaks the law must be punished. (误)

Whoever breaks the law must be punished. (正)犯法的人必受惩罚。

Who told you this was lying. (误)

Whoever told you this was lying. (正)告诉你此事的人是在撒谎。

写作指导

写工作经历和怎样制作网页

(见课本相关阐述)

同步训练

A. 基础层次

Ⅰ. 按要求做题

1. 用对应的英语填空。

_____证书	_____课程
_____受雇	_____偶然遇到
_____财政的,金融的	_____费用
_____主页	_____给……以深刻印象
_____激励,鼓舞	_____讲课,讲座
_____当地的	_____提供
_____克服	_____在海外
_____压力	_____登记
_____时间表	_____坚定地
_____供养,支持	_____学费
_____私人教师,导师	_____申请表
_____放弃	

2. 思考与问答。
(1) What courses do you like? _____.
(2) Do you know courses on child education? _____.
(3) Would you like to learn computer programming? _____.
(4) If so, would you like to sign up online? _____.
(5) What is your aim of learning the courses? _____.

Ⅱ. 按要求完成下列各题

1. What's the difference between "fare" and "fee"? (回答)→_____
2. be confident _____ doing something (介词填空)→_____
3. What does the word "homecoming" mean in Chinese? (回答)→_____
4. a uniform fare of one yuan for any distance (翻译)→_____
5. How much are your school fees? (回答)→_____

Ⅲ. 课堂效应检测:用英语在下面指定处小结你学本单元的收获体会

_____
_____
_____
_____
_____

B. 拓展层次

Ⅰ. 单项选择题

1. What I want to learn is _____ about computer programming.
   A. something new   B. new something
   C. thing new   D. new everything
2. The teaching materials in our school keep _____ the latest development in this field.
   A. race with   B. pace with   C. pace to   D. race to
3. Excuse me, do you have any _____ jobs here?
   A. part-time   B. part time   C. full time   D. alone
4. You can find our homepage on the Internet and fill in the application form _____.
   A. on-line   B. online   C. in line   D. in-line
5. Like most overseas students, I have tried a lot of jobs _____ being a Chinese tutor, a kitchen hand.
   A. for example   B. such as   C. namely   D. that is
6. Life is difficult, but I've learned _____ myself in a foreign country.
   A. supporting   B. supportive   C. to support   D. supported
7. I don't need financial help from my parents _____.
   A. no more   B. no longer   C. any more   D. not any longer

8. I don't know _____ difficulties I will have.
   A. what else   B. which else   C. what other   D. else what
9. I advised my brother to give up _____ but he wouldn't do so.
   A. to smoke   B. smoked   C. smoking   D. smoke
10. Success has been _____ us to make greater efforts.
    A. inspired   B. inspire   C. inspires   D. inspiring
11. When a guest comes in, please _____ him a cup of tea, Lily.
    A. make   B. eat   C. have   D. offer
12. While homecoming _____ differently at each school, it usually includes a parade and...
    A. celebrated   B. was celebrated   C. is celebrating   D. is celebrated
13. Which of the following sentence is right?
    A. It is true that he said at the meeting.
    B. He has been chosen made us happy.
    C. He said at the meeting encouraged us a lot.
    D. What he said at the meeting is true.
14. _____ leaves the room last ought to turn off the lights.
    A. Anyone   B. The person   C. Whoever   D. Who
15. It is generally considered unwise to give a child _____ he or she wants.
    A. however   B. whichever   C. whatever   D. whenever

Ⅱ．交际用语：补全对话题

A: __1__?
B: Yes, __2__ to borrow the novel *Silent Spring*.
A: Oh, sorry, it's on loan.
B: __3__. What else do you have by the same writer?
A: __4__ *Huck Finn*? It's a nice one, too.
B: OK, I'll take it. When must I return it?
A: Within two weeks.
B: __5__. I haven't finished reading it by then?
A: You can renew it for another two weeks.
B: Thank you.
A: You're welcome.

> A. It's a pity
> B. I'd like
> C. Can I help you
> D. What about
> E. What shall I do if

III. 阅读理解：选择题

The water level of oceans rises and falls alternately twice a day. This movement of water is called the tide. Tides are caused by the pull of the sun and the moon on the earth's surface; since the moon is closer, it affects the tides more than the sun. When the moon is directly overhead, it actually pulls on the water that is below it. This causes the water level to rise because the water is pulled away from the earth. As the moon disappears over the horizon, the pull lessens and the water level settles back towards the ocean bottom.

When the water reaches its highest level, we have high tide. And when the water comes to its lowest level, we have low tide. From its lowest point, the water rises gradually for about 6 hours until it reaches high tide. Then it begins to fall continuously for about 6 hours until it reaches low tide. Then the cycle begins again.

1. Which of the following may be the best title for the passage?
   A. The Moon and Ocean   B. The Moon and the Tide
   C. Water Levels   D. The Pull of the Moon and the Sun

2. The pull of the moon on the earth's surface is stronger than that of the sun because _____.
   A. the moon is directly over the earth
   B. the moon pulls the water away from the earth
   C. the moon is closer to the earth
   D. the moon moves around the earth

3. Water level reaches its low point when _____.
   A. the moon is hidden by clouds   B. the moon's effect is indirect
   C. the moon moves far away   D. the sun is overhead

4. High tide occurs _____.
   A. every 12 hours   B. every 6 hours
   C. every 24 hours   D. every 18 hours

5. According to the passage, which of the following statements is **TRUE**?
   A. Weather sometimes affects tides.
   B. The force directly affecting the earth's surface comes from the moon only.
   C. The effect to the sun on the ocean water can be neglected.
   D. Tides are the result of the pull of the moon and the sun.

IV. 根据括号里的中文填空

1. _____(我想要学的) is something new about computer programming.

2. It is good news to me that I can _____(网上注册).

3. It impressed me that many Australian students earn their _____(学费) in the spare time.

4. Life is difficult, but I've learned to _____(养活自己) in a foreign country.

5. I don't know _____(另外其他) difficulties I will have, but I will never give up.

V. 写作

根据中文信息写一封恭贺信:向阳毕业后通过考试准备出国深造,写信表示祝贺。

                      __1__(6月6日)

Dear Xiang Yang,

  I'm happy to have learned from our head teacher that you will go abroad for majoring in the English specialty when you __2__(大学毕业). And we think that you're very __3__(棒)and we should learn from you.

  I, together with __4__(其余同学), would like to meet you and __5__(祝贺)your success. How about holding a get-together this Sunday morning at Hilton?

  We look forward to the happy day's arriving early.

                         Sincerely yours

                            Liu Wen

Unit 4　I'll have to have my watch replaced.

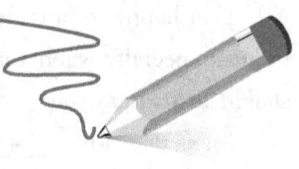

目标攻略

1. 培养良好的交际能力：表达投诉及正确处理投诉；
2. 认知本单元所有词汇；能正确运用重点词汇，如 damage, disappoint, detailed, guarantee, quality, refund 等；
3. 背诵"Everyday English"；
4. 掌握"have + 宾语 + p. p."及原因和目的状语从句等；
5. 学写投诉信。

知识解析

Ⅰ．词汇

（1）under guarantee 在保修中。
（2）be disappointed at something/in somebody or with somebody 对……感到失望。
（3）give somebody a 10% discount 给某人打百分之十的折扣。
（4）what's more 更有甚者，而且。
（5）gringo 外国佬（含贬义）；foreigner 外宾。

Ⅱ．句式

（1）I'll have to have my watch replaced because there is something wrong with the alarm. 我得去换一块手表，因为闹钟出问题了。
（2）It's still under guarantee. 仍然在保修中。
（3）We'll get this watch exchanged for you in no time. 我们将立即为你更换此表。
（4）Contact us again if you have any other problems. 如果有什么问题请再与我们联系。
（5）What's more, we will reduce the price by 10%. 而且，我们将把价格降低10%。
（6）The assembly line of our company broke down so that we couldn't finish it in time. 我们公司生产线出了故障，因此我们不能按时完成。
（7）We were disappointed at what he said. 我们对他所说的话感到失望。

解题引领

1. I'll have to have my machine _____ tomorrow.
    A. repairing   B. repaired   C. to repair   D. being repaired

答案为 B。点拨:"have + 宾语 + 过去分词"结构的意思是"让/叫某人做某事",宾语与过去分词之间有逻辑上的被动关系。

2. He didn't study hard _____ he failed in the exam.
    A. so that   B. because   C. if   D. though

答案为 A。点拨:空白处应填一个表结果的引导词,选项 A 符合,so that 既可表目的又可表结果,其区别方式是:so that 引导的从句谓语带有情态动词,则一般表目的,否则,是表结果。选项 B、C、D 分别表原因、条件和让步,故不对。

语法点睛

状语从句

状语在句中修饰谓语动词、形容词或副词。如果状语是由一个句子充当,那么就构成状语从句。状语从句种类较多,有时间、地点、原因、条件、目的、结果、方式、比较、让步等状语从句。

一、时间状语从句

引导时间状语从句的引导词有:when/as/while/after/before/since/as soon as/ever since/till/until/once/whenever/no sooner...than/hardly...when/the minute/every time/each time/next time/directly/immediately/by the time,etc.

(一)表"一……就"的句型

1. "as soon as/once..." 如:
I'll tell him about it as soon as he comes back. 他一回来我就告诉他。
Once you've been to China,you'll understand why I like it so much.
你一旦去了中国,就会明白我为什么这么喜欢中国。

2. "on + 动名词/on one's + n."如:
On arriving at the station,the robber was caught. 抢劫犯一到车站,就被抓住了。
On his arrival at the station,the robber was caught. 抢劫犯一到车站,就被抓住了。

3. "no sooner...than/hardly...when"否定词放句首时,主句要倒装。如:
No sooner had she got to the station than she was caught. 她一到车站,就被抓住了。
Hardly(scarcely)had she got to the station when she was caught. 她一到车站,就被抓住了。

4. "the moment,the minute,the second"如:
The moment I got there it began to rain. 我一到那儿,天就开始下雨。
We'll set out,the minute you are ready. 你一准备好,我们就动身。

5. 一些副词,如 directly,immediately 等。如:
It began to rain directly they came back. 他们一回来,天就开始下雨。

(二)when, while, as 引导的时间状语从句

1. when 既可指一个时间点,也可指时间段,既可表示主从句动作的同时性,也可表示动作的先后性。如:

I was short when I was a child. 当我是个小孩时,我很矮。(时间段)

She was cooking when I came back. 当我回来时,她正在做饭。(时间点)

注:when 还可作"当……这时",表示某事刚刚发生,另一件事同时发生。如:

I was watching TV, when someone knocked at the door. 我正在看电视,这时有人敲门。

2. while = during the time that 只指时间段,while 从句中不能用终止性动词。如:

I was reading a newspaper while I was waiting for a bus. 我一边等车一边看报。

注:while 还可表并列关系,意为"而"。如:

He likes swimming while she likes skating. 他喜欢游泳,而她喜欢滑冰。

3. as 引导状语从句时强调同时发生,不指先后关系,尤其是短暂动作或事情同时发生。如:

As he came back, he fell over. 他回家时,摔倒了。

注1:as 还可说明两种正在发展或变化的情况,意为"随着"(表时间的推移)。如:

As he grows older, he gets confused. 他越老越糊涂。

= The older he grows, the more confused he gets.

注2:as 作"一边……一边"。如:

He kept on looking behind as he went. 他一边走一边不断看后面。

(三)before 表示"在……之前,未来得及,趁……"时引导的时间状语从句。如:

He studied in this school before he joined the army. 他参军前在这所学校学习。

She hung up the telephone before I could answer it. 我未来得及接电话她就挂了。

You must write it down before you forget. 趁你还没忘记把它写下来。

(四)until, till(till 不可用于句首)引导的时间状语从句

1. 延续性动词(肯定式) + until,表示动作延续到……为止,意为"直到……为止"。如:

I'll wait here until he comes back. 我将一直等到他回来。

2. 终止性动词或延续性动词的否定式 + until,意为"直到……才"。如:

She didn't go to bed until her father came back. 她直到她爸爸回来才睡觉。

3. 用于强调句式:It is not until...that...(强调句中不用 till)。如:

It was not until the teacher came that we began to light the candles.

直到老师来,我们才开始点蜡烛。

4. not until 置于句首时,主句要用倒装式。如:

Not until she found his secret did she really know him.

直到发现他的秘密,她才真正认识他。

(五)since 表示"自从……"引导的时间状语从句,主句用完成时

1. since + 终止性动词过去式,时间从该动作发生起开始计算;since + 延续性动词过去式,时间从该动作结束时算起。如:

Mr. Liu has lived in this city since he came back from the countryside.

刘先生自返城以来就一直住在本市。

I haven't seen her since I lived in the school.
自从我住进这所学校以来就一直没见着她。
例外情况:I've known her since I was a boy. 我小时候就认识她了。
2. it is + 时间段 + since...句型中,时间一律以 since 从句动作结束时间算起。如:
It is five years since they moved here. 自从他们搬到这儿来已经5年了。
(六)时间状语从句中的省略问题
当主从句的主语相同,从句中又有 be 动词时,从句可以省去主语和 be 动词。另外,当从句主语是 it,含 be 时,可将 it is 省略。如:
When(it is)heated to very high temperature the wood may be burned.
木材加热到非常高的温度时会被点燃。

二、地点状语从句
(一)由 where,wherever 引导的地点状语从句
We'll go where we want to(go). 我们要去我们想去的地方。
I'll follow her wherever she goes. 无论她去哪儿,我都追随着她。
(二)地点状语从句与定语从句的区别
where 引导定语从句,从句前面应该有一个表示地点的先行词(名词)。如:
Go back where you came from. 从哪来回哪去。(地点状语从句)
Go back to your place where you came from. 回到你原来的地方。(place 为定语从句的先行词)

三、原因状语从句
由 because,as,since,now that 引导的原因状语从句。如:
She didn't come to school because she was ill. 因为她病了,所以没来学校。
Since a lot of people make mistakes in life,she wants to give him a chance.
因为很多人在生活中都会犯错,所以她想给他一个机会。
It was because he was ill that he didn't go to school. 因为他生病,所以没上学。
注1:since,as,now that 引导的原因状语从句不用于强调句中。
注2:since 比 because 的语气弱,用于说话双方都清楚的原因场合,置于主句前。如:
Since I must die,I must die,said the fisherman. 渔夫说道,既然我非死不可,我死好了。
注3:as 的语气最弱,只表明一般的因果关系。如:
As he was not well,I decided to go without him. 因为他身体不好,我决定不带他去了。
注4:now that 用来说明一种新情况,然后加以推论,置于句首时,that 可省略。如:
Now(that)it is raining outside,let's stay at home for a while.
既然外面下雨,我们在家里待一会儿再说。
注5:for 也可以表原因,但它是并列连词。它所表示的原因是对某种情况加以推论,用于补充说明理由。如:
"Get down on your knees,for I'm going to kill you" said the genie.
妖魔说:"跪下,因为我要杀死你"。

四、条件状语从句
(一)由 if/unless(= if...not),as long as(只要),suppose(假设),supposing(假如),in

case(万一……,以防……),as far as(只要),on condition that,provided that 引导的条件状语从句。如:

Come to my house if you are free. 如果你有空请来我家。

You may use my bike so long as you return it in time.
只要能准时归还,你可以借用我的自行车。

Unless you work harder at your lessons,you'll fail the examination.
除非你努力学习,否则考试会不及格。

(二)祈使句+and/or/or else etc.+单句(单句谓语用将来时)

Work hard and you'll succeed in your studies. 只要努力,你就会在学业上获得成功。

Hurry up or you'll miss the first bus. 快点,否则你会错过首班车。

注1:条件句中用一般现在时表将来。如:

I'll visit you if I'm free. 如果我有空我就拜访你。

注2:条件句与时间状语从句一样,句子成分可以有省略:从句主语是 it、从句带有 be 动词时,可以将从句主语和 be 一并省略。如:

Come to see me if you are free. 如果你有空来看看我。

Check your test paper carefully if(it is)necessary. 如果有必要,请仔细检查你们的试卷。

If so,you must go home and get it. 如果是这样,你必须回家取它。

注3:条件句中的虚拟和倒装,见虚拟语气与倒装部分。

五、目的状语从句与结果状语从句

(一)目的状语从句

由 so that,in order that,for fear that,in case,lest 引导的目的状语从句,从句谓语常用 may,might,can,could,will,would 等情感动词。如:

He got up early so that he could catch the first train. 他起床很早以便赶首班车。

She raised her voice so that every one could hear her. 她抬高声音,以便大家都能听见她。

He wrote down her address for fear that(lest)he would forget it.
他记下她的地址,以免忘记。

Please remind me of it again tomorrow in case I forget. 请明天再提醒我一下,免得我忘记。

注:当主从句主语一致时,可用 so as to/in order to 替代 so that/in order that 而变成简单句。如:

She worked overtime day and night so that/in order that she could succeed.
 =She worked overtime day and night in order to succeed.
她为了能够成功,夜以继日地工作。

(二)结果状语从句

由 so that(谓语不含情态动词),so...that,such...that,that 引导的结果状语从句。如:

She got up late so that she missed the train.
她起床晚了,结果误了火车。(so that 从句中无情态动词)

This is such a good movie that we all like it. 这是一部很出色的电影,我们都喜欢它。

There are so many students on the playground that I can't find the student who I want to find. 操场上有如此多的学生以致我找不到我要找的那个学生。

注：so/such...that 句型的区别：so + *adj.* / *adv.* + that；such + the + *adj.* + *n.* + that。另外 so + *adj.* + a/an + *n.* + that... 如：

It is so fine a day that we all go hiking. 天气很好，我们都去远足。
I have so little money with me that I can't give you any.
我身上的钱如此的少，以致一点也不能给你。
They are such little boys that we all like them. 他们是很小的男孩子，我们都很喜欢他们。
注：上述两例 little 作"少"意时用 so，作"小"意时用 such。

六、方式状语从句与比较状语从句

(一)方式状语从句

由 as/as if(though)引导的方式状语从句。如：
State the facts as they are. 如实陈述事实。
He died of cancer, as his father had done. 他与他父亲一样死于癌症。
Do as I do. 照我的做法去做。
He spoke as if he had been there before. 他讲话的样子好像他以前曾去过那儿。
He works with such enthusiasm as if he never knew fatigue.
他工作热情这么高，好像从不知疲倦似的。

(二)比较状语从句

由 as...as, not so, as...as 以及 than/the more...the more 引导的比较状语从句，常以省略形式出现。如：
This story is as interesting as that one. 这个故事和那个一样有趣。
She drove as fast as she could. 她尽可能快地开车。
They work more diligently than we. 他们工作比我们更勤奋。

七、让步状语从句

though/although/no matter + 疑问词/even if(though)/however/whatever 等可以引导让步状语从句。

(一)though/although 的用法

though 与 although 用法基本相同，只是 though 更口语化，although 更正式一些。二者均不可和 but 连用，但可以和 yet, still 连用。如：
Although the TV set is expensive, I still bought it. 尽管电视很贵，但是我仍然买了它。
Though/Although he was tired, he didn't stop working.
尽管他很累，但是他没有停止工作。

(二)as 的用法

as 引导让步状语从句时，采用倒装语序：形/副/名(零冠词)/动词(原形) + as + 主谓。如：
Child as he is, the boy is famous. 尽管这男孩还是孩子，他却很出名。
Famous as they are, they are very modest. 尽管他们很有名，但很谦虚。
Try as I might, I couldn't lift the stone. 尽管我尽力试了，但是我还是举不起这块石头。
注：在这种倒装结构中，也可以用 though，但不可用 although。如：
Famous though they are, they are very modest. 尽管他们很有名，但是很谦逊。

（三）even if(though)的用法

Even if it is raining, we'll go out. 即使天下大雨，我们还是要出去。

（四）whether...or 的用法

Whether you come or not, the party will be held as schedule.

不管你来不来，聚会都会照常举行。

（五）no matter + 疑问句的用法

疑问词 + ever = no matter + 疑问词。如：whoever = no matter who。以此类推。

二者的区别在于：no matter + wh-只引导让步状语从句，而 wh- + ever 的，除引导让步状语从句外，还可引导名词性从句。其中 whoever/whatever/wherever 引导名词性从句时，分别等于 anybody who/anything that/any place where。如：

I'll give the camera to whoever needs it. 我会把相机给需要它的人。

The prisoners had to eat whatever they were given. 囚犯必须别人给什么就吃什么。

（六）一般现在时表将来

No matter who you are, you'll be punished. 无论你是谁，你都会受到惩罚。

写作指导

投诉信

投诉信是公务信的一种，由日期、收信人、信函内容、落款 4 部分组成。它和普通信函格式相似。内容应尽量简明扼要，直达主题。用词既要讲究，又要达到所写投诉的目的。如：

July 2

Dear Sir or Madam：

The captioned goods you shipped per S. S. "Yellow River" on May 14 arrived here yesterday.

On examination we have found that many of the goods are severely damaged.

Though the cases themselves show no trace of damage. Considering this damage was due to the rough handling by the steamship company, we claimed（要求，索取，主张）to be compensated（补偿，赔偿）for the losses; but an investigation made by the surveyor（检查员）has revealed（展现，揭示）the fact that the damage is attributable to（归因于）improper packing. For further particulars（详情，细目）, we refer you to（请你们去找）the surveyor's report enclosed.

We are, therefore, compelled to claim on you to compensate us for the loss, $27,500, which we have sustained by the damage to the goods.

We trust that you will be kind enough to accept this claim and deduct（扣除）the sum claimed from the amount of your next invoice to us.

Yours truly,

Larkin Swift

A. 基础层次

Ⅰ. 按要求做题

1. 用对应的英语填空。

_____闹钟   _____很,非常
_____损坏   _____详细的,具体的
_____失望   _____担保(书),保证
_____不便   _____不妥当地
_____传单   _____(人或东西留下的)明显痕迹
_____品质   _____收据
_____退还(钱款等) _____替换
_____淋浴   _____手腕

2. 思考与问答。

(1) What does the word "prom" mean in Chinese? _____.
(2) Do you often wear a watch? _____.
(3) What does "compensation" mean in Chinese? _____.
(4) May the rates go up in heavy tourist areas in Latin America? _____.
(5) Would you like to travel abroad? _____.

Ⅱ. 按要求完成下列各题

1. Why were you late for class yesterday?（回答）→ _____.
2. Do you often take a shower?（回答）→ _____.
3. They come from Hunan.（对画线部分提问）→ _____?
4. Are you gringos?（回答）→ _____.
5. receipt(同义词)→ _____

Ⅲ. 课堂效应检测：用英语在下面指定处小结你学本单元的收获体会

_____
_____
_____
_____
_____
_____
_____
_____

B. 拓展层次

Ⅰ. 单项选择题

1. I'll have to have my car _____ tomorrow afternoon because there's something wrong with it.
   A. to repair   B. repaired   C. repairing   D. repairs

2. Excuse me, sir. I bought it one week ago and it's still _____.
   A. of guarantee   B. under guarantee   C. at guarantee   D. to guarantee

3. I'm very sorry that I am very disappointed _____ its quality.
   A. with   B. at   C. to   D. for

4. We can't sell them at the normal price and suggest that your boss _____ us a 10% discount.
   A. would give   B. should give   C. gives   D. gave

5. At present, they are short of cash but need money to invest _____.
   A. bad   B. very   C. badly   D. very well

6. The research is so designed that once _____ nothing can be done to change it.
   A. begins   B. having begun   C. beginning   D. begun

7. Hundreds of jobs _____ if the factory closes.
   A. lose   B. will be lost   C. are lost   D. will lose

8. —Did you remember to give Mary the money you owed her?
   —Yes, I gave it to her _____ I saw her.
   A. while   B. the moment   C. suddenly   D. one

9. _____ completed, this railway will join many industrial cities to seaport.
   A. Before   B. As   C. When   D. That

10. _____ it with me and I'll see what I can do.
    A. When left   B. Leaving   C. If you leave   D. Leave

11. —How soon can you finish reading the book?
    —It will be 2 weeks _____.
    A. before I will finish it   B. after I finish it
    C. since it has been finished   D. before it is finished

12. —Why was the price of bread so high that year?
    —_____ the war broke out.
    A. As   B. Since   C. For   D. Because

13. He whispered to his wife _____ he might wake up the sleeping baby.
    A. so that   B. on condition   C. for fear that   D. as long as

14. He was unable to make much progress, _____.
    A. as he tried hard   B. as hard he tried
    C. so hard he tried   D. hard as he tried

15. We put the corn _____ the birds could find it easily.
    A. such   B. where   C. of which   D. there

Ⅱ．交际用语：选择题

1. —What's the trouble, young boy?
   —_____.
   A. With pleasure　　B. No problem　　C. I've got a fever　　D. Thank you

2. —Sorry, I'm late for the meeting.
   —_____.
   A. That's nothing.　　B. Really?　　C. Why not?　　D. OK.

3. —What can I do for you, sir?
   —_____.
   A. Yes, I want a coat　　　　　　B. No, I want another one
   C. I want to buy a coat　　　　　D. All right, thanks

4. —What's the weather like today?
   —_____
   A. You don't know?　　　　　　B. I don't know, too.
   C. Rather warm, isn't it?　　　　D. Tomorrow is fine.

5. —What would you like to eat?
   —_____.
   A. Some beer　　B. Some coffee　　C. Some soup　　D. None of the above

Ⅲ．阅读理解：简答题

I'm usually fairly doubtful about any research that concludes that people are either happier or unhappier or more or less certain of themselves than they were 50 years ago. While any of these statements might be true, they are practically impossible to prove scientifically. Still, I was shocked by a report which concluded that today's children are significantly more anxious than children in the 1950s. In fact, the analysis showed, normal children aged 9 to 17 show a higher level of anxiety today than children who were treated for mental illness 50 years ago.

Why are America's kids so stressed? The report provides two main causes: increasing physical separation—brought on by high divorce rates(离婚率) and less involvement in community (社团), among other things—and a growing opinion that the world is a more dangerous place.

Given that "we can't turn the clock back", adults can still do plenty to help the next generation.

At the top of the list is nurturing(培养) a better appreciation of the limits of individualism. No child is an island. Strengthening social ties helps build communities and protect individuals against stress.

Help kids build stronger connections with others, you can turn off TVs and computers. Your family will thank you later. They will have more time for face-to-face relationships, and they will get more sleep.

Limit the amount of virtual(实际的) violence your children are exposed to. It's not just video games and movies; children see a lot of murder and crime on the local news.

Keep your expectations for your children reasonable. Many highly successful people never attend Harvard or Yale.

Make exercise part of your daily work. It will help you deal with your own anxieties and provide a good model for your kids. Sometimes anxiety is unavoidable. But it doesn't have to ruin your life.

1. How does the author think that the conclusions of any research about people's state of mind are?
_____

2. What does the author mean when he says "we can't turn the clock back" in Paragraph 3?
_____

3. What is the first and most important thing parents should do to help their children?
_____

4. What conclusion can be drawn(做出什么结论)from the passage?
_____

5. Did the highly successful people certainly enter the famous universities?
_____

Ⅳ. 根据括号里的中文填空

1. They want to _____(向她出价)5,555 yuan for the old antique.

2. I'll have to have _____(换台机器)tomorrow.

3. I bought it one week ago and it's still _____(在保修中).

4. They said that they were very _____(对……感到失望)its quality.

5. We can't sell them at the normal price and suggest you give us _____(打八折).

Ⅴ. 写作

Complete the following complaint letter.

Dear sir,

  I am writing to let you know the deplorable(应受谴责的,糟糕的) attitude of one of your ___1___(全体职员). I received my telephone bill for the previous(先前的)month from you and thought there were some errors in calculation: I had been overcharged(要价太高)for two overseas calls. However, when I called your ___2___(投诉部), the girl who answered my phone was ___3___(非常粗鲁). For one thing she interrupted me continually, for another she even said that the fault was my own. Needless to say, such a way of dealing with customers is unacceptable. I would like to suggest that the girl who is ___4___(成问题的)should be disciplined, and instructed on the proper way to deal with clients. And I hope she can ___5___(正式道歉). An early response will be appreciated.

Sincerely yours
Mary

Unit 5 We are going to work as packagers on the assembly line.

目标攻略

1. 培养良好的交际能力:谈论获取工作任务等;
2. 认知本单元所有词汇;能正确运用重点词汇,如 assembly line,cooperation,improve,divide...into 等;培养兴趣爱好;
3. 背诵"Everyday English";
4. 掌握动词时态:直接引语和间接引语;
5. 学习书写社会实践报告。

知识解析

Ⅰ. 词汇

(1) in charge of 负责……;in the charge of 由……负责。
(2) package/pack/pocket/sack 的区别:package 指中型大包;pack/pocket 指小包;sack 指大袋,麻袋。另外 pack something into... 表示"把某东西装进……"。
(3) improve 改善,提高;improve relations with somebody 改善与某人的关系。
(4) TPP Trans-Pacific Partnership 跨太平洋伙伴。
(5) seal(v.) 给……封口,(n.) 封条,封铅;印记,图章。
    break/take off the seal 启封,拆封;seal one's mouth/lips 封嘴。
(6) maximum 最大量,最大值;minimum 最小量,最小值。
(7) come true vi.;realize vt. 实现。
(8) cooperate with somebody 与某人合作。

Ⅱ. 句式

(1) We are going to work as packagers on the assembly line. 我们要上生产线做打包工。
(2) Who is in charge of the work? 谁负责这个工作?
(3) And it is the second time they have cooperated with Pepsi.
    这是他们第二次与百事可乐合作。

(4) Children are not legally allowed to work until they are 13 in Britain.
在英国,雇用 13 岁以下儿童工作是违法的。

(5) We'll be divided into groups. 我们将被分成几个小组。

(6) We can't wait to have a try. 我们迫不及待想试试。

解题引领

1. We are going to work _____ packagers on the assembly line.
   A. on　　　　　　B. to　　　　　　C. in　　　　　　D. as

答案为 D。点拨:词组 work as 是"担任,当"之意。其他搭配不当。

2. Vocational-school students should _____ some social practice programs.
   A. participate with　　B. participate on　　C. participate in　　D. take part

答案为 C。点拨:participate 作不及物动词时,搭配 in/with,而搭配 in 时,是"参加(某活动)"之意;搭配 with 时,是"分享,分担"之意。

语法点睛

直接引语和间接引语

(略)

写作指导

调查报告的书写方法

实践调查由四部分构成。第一部分:调查报告的事由,说明为什么要写这篇报告,写作的意义、目的等。第二部分:调查对象的基本情况,包括现状、趋势、存在问题。有时也根据写作目的来介绍相关方面的意见。第三部分:针对存在的问题,分析问题形成的原因。第四部分:针对问题,提出建议或相关意见。

调查报告是人们对某一情况、事件、经验或问题经过深入细致的调查研究而写成的书面报告。它反映了人们通过调查研究找出某些事物的规律,并提出相应的措施和建议,是社会调查实践活动的成果。学习撰写调查报告,有助于学生进一步认识社会、参与社会,把所学知识与社会实践结合起来,全面提高自身素质。

怎样撰写调查报告?

[例题]以"发扬勤俭美德,树立正确的消费观"为主题,以周围学生为调查对象,根据他们的生活态度和表现,写一份调查报告,题目自拟。

撰写调查报告,要做到以下几点:

1. 着力点要明确

首先,要深入调查,占有材料。这是写好调查报告的基础和先决条件。为此,就应该亲自了解第一手材料。既要了解"面"上的材料,又要了解"点"上的材料;既要了解正面材料,又要了解反面材料;既要了解现实材料,又要了解历史材料。如例题中,要求学生认真回顾平时手头搜集到的有关"勤俭是美德,是事业成功的重要因素,奢侈浪费导致事业失败"方面的详细资料。

其次,要认真分析,找出规律。这是调查的目的。在占有大量材料的基础上,要"去粗取精、去伪存真、由此及彼、由表及里"地总结出事物的规律。如例题中,除了要有具体的事例或数据外,还要对占有的资料分门别类地加以总结,如以"盲目攀比,铺张浪费""勤劳节俭、合理消费"为门类加以归纳,从中找出规律性。

再次,要立场正确,观点鲜明。调查报告要站在客观的立场上,透过现象看本质,对事物做出正确的判断和评价。如例题中,调查的目的是帮助学生树立勤俭节约是美德的观念,结合学生的生活实际,解决乱花钱、互相攀比、超前消费等不良习惯和问题。

最后,要概括事实,有叙有议。不能只罗列现象,而要适当地进行分析、议论,阐述观点。如例题中,在做到有事例和数据的基础上,运用所学的社会原理进行理性分析,观点要全面。

2. 报告格式要规范

(1)标题。①单标题,如例题中,标题可拟成《中学生合理消费的调查报告》,以清楚交代调查的内容。②双标题,可拟成《合理消费——××中学调查报告》。③标题若不用"调查报告"字样,也可用一般文章题目形式,如可拟成《中学生应该养成合理消费的好习惯》。

(2)前言。这部分内容往往是对调查的时间、地点、对象、范围的必要交代,总领全文。如例题中,调查对象可以是××中学整所学校的学生,也可以是初一年级的学生,还可以是随机抽查的学生;调查内容主要是学生的生活态度和表现两个方面。

(3)主体。主体是叙述具体调查内容、列举事例和数据并做出恰当的议论和分析,概括出经验或规律。这是表现调查报告主旨的关键部分。在材料的安排上,要把调查得来的大量材料归纳整理出若干条目,采用小标题式写法,要注意层次清楚,条理分明。有的可按问题的几个方面或几个问题并列安排材料,即采用"横式结构";有的可按事物发展的过程来写,即采用"纵式结构"。

(4)结尾。结尾是调查报告的结束语,可归纳、说明或总结全篇的主要观点,也可指出存在的问题,提出建议。

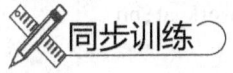

A. 基础层次

I. 按要求做题

1. 用对应的英语填空。

_____生产线	_____合作
_____主任	_____把……分成
_____进步	_____组织
_____包装	_____包,包裹
_____塑料的,塑料制品的	_____实践
_____封口	_____技巧,技能
_____社会的	_____玩具

_____车间 _____把……包起来
_____例如 _____参加

2. 思考与问答。
(1) Are you going to work as packagers on the assembly line? _____.
(2) Are you in charge of the work? _____.
(3) Don't shout, will you? _____.
(4) What's your favorite course? _____.
(5) What sports do you like best? _____.

Ⅱ. 按要求完成下列各题
1. "I am feeling ill."Tom said. (合成一个句子)→_____.
2. "Let's have fish for lunch."Mother said. (合成一个句子)→_____.
3. improve relations with somebody(翻译)→_____
4. How old are children allowed to work in Britain? (回答)→_____.
5. Lily goes to school by bus every day. (变一般疑问句)_____?

Ⅲ. 课堂效应检测：用英语在下面指定处小结你学本单元的收获体会
_____
_____
_____
_____
_____

B. 拓展层次

Ⅰ. 单项选择题

1. We are going to _____ packagers _____ the assembly line.
   A. work as; on   B. work as; in   C. work out; on   D. work at; on
2. Mr. Smith said we should _____ at least three groups.
   A. divided into   B. be divided into   C. be divided in   D. divided in
3. Do you know who is _____ the work?
   A. into charge of   B. in the charge of
   C. in charge of   D. into the charge of
4. And it is the second time that the boy _____ Pepsi.
   A. cooperated with   B. cooperated in
   C. has cooperated in   D. has cooperated with
5. The bus was packed _____ people, old and young, men and women.
   A. of   B. in   C. for   D. with
6. How long have you _____ the army, young man?
   A. joined   B. taken part in   C. been   D. been in

7. He had a heavy _____ on his back, so he can't walk fast.
   A. pocket   B. schoolbag   C. pack   D. package
8. The teacher asked his students _____ harmoniously with him these school terms.
   A. cooperated   B. cooperate   C. to cooperate D. cooperating
9. The working week is, _____, the longest of any country in Europe.
   A. in average   B. on average   C. to average   D. of average
10. In Britain, children are not legally allowed to work _____ they are 13.
    A. until   B. after   C. when   D. if
11. Do you think Mr. Brown's dream will _____?
    A. come true   B. realize   C. is coming true D. realized

Ⅱ. 交际用语：选择题

1. —Doctor, I feel terrible!
   —_____.
   A. Let me take your temperature   B. Are you sure you feel terrible?
   C. Let me examine you   D. A or C
2. —Is there anything to eat, madam?
   —_____.
   A. Yes. Here are some drinks and food, and help yourself to them
   B. No delicious food here
   C. With pleasure
   D. No problem. Help yourself to some food
3. —Do you have the time?
   —_____.
   A. Yes, nine five   B. A quarter to nine
   C. No, half past ten   D. A quarter past nine
4. —Who is on duty today?
   —_____.
   A. Yes, I am   B. I am   C. This is me   D. It's I
5. —Shall we go hiking tomorrow, Tom?
   —_____
   A. Good idea.   B. Why not?
   C. Sorry, I'm very busy.   D. A, B or C

Ⅲ. 阅读理解：判断题

Do you know when and where ice cream got its start? It's an international favorite with a long and interesting history. The earliest ices were eaten in China many years ago. The people would put orange juice on ice. Later, this idea traveled to Italy. Nero, the emperor of Rome between 37 and 68 A. D. liked to eat ice as a special treat between violin lessons. He ordered runners to run to the mountains, get snow, and run back quickly to the palace. The snow was mixed with fruit juices and nuts.

Around 1660, coffee shops serving ice cream were very popular in Paris. Italians owned most of the coffee shops. A man from Sicily named Francesco Procopio opened the first successful one. Before ice cream was sold in stores, it was made and frozen at home. It took a lot of work to mix cream, eggs, fruit, ice, and salt, and then to freeze it. Nancy Johnson, an American woman who was good at machines, invented the hand-turned ice cream freezer in 1846. Five years later, Jacob Flusell opened the first ice cream business in Baltimore, Maryland.

His business quickly spread to other states.

1. Ice cream is an international favorite with a long and interesting history.

2. Nero, the emperor of Germany between 37 and 68 A. D. liked to eat ice as a special treat between violin lessons.

3. The snow coming from the mountains was mixed with fruit juices and nuts.

4. Around 1660, coffee shops serving ice cream were very popular in Italy.

5. Nancy Johnson, an Italian woman being good at machines, invented the hand-turned ice cream freezer in 1846.

Ⅳ. 根据括号里的中文填空

1. We are going to work as packagers on the _____(生产线).

2. Sounds easy. The students will _____(分成) a number of groups.

3. Could you tell me who is _____(负责) the work?

4. And it is the second time that they _____(合作) with Pepsi.

5. Children are not legally allowed to work _____(直到) they are thirteen years old.

Ⅴ. 写作

Complete the following composition of shopping at a supermarket. (完成下面有关超市购物的作文。)

"Can I help you?" a shop assistant said to me when I went into __1__ (一家超市). I answered her that I would like to buy a lot of __2__ (东西) because the festival was __3__ (要来了). The assistant showed me around __4__ (整个超市). "Wa! The supermarket is __5__ (真大)." I __6__ (自言自语). "Also there are a lot of things that there are in other supermarkets and that there aren't in __7__." I sought the goods that I liked for a long time, but I __8__ (不知道该买什么). At last I sought and bought many things __9__ I liked. When I came home, I felt that I was __10__ (太累而不能走动).

Unit 6 Would you mind saying something about your work experience?

目标攻略

1. 培养良好的交际能力：找工作和参与面试；
2. 认知本单元所有词汇；能正确运用重点词汇，如 apply, application, contact, full-time, part-time, interview 等及面试的方法；
3. 背诵"Everyday English"；
4. 掌握语法：定语从句；
5. 学写申请信。

知识解析

Ⅰ. 词汇

(1) mind doing something 意为"介意做某事"，mind 后面要跟动名词作宾语。

(2) HRD = Human Resources Department 人力资源部。

(3) deal with/do with 对付，处理。

(4) experience 既可作可数名词表"经历"，又可作不可数名词表"经验"。如：
some experiences 一些经历；some experience 一些经验；experienced 经验丰富的，有经验的；be experienced in/at 对做……有经验。如：
Mr. White is experienced in/at teaching. 怀特先生对教学很有经验。

(5) fair *adj.* 公平的，公正的 *n.* 市场，交易会，展览会。
be fair to/on somebody 对某人公平；be fair in doing something 公平地做某事。

(6) I am a trend-spotter. 我是一个时尚观察员。

(7) Broadway 百老汇大街(美国纽约市的一条大街，为戏剧、夜总会的集中地区)。

(8) play the role of 扮演……的角色。

(9) a world fair 世界博览会。

Ⅱ. 句式

(1) Would you mind saying something about your work experience?

能说说你的工作经历吗？

（2）We should be fair in buying and selling. 我们应买卖公平。

（3）I play the role of a patient for medical students. 我为学医的学生扮演病人角色。

（4）You might be just the person whom we've been looking for.

你可能正是我们一直在找的那个人。

（5）And I believe that I am quite qualified for it. 而我认为/相信我能胜任它。

（6）I'd like to find a job that is suitable for me. 我想找一份适合我的工作。

解题引领

1. Would you mind _____ next to you, Mrs. Black?
   A. to sit   B. my sitting
   C. having been sat   D. sat

答案为 B。点拨：mind 后跟动名词，动名词的逻辑主语由物主代词或名词所有格充当（不在句首时也可用宾格代词或名词通用格来充当）。选项 C 是动名词完成时的被动式，故不对。

2. The job your company offered is exactly _____ that I am looking for.
   A. ones   B. the one
   C. those   D. the ones

答案为 B。点拨：空白处需填先行词，that I am looking for 是定语从句，且根据已知条件应用单数。

语法点睛

定语从句

一、概念

主从复合句中修饰主句中某一名词或代词的从句叫定语从句。被定语从句所修饰的名词或代词叫先行词。定语从句须后置。如：

The woman who/that is sitting on the chair is her mother. 坐在椅子上的那个女人是她妈妈。

定语从句分为限定性定语从句和非限定性定语从句两种。限定性的无逗号，非限定性的有逗号隔开，且不用 that 引导。如：

The book which/that you are reading is mine.

你在阅读的这本书是我的。（限定性定语从句）

Yesterday I met Li Ping, who looked tired.

昨天我见到了李平，她看上去很累。（非限定性定语从句）

二、引导定语从句的关系代词和关系副词

（一）关系代词：that/which/who/whom/whose

关系代词在定语从句中充当一个成分。

that 的先行词可以是人，也可以是物；which 的先行词只能是物；who 指人；whose 指人/

物,在定语从句中作定语;whom 指人,作宾语。如:
The book that you read is his.(作宾语)你读的那本书是他的。
The noodles that/which I cooked were delicious.(作宾语)我下的面条好吃。
Let's ask the man that/who is reading.(作主语)让我们问问那个读书的人。
They planted the trees which/that didn't need much water.
(作主语)他们种的那些树不需要很多水。
The boy who broke the window is called Mike.(作主语)打碎玻璃的男孩叫迈克。
Harry is the boy whose mother is our English teacher.
(作定语)哈利的妈妈是我们的英语老师。

注1:that/which 在从句中作主语时,不能省略;作宾语时在口语和非正式文体中常省略,whom 也常省略。
注2:which/whom 作介词宾语时,可一并提到从句前。如:
The man to whom you talked is a famous writer. 那个与你交谈的人是一个著名作家。
The factory in which he work caught fire yesterday. 他上班的那家工厂昨天着火了。

(二)关系副词:when/where/why
when 指时间;where 指地点;why 指原因。如:
I still remember the day when I first came here. 我仍然记着我刚来的那天。
This is the house where we lived last year. 这是我们去年住的房子。
There are some reasons why we can't do that. 这些是我们不能做的原因。

(三)限定性定语从句和非限定性定语从句
1. 限定性定语从句是先行词在意义上不可缺少的定语。如去掉,主句意思就不完整或失去意义,限定性定语从句和主句的关系密切。如:
She has found the watch(that)she lost two days ago. 她找到了她两天前丢的表。
The accident happened on the day when I lost my job. 事故发生在我失业那天。

2. 非限定性定语从句和主句的关系不十分密切,只是对先行词做些附加说明。如果去掉,主句意思仍然很清楚。非限定性定语从句和主句之间常用逗号隔开,不用 that 引导。如:
Helen,who is sitting on my left,said that she would go back to the U. S. A.
坐在我左边的海伦说她将回美国去。
Dinner starts with a small dish,which is called a starter.
正餐以一小碟菜开始,这碟菜叫开胃菜。
Hunan,where I was born,is a developed province.
湖南,我所出生的地方,是一个发达省份。

拓展1:as 作关系代词引导定语从句,与 as/so/such/the same 搭配连用。如:
We'll meet at the same place as we did. 我们将在老地方见面。
Changsha is not the same as it used to be. 长沙不是过去的长沙了。
We have never seen such a thing as we met. 我们从未见过这等事。

拓展2:句型 the same...as(表类似)/the same...that(表同一人/物)。如:
That is the same bag as she lost. 那个包与她所丢失的包类似。(与丢失的类似)

That is the same bag that she lost. 那个包就是她所丢失的那个。（同一个包）

拓展3：such...as 与 such...that。如：

It is such a simple problem as I can solve. 这是我能解决的简单的问题。（定语从句）

It is such a simple problem that I can solve it. 这问题如此简单，我能解决。（状语从句）

拓展4：as 和 which 可以引导一个句子，作定语从句的先行词。which 在非限定性定语从句中可代替前面整个句子，只能放在主句后面，但 as 更灵活，可放主句前或主句后。如：

As we all know, the earth is round.

我们大家都知道，地球是圆的。（非限定性定语从句，as 代替 the earth is round 这一内容）

Lin Tao was late again, which/as was natural.

林涛又迟到了，这一点是自然的。（which/as 代替 Lin Tao was late again 这一内容）

拓展5：当先行词为 way 表示方式方法时，可用 in which 或 that 引导，that 可省略。如：

This is the way in which/(that) he has succeeded in training.

这就是他在训练中取得成功的方法。

拓展6：先行词与引导词的定位：Is it/this + the 先行词 + that 从句/名词 + 先行词。如：

Is this hotel the one that you visited/where/in which you stayed?

这是你旅游时留宿的那个酒店吗？

此句有点复杂，其实还原成陈述句便一目了然，即：

This hotel is the one that you visited/where/in which you stayed.

拓展7：强调句与定语从句的区别：如果将 it is/was...that/who... 抽掉，剩下的还是个完整句子，则一定是强调句，因为强调句是把 it is/was...that/who... 安插到一个完整句子中去，强调各个部分的，所以抽掉后句意仍完整。如：

①It is I who am looking for you. 我正在找你。

②It is the place that she was born in. 这就是她出生的地方。

很明显，例①是强调句，因去掉 it is...who 后，剩下 I am looking for you. 是个完整句子；例②则是定语从句，去掉 it is...that 后不成立。

拓展8：关系代词 that/which，关系副词 who/whom 等的特殊用法。

(1)先行词为不定代词 all, much, something, nothing, the one 等时，只能用 that。如：

I'll tell you something that happened just now. 我要告诉你刚刚发生的事情。

(2)先行词被 the only, very, no, little, few, any one of, last 等修饰时，只能用 that。如：

The only thing that he can do is to leave the place. 他唯一能做的事是离开这个地方。

(3)先行词被序数词和最高级所修饰或本身就是序数词或最高级时，只能用 that。如：

This is the first/last foreign novel that I have read.

这是我读过的第一本/最后一本外国小说。

(4)先行词既有人又有物时，只能用 that。如：

We are talking about the person and things that happened in the film.

我们正在谈论影片里发生的人和事。

(5)在含 who 等的问句中，只能用 that 引导定语从句。如：

Who is the man that is looking for you? 正在找你的那个人是谁？

(6)被修饰的词为数词时，只能用 that。如：

He has two sons;people often see the two that quarrel about toys.
他有两个儿子,常因为玩具而争吵。

(7)主句是 there be 结构,定语从句的主语是物时,只能用 that。如:
There are some beautiful pictures that are on sale in that shop.
那个商店有很多漂亮的画在促销。

(8)如果两个定语从句,其中一个用了关系代词 which,另一个则用 that 以避免重复。如:
They are running a company which sells marble tables that are famous in China.
They are running a company that sells marble tables which are famous in China.
他们在经营一家销售大理石桌子的公司,他们的大理石桌子在中国很有名。

(9)定语从句中用 which,而不用 that 的情况。关系代词前有介词时,只用 which,不用 that,如 in which。如:
This is that factory in which workers make marble tables.
这就是工人们制造大理石桌子的工厂。

(10)非限定性定语从句中,只能用 which,且 which 前用逗句将主句与从句分开。如:
The boy has passed the exam,which made his family very happy.
男孩通过了考试,这让全家都很高兴。
This is her house,which was built last year. 这就是她去年修建的房子。

(11)先行词是 that,those 时,只能用 which。如:
What's that which glitters in your pocket? 你口袋里闪亮的东西是什么?

(12)定语从句中,先行词为 one/ones/anyone/all/those 时,用 who,不用 that。如:
Anyone who works hard will get his own back. 任何努力耕耘的人将获得回报。

(13)There be 句型,主语是人时,用 who(whom)。如:
There is a stranger who wants to see you. 这儿有一个陌生人想见你。

(14)两个定语从句(先行词指人)一个用了 that,另一个用 who 避免重复。如:
The teacher that was praised at the meeting who is our English teacher will go abroad.
会上受到表扬的那个老师是我们的英语老师,她将要出国了。

(15)先行词是人称代词时,用 who。如:
He who makes no mistakes makes nothing. 什么事都不干,当然不会犯错误。

(16)介词 + 关系代词:定语从句中只有两个关系代词 which 和 whom 可与介词搭配,介词可前置,也可后置。后置时,可替换成其他关系代词。如:
We've come to the city in which they live. 我们来到了他们所居住的城市。(in which = where)
The novel about which we talk is on sale. 我们谈论的那本小说正在促销。
He is the teacher from whom we have learned a lot.
他就是那位我们从他那学到很多东西的老师。

(17)定语从句可由"名词/代词/数词 + 介词 + which/whom"引出。如:
The car the door of which was damaged is being repaired. 车门受损的那辆车正在修理中。

写作指导

写求职信

求职信是日常生活中较为常用的一种应用文体。求职信是以书信的方式,介绍、推销自己,从而达到谋职的目的。求职信属于商业信函(Business Letters),写信的态度应是严肃认真的。具体应注意:

第一,简洁、明了。求职信要突出求职主题,开场应直截了当。介绍个人情况时除年龄、学历、所学专业、工作经历及特长等必须说明以外,尽可能不要写与求职无关的事情。

第二,求实、自信。写求职信时应如实介绍自己的情况,实话实说。千万不要夸夸其谈,过分渲染自己,否则会给人留下浮躁不踏实的感觉。当然,故作谦卑也是不可取的,应充满自信。

第三,工整、美观。英语中有句谚语:Dress makes the man.(佛要金装,人要衣装。)因此,求职信的"外表"也很重要。一封书写工整、字迹美观的求职信无疑会给人留下深刻的印象。这一点与高考对书面表达卷面的要求是吻合的。

第四,求职信属于正式文体,在语言的运用上应尽可能避免使用口头语。

下列一些常见表达法可供参与:

1. 开头。说明写求职信的缘由与动机。如:

(1) I wish to apply for the job you are offering in... 本人希望获得贵单位在……上所提供的工作。

(2) Learning from... that you are looking for..., I should like to apply for the post. 从……那里获悉,贵处正在招聘一名……,本人愿应聘此职。

(3) I'm writing in the hopes that you will be able to offer me a summer job. 本人写此信,希望贵公司能提供给我一份暑假工作。

2. 中间。介绍个人情况。如:

(1) I graduated from... in... 本人于××年毕业于××(学校)。

(2) I am majoring in.../My major is... 本人主修(我的专业是)××。

(3) I am experienced in operating computers. 本人熟悉计算机操作。

(4) I'm twenty-eight and have had four years' experience in my present post as a... 本人今年28岁,曾有4年……(岗位)的经验。

3. 结尾。询问参加面试的时间或说明联系方式。另外,在结尾处要加上一句客套话。如:

(1) I shall be glad to call for an interview at any time. 本人很乐意在任何时候前来面试。

(2) I hope to have the pleasure of an interview. 本人希望有幸获得面试机会。

(3) I look forward to your call at 123456789./I would appreciate your call at 123456789. 恭候您的电话。我的电话号码是123456789。

(4) Yours respectfully/faithfully/truly... ××× 敬启

如:

假如你叫刘梅,是上海市五一路一家工厂的秘书。2017年3月19日,你在《人民日报》

上看到了某企业刊登的招聘英语秘书的广告。请根据下列提示,用英语写一封求职信。

出生日期:1996年8月5日　　　　　　健康状况:良好

教育程度:本科　　　　　　　　　　　学校:上海大学　2013年至今

外语水平:擅长英文写作;英语口语好,在校期间获全校英语竞赛一等奖。

业务爱好:读书、写作、听音乐。

联系电话:123456789

注意:(1)要点齐全,切忌逐字翻译;(2)词数:100;(3)生词提示:apply for 申请;post 工作;职位。

Wuyi Road,Shanghai
March 19th

Dear Sir,

　　Today I read your advertisement in *People's Daily*. I'd like to apply for the post as an English secretary.

　　I was born on August 5th, 1996. I went to Shanghai University in 2013 and I am studying there. Now I want to work as a secretary in your company. I'm in good health.

　　I can write well in English and my oral English is excellent. I once won the first prize in an English contest held in our university. In my spare time I enjoy reading, writing and listening to music.

　　If you think I am the right person, please give me a telephone call. My number is 123456789. I hope to have the pleasure of an interview.

Yours sincerely,
Liu Mei

A. 基础层次

Ⅰ. 按要求做题

1. 用对应的英语填空。

_____	另外的,附加的	_____	做广告
_____	申请	_____	申请,求职
_____	欣赏,感激	_____	可用的
_____	具有挑战性的	_____	联系
_____	合作的,协作的	_____	合作的,协作的
_____	经验丰富的,有经验的	_____	公平的,公正的;展览会
_____	全职的(地)	_____	招聘广告
_____	指示,说明书	_____	面试
_____	主要的;专业	_____	机会,时机
_____	好交际的,外向的	_____	加班时间
_____	兼职的(地)	_____	个人的,私人的

_____ 个性,性格　　　　　　_____ 职位
_____ 个人简历　　　　　　　_____ 能胜任……
_____ 处理　　　　　　　　　_____ 取得成功
_____ 努力工作的,勤奋的

2. 思考与问答。
(1) Do you have any work experience? _____.
(2) What job do you like best? _____.
(3) How many fans do you have? _____.
(4) What are you going to do after graduation? _____.
(5) Do you know the world fair? _____.

Ⅱ．按要求完成下列各题
1. This is the house which I bought last year. (翻译)→_____
2. This movie is as interesting as that one. (翻译)→_____
3. Is there anything _____ (关系代词填空) I can do for you?
4. I long for a moment _____ (关系副词填空) I can have a good rest.
5. They have found a good place _____ (关系副词填空) they can do some exercise.

Ⅲ．课堂效应检测:用英语在下面指定处小结你学本单元的收获体会
_____
_____
_____
_____
_____
_____
_____

B. 拓展层次

Ⅰ．单项选择题
1. Would you mind _____ a little English at the interview about your work experience?
   A. speaking　　B. saying　　C. to speak　　D. said
2. I can work overtime and I'm sure that I can get along _____ others.
   A. well in　　B. well with　　C. good with　　D. good in
3. You may be just the person _____ we've been looking for.
   A. whom　　B. which　　C. what　　D. whose
4. I'm writing to _____ the position of secretary to general manager that you advertised in it.
   A. apply to　　B. apply for　　C. application for　　D. wish
5. I graduated _____ Shanghai Technical Institute of Tourism & Commerce in 2013, majoring in English.
   A. from　　B. in　　C. at　　D. to

6. What have you _____ with the dispute(纠纷) between them?
   A. dealt　　　　B. had　　　　C. working　　　　D. done
7. I believe that I am qualified _____ this work.
   A. at　　　　B. in　　　　C. for doing　　　　D. to
8. I hope to have an opportunity to meet with you for a personal interview and look forward to _____ me.
   A. reply to　　　　B. reply　　　　C. replies to　　　　D. replying to
9. These young teachers are experienced _____ teaching and working.
   A. on　　　　B. at　　　　C. of　　　　D. with
10. If you go to New York and want to enjoy plays or night clubs, you may go to _____.
    A. London　　　　B. Paris　　　　C. Broadway　　　　D. Shanghai
11. The film brought the hours back to me _____ I was taken good care of in that far away village.
    A. until　　　　B. that　　　　C. when　　　　D. where
12. It was about 200 years ago _____ the first clock with a face and an hour hand was made.
    A. that　　　　B. until　　　　C. before　　　　D. when
13. Can you see a man and his horse _____ are crossing the bridge?
    A. which　　　　B. who　　　　C. that　　　　D. they
14. There are several story books _____ *Red Star* is the best one _____ I have ever read.
    A. whose; that
    B. which; that
    C. of which; that
    D. of which; as
15. All of the flowers now raised by her have developed from those _____ in the forest.
    A. once they
    B. they grew once
    C. that once grew
    D. once grew
16. So I act in hospitals and I play the _____ a patient for medical students.
    A. parts of　　　　B. models of　　　　C. stick of　　　　D. role of

Ⅱ. 交际用语:选择题
1. —Will you be free tomorrow?
   —_____.
   A. I think this
   B. All right, I think so
   C. OK, I'll be free then
   D. Yes, I think so
2. —Would you like some more vegetables?
   —_____.
   A. Thank you. I've had enough
   B. Yes, please
   C. They are delicious
   D. Do please
3. —I'm sorry I can't follow you. Would you please speak more slowly?
   —_____

A. Why say so? B. Really?
C. OK. I will. D. It's impossible.

4. —No smoking, please.
   —_____
   A. Tell me the reasons. B. Why so?
   C. OK, we won't. D. It's impossible.

5. —Thank you all the same.
   —_____
   A. OK. B. Sorry. C. It's nothing. D. Really?

Ⅲ. 阅读理解：判断题

Today we are going to talk about the climate of the United States. The United States has many different kinds of climates. On the west coast, the temperature changes very little between summer and winter. In the north central states, people wear light clothing in the winter. In the southwest, the climate is pleasantly warm during winter, but summer is hot. In the eastern part of the United States, summer is usually hot and winter is usually cold. Spring is comfortably warm and autumn is pleasantly cool. Years ago, people in the cold parts of the United States did not often eat fresh vegetables and fresh fruits during winter. Today, however, trucks and trains carry fruits and vegetables very quickly to all parts of the United States. In this way, Americans send their climates to people in other states.

1. The United States has quite a few different kinds of climates.

2. On the west coast, the temperature changes very much between summer and winter.

3. In the southwest, the climate is pleasantly warm during winter, but spring is hot.

4. Years ago, people in the cold parts of the United States often ate fresh vegetables and fresh fruits during winter.

5. Today, however, trucks and trains carry fruits and vegetables very quickly to all parts of the United States.

Ⅳ. 根据括号里的中文填空

1. The bus was _____(挤满)a lot of people that day.

2. Would you mind _____(说点什么)about your work experience?

3. Well, you might be _____(正是其人)whom we've been looking for.

4. He is writing to _____(申请)the position of secretary to general manager.

5. They are all looking forward to _____(你的到来)at the party.

Ⅴ. 写作

Write an application letter.

_____
_____
_____

Unit 7　The convenience store is over there.

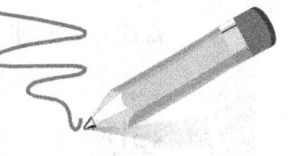

目标攻略

1. 培养良好的交际能力：社区服务交际等；
2. 认知本单元所有词汇；能正确运用重点词汇，如 aid，apartment，clinic，educational，equip，service，community center，get used to，be involved in 等及相关电话用语；
3. 背诵"Everyday English"；
4. 掌握语法：定语从句；
5. 简单介绍社区情况。

知识解析

Ⅰ．词汇

(1) on/at/weekends 在周末。
(2) used to do something 过去习惯做某事；be/get used to + n./doing something 现在习惯（做）某事。
(3) require/want/need + doing something 需要被做……
(4) aid 帮助。aid earthquake victims 救助地震灾民；come to somebody's aid 帮助某人；aid somebody with money 资助某人。
(5) equip with 装备，设备，配备。
(6) follow the rules 守规。
(7) be responsible for 对……负责。

Ⅱ．句式

(1) The convenience store is over there. 便利店就在那边。
(2) He was appointed manager. 他被任命为经理。
(3) All the classrooms are equipped with a new color TV set.
　　所有教室都配备了一台新彩电。
(4) The girl is similar to Lily in many ways. 这个女孩和莉莉很多方面类似。

(5) Residents agree to follow the rules when they buy their homes.

业主买房时同意遵守规矩。

(6) The committee of the body corporate is elected by the owners each year.

业主委员会每年由业主选择一次。

(7) It's about a ten-minute walk from here.

离这儿大约步行 10 分钟的路程。

解题引领

1. What I like most is the community high school _____ my daughter studies.
   A. that　　　　B. which　　　　C. in which　　　　D. whose

   答案为 C。点拨：先行词是表地点的词(the community high school)，关系词用 where 或介词 + which 来引导定语从句。

2. Could you tell me the time _____ the community center opens?
   A. in that　　　B. that　　　　C. which　　　　D. at which

   答案为 D。点拨：先行词是表时间的词(the time)，关系词用 when 或介词 + which 来引导定语从句。(注：定语从句中引导词没有介词 + that 这种说法)

3. He, as well as I _____ often kept in the classroom after school.
   A. am　　　　B. is　　　　　C. are　　　　　D. were

   答案为 B。点拨：由 as well as 连接两个主语时，谓语动词要与前面主语保持一致。

语法点睛

定语从句(续)

参见前面单元的阐述。

写作指导

说明文

阐述(略)

描写你或你朋友所在社区的一些常规情况。

同步训练

A. 基础层次

Ⅰ．按要求做题

1. 用对应的英语填空。

＿＿＿＿＿＿帮助,援助	＿＿＿＿＿＿公寓
＿＿＿＿＿＿任命,委派	＿＿＿＿＿＿咖啡馆,小餐馆
＿＿＿＿＿＿诊所	＿＿＿＿＿＿小区,群体
＿＿＿＿＿＿课程	＿＿＿＿＿＿教育的
＿＿＿＿＿＿装备,配备	＿＿＿＿＿＿设施,装备
＿＿＿＿＿＿自由的,免费的,空闲的	＿＿＿＿＿＿功能,作用
＿＿＿＿＿＿食品杂货(店)	＿＿＿＿＿＿体育馆,健身房
＿＿＿＿＿＿理想的	＿＿＿＿＿＿改善,改进
＿＿＿＿＿＿图书馆	＿＿＿＿＿＿邻居
＿＿＿＿＿＿项目,工程	＿＿＿＿＿＿休息,放松
＿＿＿＿＿＿需要,规定	＿＿＿＿＿＿服务
＿＿＿＿＿＿相似的	＿＿＿＿＿＿成人学校
＿＿＿＿＿＿和,也,又	＿＿＿＿＿＿参与
＿＿＿＿＿＿小区活动中心	＿＿＿＿＿＿习惯于
＿＿＿＿＿＿野餐	＿＿＿＿＿＿邮局

2. 思考与问答。

(1) Do you remember the day when we have been friends? ＿＿＿＿＿＿＿＿＿＿＿＿＿＿．

(2) Are you living in a big neighborhood? ＿＿＿＿＿＿＿＿＿＿＿＿＿＿＿＿＿＿＿＿＿．

(3) Do you like your neighborhood? ＿＿＿＿＿＿＿＿＿＿＿＿＿＿＿＿＿＿＿＿＿＿＿．

(4) Would you please tell me something about your community? ＿＿＿＿＿＿＿＿＿＿．

(5) Do you get on well with your neighbors? ＿＿＿＿＿＿＿＿＿＿＿＿＿＿＿＿＿＿．

Ⅱ．按要求完成下列各题

1. What I like most is the community high school. (翻译)→ ＿＿＿＿＿＿＿＿＿＿＿＿＿

2. What I like most is the community high school ＿＿＿＿＿＿ my daughter studies. (填空)

3. Sometimes we have a picnic on weekends ＿＿＿＿＿＿ we are free. (填空)

4. He, as well as I ＿＿＿＿＿＿ kept in the classroom after school. (填空)

5. body corporate (翻译)→ ＿＿＿＿＿＿＿＿＿＿＿＿＿＿＿＿＿＿＿＿＿＿＿＿＿＿＿

Ⅲ．课堂效应检测:用英语在下面指定处小结你学本单元的收获体会

＿＿＿

＿＿＿

＿＿＿

B. 拓展层次

Ⅰ. 单项选择题

1. Walk along this road to the end and the convenience store is _____.
   A. coming over   B. on the way   C. here   D. over there
2. Is there any place _____ I can exercise, Mr. White?
   A. which   B. what   C. where   D. when
3. By the way, could you tell me the time _____ the community center opens?
   A. where   B. how   C. which   D. when
4. When an earthquake happens, we should _____ the quake victims.
   A. give up   B. aim at   C. be helpful   D. aid
5. _____ I like most is the community high school _____ my daughter studies.
   A. Which; which   B. Where; which   C. What; where   D. How; which
6. They suggested that they _____ a place to exchange the working experience.
   A. appointing   B. appoint   C. appointed   D. would appoint
7. In our school all the classrooms are equipped _____ a color TV set.
   A. of   B. to   C. with   D. on
8. We shouldn't _____ our attention to our studies.
   A. pay   B. relax   C. throw   D. give in
9. Look! Those flowers require _____ at once.
   A. to water   B. watering   C. watered   D. to be watering
10. She, as well as you _____ kind and beautiful.
    A. are   B. are to be   C. is   D. is to be
11. The persons and the things _____ they are talking about made us interested.
    A. which   B. who   C. whom   D. that
12. This is the last house _____ the soldiers searched last night.
    A. which   B. that   C. whom   D. what
13. Miss Lee is one of the beautiful girls _____ English well in this university.
    A. who speaks   B. who speak   C. who is speaking   D. which speak
14. Miss Lee is the only one of the beautiful girls _____ English well in this university.
    A. who speak   B. who speaks   C. who are speaking   D. that speak
15. It is the little mountain village _____ she has ever worked with the farmers.
    A. which   B. in which   C. that   D. on which

Ⅱ. 交际用语：选择题

1. —I got the first place in the math contest.
   —_____
   A. Good luck.   B. Congratulations.   C. Good idea.   D. Really?
2. —I want to see a doctor, Mr. Smith.
   —_____

A. What's wrong with you?   B. What?
C. Oh, really?   D. What a shame!

3. —Shall we go swimming this afternoon?

   —_____.

   A. What's wrong with you?   B. All right.
   C. It doesn't matter.   D. Sorry, I don't think.

4. —How are you getting along with your studies?

   —_____.

   A. Not too bad.   B. Why asking so?
   C. Don't ask me.   D. Oh? I don't know.

5. —May you succeed in your studies.

   —_____.

   A. Don't say so   B. I'm sorry I can't   C. Thanks to you   D. Thanks

Ⅲ. 阅读理解：判断题

The music business is very difficult to succeed in 9 out of 10 bands that have made their first record fail to produce a second. Surviving in the music industry requires luck and patience, but most of all it requires a full knowledge of how a record company functions. The signing of a recording contract(合同) is a slow process. The record company will spend a long time investigating the band and current tide in popular music; during this period, it is important that a band exchange an investigation of its own, learning as much as possible about the company and making personal connections within the different departments that will handle their recordings. A record company's search for new talent usually begins by sending a representative of the Artists and Repertoire(A&R) department to visit bars and night clubs scouting for young, talented bands. When the representative finds a promising band, he or she will work to negotiate(谈判) a contract and make the recording arrangements. Once a band has finished recording the album, the Publicity and Promotions department takes over and decides whether or not to mass produce and market the band's album. This is where many bands go wrong. They fail to make personal connections in this second department, thus losing their voice in the final process of producing and marketing their album. This loss of voice often contributes to the band's failure as a recording group.

1. In the writer's opinion, most bands fail in the music industry because they don't fully understand how a record company functions.

2. The band must try to get in touch with different departments.

3. The phrase "scouting for" is close to "searching for" in meaning.

4. Many bands still fail after they finished recording albums because they are found not promising in the end.

5. The band must wait patiently without doing anything.

Ⅳ. 根据括号里的中文填空

1. I like the adult school, where I can go to _____(提高英语) or learn some job skills.

2. It is only _____ (5分钟的步行路程) from my apartment.

3. What I like most is the community high school _____ (在那里) my daughter studies.

4. When the earthquake happened, all the people were _____ (拯救) earthquake victims.

5. Lily is _____ (同……相似) Rose in many ways.

V．写作

Complete a weather forecast according to the Chinese information.

天气是英美人士喜爱谈论的话题之一，一是因为它与人们日常活动密切相关；二是因为它是一个安全的话题：不涉及政治、宗教和隐私。下面请你为湖南省气象台播报相关天气情况。湖南气候特征：冬冷夏热，典型的亚热带气候，冬季平均气温 11.6 ℃，最低气温达零下 12 ℃，最高气温达 43 ℃。年平均降雨量 1 500 mm，年平均降雨日 150 天左右。

Good morning, everyone. The climate in Hunan is being forecasted as follows：

Hunan, which lies in the inland, belongs to the typical subtropical zone/semi-tropics, and so it's cold in winter with __1__ of 12 ℃ below zero and hot in summer with __2__ of 43 ℃, __3__ is 11.6 ℃ in winter. Hunan is also humid, with __4__ on the average every year and the __5__ of 1,500 mm.

Unit 8　That's how most accidents happen.

目标攻略

1. 培养良好的交际能力：提建议、警告、询问和获取安全信息；
2. 认知本单元所有词汇；能正确运用重点词汇，如 absent-minded, belongings, traffic signs, break into, license 等及预防车祸；
3. 背诵"Everyday English"；
4. 掌握语法：表语从句；
5. 学写安全说明。

知识解析

Ⅰ．词汇

(1) basic 基本。some basic facts 一些基本事实；basic requirements 基本要求；basic pay 基本工资；get back to basics 回到基本事实上来。

(2) alert 警惕的。be alert to 对……保持警惕；on alert 处于警戒状态；on the alert 警惕着。如：

We should be alert to danger. 我们应当对危险保持警惕。

(3) inform 通知。inform somebody of something 通知某人某事；inform somebody that clause... 通知某人……

(4) management 管理。personnel management 人事管理；household management 家务处理。

(5) pay attention to 注意……（其中 to 为介词）。

(6) the more... the better... 是比较级 + 比较级的用法，表示"越……就越……"。

(7) keep... in mind 牢记。

(8) speed up 加速。

(9) result in 导致，结果，产生，发生；result from 发生，产生。

Ⅱ．句式

(1) That's how most accidents happen. 大多数车祸都是由此发生的。

(2) The more you know about driving, the better you can control your car in a dangerous road situation. 驾驶知识你了解得越多,你就越能在危险路况下控制好你的车子。

(3) If you keep some of this advice in mind when you are on the roads, you can avoid most car accidents. 如果当你开车上路时能牢记这些建议,你就能避免多数车祸。

(4) Please pay attention to your pronunciation. 请注意发音。

(5) Did you inform him his uncle's coming back? 你把他叔叔回来的事告诉他了吗?

(6) Watch out for falling objects, please. 请注意坠物。

(7) You can't pass if you go on like that. 如果你这样下去是不会通过的。

(8) Will you keep an eye on my child for a while? 替我照料一下孩子好吗?

(9) So we have put together some useful advice to help you prevent a car accident. 因此,我们已整理了一些有益建议帮助你防止车祸发生。

(10) Floods resulted from heavy rains. 洪水因大雨造成。

(11) Regularly check if your brakes are working well. 定期检查你的刹车是否灵验。

(12) We believe that if you keep some of this advice in mind when you are on the roads, you can avoid most car accidents. 我们相信如果你在公路上行驶时能牢记这些建议,你就会避免多数车祸。

解题引领

1. That's _____ most accidents happen at present.
   A. when   B. what   C. how   D. which

答案为 C。点拨:表语从句中的 happen 为不及物动词,不带宾语,故排除 B、D 选项;at present 已经表述了时间,故排除 A。

2. Copies of keys are just _____ thieves use to break into an apartment.
   A. how   B. whom   C. what   D. why

答案为 C。点拨:表语从句中 thieves 为主语,use 为谓语,并且是及物动词,须有宾语;to break into an apartment 是动词不定式作状语。因此,空白中应填一个代替 keys 的词,用 keys 来开门,故选 C。

语法点睛

表语从句

表语从句属于名词性从句的一种。详细情况请参见前面单元的阐述。

写作指导

标示用语简介

带客人参观某地时,一般是边走边介绍,尤其是有特色的建筑物。

根据课文要求写一段带客人参观某地的短文。
_____
_____
_____
_____

同步训练

A. 基础层次

Ⅰ．按要求做题

1. 用对应的英语填空。

_____不在意的,心不在焉的	_____事故
_____属于	_____交通标志
_____附属品,物品	_____紧急情况,突发事件
_____出口	_____通知,告知
_____执照	_____管理
_____两个,几个	_____闯入,破门而入
_____留神,注意	_____保证,确保
_____速度限制	_____基本的

2. 思考与问答。

(1) Is that how most accidents happen? _____.
(2) Did you watch TV last night? _____.
(3) Do you often use the zebra crossing when you cross the road? _____.
(4) Do you often stay alert when you enter your apartment? _____.
(5) Do you leave notes for roommates or guests on your door? _____.

Ⅱ．按要求完成下列各题

1. Don't talk on your cell phone or look absent-minded when walking to your building after dark. (翻译)→_____
2. Will you keep _____ (an eye/eye/eyes) on my child for a while? (选词填空)
3. in case of emergency (翻译)→_____
4. be alert to danger (翻译)→_____
5. Do you often talk to strangers? (回答)→_____.

Ⅲ．课堂效应检测：用英语在下面指定处小结你学本单元的收获体会

_____
_____
_____
_____

B. 拓展层次

I. 单项选择题

1. That's _____ most accidents happen.
   A. which   B. how   C. whenever   D. what
2. Remember, copies of keys are what thieves use to _____ an apartment.
   A. break through   B. break into   C. break out   D. rush in
3. Will you keep _____ on my child for a while, Mrs. White?
   A. eye   B. an ear   C. an eye   D. a nose
4. Did you _____ Mr. Zhang of his daughter coming back from the U.S.A?
   A. inform   B. notice   C. speak   D. know
5. The more you know about driving, _____ you can control your car in a dangerous road situation.
   A. better   B. worse   C. the better   D. the worse
6. If you keep some of the advice _____, you can avoid most car accidents.
   A. on mind   B. in your mind   C. in mind   D. at mind
7. Your hands should be at 9:00 and 3:00 on the wheel _____ you can have a good control in danger.
   A. because   B. unless   C. so that   D. or else
8. Sorry I can't go there with you because I have a _____ visitors to meet this afternoon.
   A. some   B. little of   C. couple of   D. several
9. This is _____ she always came late to school.
   A. that   B. what   C. why   D. when
10. He told us that it was _____ he used to live 28 years ago.
    A. when   B. where   C. that   D. what

II. 交际用语：选择题

1. —Would you like to join us in the party?
   —_____.
   A. With pleasure   B. I'd like to, but I'm busy
   C. Thanks for your invitation   D. Good idea
2. —We are all going to take part in the contest.
   —_____.
   A. Well done   B. Good luck
   C. Congratulations   D. Enjoy yourself
3. —We had a good time at your party.
   —_____.
   A. I'm glad that you enjoyed it   B. Thank you
   C. Good party   D. Well done

4. —How beautiful it is!
   —_____.
   A. You are right　　B. Me, too　　C. I agree with you　　D. A or C

5. —You look so unhappy! Why?
   —_____.
   A. I lost some money　　　　　　B. No, I don't
   C. No doubt that I'm happy　　　D. You, too

Ⅲ. 阅读理解：判断题

In the United States in recent years, camping has become very popular. Every summer, thousands of families leave the cities behind to spend weekends or vacations outdoors. Some families take along trailers. Others load their cars with tents, small stoves and air-filled mattresses. Then they drive to one of the country's campgrounds.

Most campgrounds in the United States are publicly owned. The national parks and many national monuments and national forests have land for campers. State governments also run campgrounds in state-owned parks and forests.

A few years ago, campers could always find room to camp in a public campground. But today, state-owned campgrounds are often overcrowded. To meet the needs of the every-growing number of campers, some businessmen are opening private campgrounds to campers. The campers usually pay more money than they pay at state-owned grounds. But many private parks offer more services and give more people the chance to enjoy camping.

1. In the United States in recent years, camping has become very popular.

2. Thousands of families leave the cities behind to spend weekends or vacations outdoors per fall.

3. Most campgrounds in the United States are publicly owned.

4. The national parks and many national rivers and national forests have land for campers.

5. To meet the needs of the every-growing number of campers, some businessmen are opening public campgrounds to campers.

Ⅳ. 根据括号里的中文填空

1. That's _____（大多数[车祸]由此[引起]）accidents happen.

2. You should _____（注意）the traffic lights and the traffic signs on the road.

3. Remember, in many cases, copies of keys are what thieves use to _____（破门而入）an apartment.

4. Stay _____（警惕）danger when you enter your apartment.

5. Did you _____（通知/告诉他）of his uncle coming back?

Ⅴ. 写作

Complete the following poster.

海报：篮球友谊赛

下周星期六（6月6日）下午3:00 学校将在校篮球场举行高三年级对高二年级的篮球

赛,欢迎全体同学观赏。

        __1__(海报:篮球友谊赛)
          __2__(6月6日,星期六)
  __3__(由我校组织)our school, a friendly basketball match __4__(将被举行)between the Teams of Grade 3 and Grade 2 on the basketball court at 3:00 p.m. on Saturday, June 6th. All the students __5__(受欢迎).

                     The School Office

Unit 9　Is your company going to the fashion fair in Shanghai?

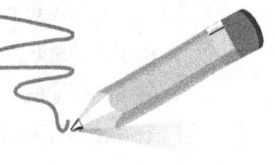

目标攻略

1. 培养良好的交际能力：申请加入时装展览等；
2. 认知本单元所有词汇；能正确运用重点词汇，如 arrangement，ceremony，committee，international，fashion fair，opening ceremony，media 等及加入时装展览会的方法等；
3. 背诵"Everyday English"；
4. 掌握语法：分词作定语；
5. 学写时装表演说明。

知识解析

Ⅰ．词汇

(1) be going to do something 计划做……，打算做……。

(2) not only...but also 不但……而且……，其中的 but 和 also 可省略其中一个。

(3) contest/match 比赛。contest 多指知识方面的比赛，match 多指运动方面的比赛。如：
math contest 数学竞赛；basketball match 篮球比赛

(4) fashion/trend/style 时尚。be in(the)fashion/style/trend 合乎时尚；
be out of(the)fashion/style/trend 不合时尚；
follow(the)fashion 赶时髦。

(5) trend 趋势，走向，倾向，动向，动态。如：
an upward trend of prices 物价上涨趋势；
trends in the teaching of foreign language 外语教学的趋势。

(6) casual 偶然的，不定期的。a casual meeting 巧遇；a casual visitor 不速之客。

(7) the forefront of fashion 时尚最前沿；UV protection 紫外线保护（UV = ultraviolet）；
infrared rays 红外线。

(8) as well/too/also/either 也。

(9) be born to 生来就处于……状况。

(10) stick out 伸出，突出，显眼；坚持要求。

Ⅱ．句式

（1）Is your company going to the fashion fair in Shanghai?
你们公司计划参加上海的服装展览会吗？

（2）Yes, I have just reserved a booth. 是的,我刚刚订了一个展位。

（3）...which lead the latest fashion trends not only in clothing, but also in jewelry and shoes in the Asia-Pacific region. 在亚太地区不仅在服装方面而且在珠宝和鞋业方面均引领最新时尚。

（4）Today's trend is toward less formal clothing. 时下流行穿便装。

（5）The trend of the coastline is to the south. 海岸线向南延伸。

（6）Fewer children are born to older parents nowadays.
如今很少有孩子出生在老年父母家里了。

（7）The kids were born to wealth. 这些孩子生来就富有。

（8）Besides, they cooperate very well with various media organizations.
加之,他们同各种媒体合作得非常好。

（9）The China International Fashion Fair is an international trade event taking place every summer. 中国国际时装交易会是一项国际性贸易活动,每年夏天举办一次。

（10）Famous designers such as Giorgio Armani, FENDI lead the masses in this historic city.
著名设计师,如吉奥吉奥·阿玛尼、芬迪,在这个历史悠久的城市里引领大众。

（11）Italy is home to the world's great designers, and now she is boldly taking her place to the forefront of fashion. 意大利是全球伟大设计师的摇篮,而现在她正大胆地把自己置于时尚最前沿。

解题引领

1. There _____ a fashion design contest and a modeling contest.
　　A. are going to be　　B. are　　　　C. is going to have　　D. is going to be
答案为 D。点拨:there be 句型中 be 是用 is 还是 are 决定于后面第一个名词,其中选项 C 句型不对,若去掉 is going to 后,就成了 there have 了。

2. About 70 _____ designers are showing their recent designs.
　　A. led　　　　　　B. leads　　　　　C. leading　　　　　D. being led
答案为 C。点拨:分词分为现在分词和过去分词两种;现在分词表主动和进行这个含义;过去分词则表被动和完成这个含义。

语法点睛

分　词

分词有现在分词和过去分词两种。现在分词加-ing 构成,和动名词相同;过去分词加-ed 构成,部分动词的过去分词有不规则变化。现在分词表主动与进行;过去分词表被动与完成。分词有形容词、副词和动词的功能,在句中可作定语、表语、状语、补语等。

现在分词有一般式和完成式及语态变化,过去分词只有一种形式,无时态和语态变化。如:

falling leaves 落叶(正在飘落的叶子);fallen leaves 落叶(已经落地的叶子)。
boiling water 开水(正在沸腾的开水);boiled water 开水(已开的水,可能凉了)。
developing country 发展中国家(正在发展);developed country 发达国家(发展完了)。

在语态方面,现在分词有主动含义,过去分词则有被动含义。如:

a moving story 动人的故事(故事本身具有动人的特征,能感动读者,故用现在分词);some moved audiences 一些被感动了的观众(观众被所看的内容感动了,有被动意义,故用过去分词)。

I saw someone entering the room. 我看到有个人(正在)进房间了。(主动)
I saw someone hit by a car. 我看到有个人被车撞了。(被动)

1. 分词作定语

(1)单个分词作定语一般前置,个别的过去分词作定语须后置。如:

She told us a very moving story. 她给我们讲述了一个非常动人的故事。(前置)
The frightened children couldn't help crying. 受惊的孩子们忍不住哭了起来。(前置)
There's a little time left. 时间所剩无几。(后置)

(2)分词短语作定语一般后置,相当于一个定语从句。如:

The book written by her sells well. 由她所著的这本书销量很好。(分词短语后置)
= The book which was written by her sells well.
The man talking with our headmaster is my brother. 与我们校长谈话的人是我哥哥。
= The man who is talking with our headmaster is my brother.

(3)分词修饰复合不定代词 something/anything/anybody 等及指示代词 those 时,须后置。如:

I have something interesting to tell you. 我有有趣的事要告诉你。(后置)
She is the last one of those hired. 她是雇佣人中的最后一名。

(4)现在分词一般不用作定语,但可作宾语补足语、状语。如:

Those being back at 11:00 in the evening must register. (×)
Those who are back at 11:00 in the evening must register. (√)
那些晚上11:00后回来的人必须登记。

2. 分词作表语

现在分词作表语,表示主语的特征;过去分词作表语,表示主语的状态。如:

The book is very interesting. 这本书很有意思。
I'm interested in the book. 我对这本书很感兴趣。
Jane felt very tired. 简感到很累。

注:现在分词作表语,表示"令人感到……";过去分词作表语,表示"感到……"。换言之,只有表示人的词作主语时,才可用过去分词作表语。

3. 分词作补语

现在分词作补语,表示动作正在进行;过去分词作补语,表示被动或动作完成。如:

I heard her singing in the room. 我听到她在房间里唱歌。(在进行)

I saw the thief taken away by the police. 我看到小偷被警察带走了。(动作完成)
He had his camera repaired. 他叫人修相机了。(被动)
He got the house painted. 他让人油漆房子了。(被动)

注1：have/get/leave 后既可接现在分词作补语，表示动作正在进行，也可接过去分词作补语，表示动作由别人完成。如：
He left his child taken care of. 他把孩子照顾好了。
They can't get the machine starting. 他们无法让机器运转。
He had his light burning all night long. 他的灯整夜亮着。(一直亮着)
She had her clothes washed. 她洗了衣服。

注2：一些感官动词，如 see/hear/watch/feel/listen/notice 等后既可接 doing，又可接(to) do，但有区别：不定式作补语强调不定式动作已完成，现在分词作补语表示动作正在进行。如：
We saw her come down. (已下来)
We saw her coming down. (正在下来)
I heard the baby cry. (哭过)
I heard the baby crying. (正在哭)

4. 分词作状语

现在分词作状语，句中主语为现在分词的动作执行者；过去分词作状语，句中主语为过去分词的动作承受者。现在分词作状语可表时间、原因、方式、伴随和结果，过去分词作状语可表时间、原因、条件、让步。这些表示时间、原因、条件的分词或分词短语相当于对应的状语从句。如：
Not believing what he said, I went out to investigate into it.
由于不相信他所说的话，我出去做调查了。
= Because I didn't believe what he said I went out to investigate into it.
Passing by the house he saw a woman playing the guitar.
他经过那所房子时，看见一个妇女在弹吉他。
= When he was passing by the house he saw a women playing the guitar.
Seeing the photo I couldn't help recollecting my childhood days.
看到这张照片，我情不自禁地想起我的童年岁月。
= When/After I saw the photo I couldn't help recollecting my childhood days.
Seen from the top of the hill, the village looks more beautiful.
从山顶看去，这村子显得更美丽。
= When/If the village is seen from the top of the hill, it looks more beautiful.

(1)现在分词作时间状语。如：
Hearing what she said, he couldn't help laughing walking out of the hotel, and I found my bike gone. 听到她说的话，他忍不住笑着走出了宾馆，我发现我的自行车不见了。
注：在由 when/while 引导的从句及条件句中，若从句主语与主句主语相同，又含有 be 动词的话，可省去从句主语和 be 动词，只保留连词与分词。如：
I must look out when crossing the road. 过马路时我必须小心。

When cooking in the kitchen he often listened to music. 当他在厨房做饭时常常听音乐。
I got to know him while working with him. 我和他一起工作时认识了他。
(2)现在分词作原因状语。如：
Being ill he didn't go to school yesterday. 因为生病,他昨天没去上学。
Not knowing how to go to the station he had to ask the policeman for help.
由于不知道怎么去车站,他只好向警察求助。
Learning that he was at home I went to meet him at once.
获悉他正好在家,我连忙去见他。
(3)现在分词作伴随/方式状语。如：
She sat on the bench reading. 她坐在长凳上阅读。(伴随)
They came to the sea talking in loud voices. 他们高声谈着来到海边。(伴随)
The boy came to school running. 这男孩是跑步到校的。(方式)
(4)现在分词作结果状语。如：
He died from the accident leaving his wife three poor children.
他死于车祸,给他妻子留下3个可怜的孩子。
He went out in a hurry forgetting to take the purse. 他急匆匆出门,结果忘了带钱包。
拓展：现在分词作状语的固定结构：
①judging from/by...从……判断；②generally speaking 一般说来；③turning to...转向；
④considering...考虑到……。如：
Judging by/from his appearance he can't be a worker. 从表面判断,他不可能是工人。
(5)过去分词作时间状语。如：
Heated to about 1,500 ℃, iron will be melted. 当铁加热到1 500 ℃左右,就会熔化。
(6)过去分词作原因状语。如：
Criticized by his father, he felt terrible. 由于受父亲批评,他感觉不舒服。
Inspired by the hero these students decided to do some good deeds.
受到英雄的鼓舞,这些学生决定做些好事。
(7)过去分词作条件状语。如：
Given more time, I would make much better achievement.
如果给我更多时间,我就会取得更好的成绩。
(8)过去分词作让步状语。如：
Hurt in the accident he insisted on going on working.
尽管在事故中受伤,他仍坚持继续工作。
(9)过去分词与现在分词作状语的区别在于：过去分词表被动完成的动作,现在分词表主动进行的动作。如：
Seen from the top of the hill the river looks like a snake.
从山顶上看,这条河看起来像条蛇。
(句子主语是the river,不能执行see的动作,所以只能是被看,seen 表被动与完成)
Seeing the river, I always recall a lot about my hometown.
看到这条河,我总会回想起许多与我家乡有关的事。

(句子主语是 I,是 seeing 动作的执行者,故用现在分词)

时装展、时装表演说明

写作范例:

学校周末时装表演

时间:2016 年 11 月 21 日,晚上 8:00
地点:大礼堂
主办:时装协会
时装特点:全部由本校服装爱好者设计,今冬明春最新款式,所有模特均由本校师生担任。
Notes:1. exhibition 展览;2. association 协会。

Fashion Show Weekends

How do you spend this weekend of yours? Do you have some special plan? If not, please come to our Fashion Show Exhibition! The latest styles of this winter and the next spring(今冬明春)will be exhibited. All the fashionable dresses are designed by the fashion lovers of our school and all models are from the staff members and the students.

Time:8:00 p.m. November 21,2016
Place:Big Hall
Organized by the Fashion Association

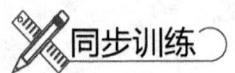

A. 基础层次

Ⅰ. 按要求做题

1. 用对应的英语填空。

_____安排	_____种类,类别
_____仪式	_____服装(总称)
_____委员会	_____比赛
_____事件	_____展览
_____参展商	_____国际的
_____牛仔服装	_____针织服装
_____媒体	_____新闻
_____专业人员	_____预订
_____研讨会	_____运动装
_____趋势	_____休闲装

_____儿童服装　　　　　　　　_____男士正装
_____闭幕式　　　　　　　　　　_____时装设计比赛
_____时装设计师　　　　　　　　_____时装博览会
_____时装表演　　　　　　　　　_____开幕式
_____记者招待会　　　　　　　　_____女士服装
_____国际展览中心

2. 思考与问答。
（1）Is their company going to the fashion fair in Shanghai? _____.
（2）Do you like being a model? _____
（3）Could you do me a favor? _____
（4）How many visitors has the fair attracted according to the text? _____
（5）Are you going to the fashion fair? _____

Ⅱ．按要求完成下列各题

1. I was awakened by a barking dog this morning.（翻译）→_____
2. The piano played at the concert is made in China.（改为定语从句，played：p. p）→_____
_____
（注：p. p. 过去分词；p. pr. 现在分词；p. v. 谓语动词）
3. contest 比赛，竞赛（同义词）→_____
4. press 出版社（同义词）→_____
5. be in(the)fashion 合乎时尚（反义词）→_____
6. be born to wealth（翻译）→_____

Ⅲ．课堂效应检测：用英语在下面指定处小结你学本单元的收获体会

_____
_____
_____
_____
_____
_____

B. 拓展层次

Ⅰ．单项选择题

1. Is your company going to _____ the fashion fair in Shanghai?
　　A. take part in　　　B. join　　　C. take part　　　D. will join
2. The fashion fair? Yes, we have just reserved _____ .
　　A. a boot　　　B. a booth　　　C. a post　　　D. a country
3. There is going to _____ a fashion design contest and a modeling contest.
　　A. have　　　B. are　　　C. be　　　D. has

4. I think they are very professional and _____ they cooperate very well with media.
   A. except   B. except for   C. beside   D. besides
5. It _____ a perfect trading platform for fashion traders.
   A. serves for   B. acts for   C. has as   D. serves as
6. Their recent designs lead the latest fashion trends _____ in clothing but in jewelry and shoes.
   A. only   B. not only   C. not more   D. no only
7. There are more than 3,000 companies making _____ clothing.
   A. branding   B. branded   C. to brand   D. brands
8. At present, most of young people _____ the fashion and they are often in the style.
   A. follow   B. rush   C. copy   D. run
9. Today's _____ is toward less formal clothing.
   A. trends   B. trend   C. styles   D. event
10. Fewer children are _____ older parents nowadays and it means more money is spent on each child.
    A. born to   B. born in   C. borne to   D. born for

Ⅱ. 交际用语:补全对话题

A:Good morning, sir.

B:Good morning. How should I call you?

A: __1__

B:Nice to meet you, Miss Liu.

A: __2__

B:Do you have any experience?

A: __3__

B: __4__

A:Yes, I can type 80 words a minute.

B:Great! It happens we want a person like you. What about a secretary?

A:It sounds very good.

B: __5__

A:OK. I will. Thank you, sir. Bye.

> A. Bye.
> B. Oh, I forgot to introduce myself. I'm Miss Liu.
> C. Me, too. I want to find a job.
> D. I graduated just now.
> E. Can you type and operate a computer?
> F. You can come to work tomorrow if you like.

Ⅲ. 阅读理解:判断题

Happiness is for everyone. In fact, happiness is always around you if you put your heart into it. When you are in trouble at school, your friends will help you; when you study hard at your lessons, your parents are always taking good care of your life and your health; when you get success, your friend will congratulate you; when you do something wrong, people around you will help you to correct it. And when you do something good to others, you will feel happy, too. All these are your happiness. If you notice a bit of them, you can find that happiness is always around you.

Happiness is not the same as money; it's a feeling of your heart. When you are poor, you can also be very happy, because you have something else that can't be bought with money.

When you meet with difficulties, you can say loudly you are very happy, because you have more chances to challenge yourself. So you cannot always say you are poor and you have bad luck. If you take every chance you get, you can be a happy-and-lucky person.

1. In fact, happiness is seldom around you if you put your heart into it.

2. When you study hard at your lessons, your teachers are always taking good care of your life and your health.

3. When you do something wrong, people around you will help you to correct it.

4. Happiness is not the same as cash; it's a feeling of your heart.

5. When you meet no difficulties, you can say loudly you are very sad, because you have more chances to challenge yourself.

Ⅳ. 根据括号里的中文填空

1. Is your company going to the _____(服装展览会)in Shanghai?

2. I have just _____(订了个展位)because our company is going to it.

3. There will be _____(记者招待会)and lectures on fashion trends.

4. The China International Fashion Fair is an international trade event _____(举办)per year.

5. It seems that these clothes are _____(不合时尚)now.

Ⅴ. 写作

Complete the following "Fashion Show Weekends."

时间:10月21日,晚上8:00

地点:大礼堂

主办:时装协会

时装特点:全部由本校服装爱好者设计,今冬明春最新款式,所有模特均由本校师生担任。

____1____(周末时装表演)

How do you spend this weekend of yours? Do you have some special plan? If not, please come to our __2__(时装表演展)! The latest styles of __3__(今冬明春)will be exhibited. All the fashionable dresses __4__(由……设计)the __5__(服装爱好者)of our school and all __6__(模特)are from the __7__(教职人员)and the students.

Time: __8__(10月21日,晚上8:00)

Place: __9__(大礼堂)

Organized by __10__(服装协会)

Unit 10 That's what has been my dream work.

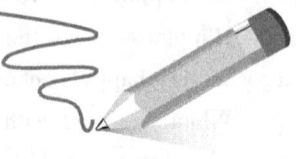

目标攻略

1. 培养良好的交际能力:表达自己的理想、愿望及计划;
2. 认知本单元所有词汇;能正确运用重点词汇,如 achieve, create, creativity, patient, reward, economy 等及拓开学英语的途径;
3. 背诵"Everyday English";
4. 掌握语法:分词作状语等;
5. 介绍自己的理想和计划。

知识解析

Ⅰ. 词汇

(1) surely 想必。
(2) occur 发生,被发现。如:
  Don't let the mistake occur again. 不要让错误再次发生。
(3) study n. 学习; studies n. 学业。
(4) achieve 完成,达到。achieve one's aim 达到目的; achieve a gradual increase in studies 实现学业上的逐步上升。
(5) create 创造,创作。create a role/part in the TV play 创造电视剧中的角色; create a friendly atmosphere 创造友好气氛。
(6) economy n. 经济→economize v. 节约→economical adj. 经济的;节约的。national economy 国民经济; practice economy 厉行节约; politics and economy 政治与经济。
(7) unexpected 出乎意料的。如:
  an unexpected guest(visitor) = a casual visitor 意外之客。
(8) whereas(公文用语) 鉴于;而,却,反之。如:
  He's ill whereas I am only a little tired. 他病了,而我只是有一点累罢了。
(9) earn a living = make a living 谋生。
(10) incorporate something into 把……合并。

Ⅱ．句式

（1）That's what has been my dream work. 这就是我一直梦想的工作。

（2）Having that dream for so long, you surely will make it.
怀揣那个梦想那么久/梦寐以求那么久,你肯定会成功的。

（3）It is necessary to master a foreign language. 掌握一门外语是必要的。

（4）May you make even greater progress. 祝你取得更大进步。

（5）Wish you great success. 祝你成功。

（6）You are supposed to choose one career based on your own interest.
你应选择一门基于自己兴趣上的职业。

（7）In the corporate world, a job is something handed over to you by your employer, whereas a career is more like your personal belongings. Employers will look for a candidate to fill up a job opening but you will search for a job that matches your career path.
在这个相互联系的世界上,工作是你的雇主给你的,而职业却是属于你个人的。老板要找一个求职者来填充工作空缺,但你却要寻找与你的职业路径相吻合的工作。

（8）Do you earn a living by having a job or pursuing a career?
你是靠工作为生还是为追求职业而生存呢?

解题引领

1. That's _____ has been my dream work.
   A. when   B. where
   C. that   D. what

答案为 D。点拨:表语从句中差主语,在四个选项中,唯有 D 是连接代词,能作主语。选项 C 作引导词用时,仅仅引导定语从句时才是关系代词。

2. Once _____ skills necessary for a new career, you'll find both work and financial satisfaction along your career journey.
   A. master   B. mastered
   C. mastering   D. being mastered

答案为 C。点拨:本题的句子主语是 you,能执行 mastering 动作,具有逻辑上的主谓关系,故选现在分词。

分词(续)

参见上一单元的阐述。

 **写作指导**

名人简介

设计一份海报介绍你所喜爱的名人。

_____
_____
_____
_____
_____

 **同步训练**

A. 基础层次

Ⅰ．按要求做题

1. 用对应的英语填空。

_____完成,达到	_____事业
_____创造	_____创造力
_____经济	_____目标
_____掌握	_____耐心
_____耐心的	_____回报,报酬
_____出乎意料的	_____对……厌烦
_____长期的,长久的	

2. 思考与问答

(1) Is Italy the world's fashion capital? _____.

(2) Are there a lot of designers in Italy? _____.

(3) Is that what has been your dream work? _____.

(4) Do you often do health care? _____.

(5) Will you choose your career based on your interest after graduation? _____

Ⅱ．按要求完成下列各题

1. What do you think is the best career for the future? (回答)→_____.

2. You'd choose a career based on your own interest. (翻译)→_____

3. either "也" (同义词)→_____

4. occur "发生" (同义词)→_____

5. Heated, ice will change into water. (翻译)→_____

6. Given more attention, the trees could have grown better. (翻译)→_____

Ⅲ. 课堂效应检测：用英语在下面指定处小结你学本单元的收获体会

_____
_____
_____
_____
_____
_____

B. 拓展层次

Ⅰ. 单项选择题

1. Working hard for your company is _____ has been my dream work.
   A. when   B. how   C. what   D. why

2. I always have to work late at night and the company keeps me _____ in the office.
   A. to work   B. worked   C. relax   D. working

3. _____ that dream for so long, you surely will succeed.
   A. Have   B. Had   C. Having   D. Having been

4. They may not be the best paid careers _____.
   A. too   B. also   C. as well as   D. either

5. You are supposed to choose one _____ on your own interest.
   A. base   B. basing   C. to base   D. based

6. The good careers for the future are those _____ will reward you with long term joy and fulfillment.
   A. which   B. how   C. who   D. what

7. Then you will _____ look for other jobs, and use all your gifts in your found career.
   A. no longer   B. not longer   C. not any longer D. any longer

8. It includes a set of careers _____ you can reach your goal of life.
   A. when   B. which   C. where   D. whom

9. Once _____ skills necessary for a new career, you'll find both work and financial satisfaction.
   A. mastered   B. mastering
   C. being mastered   D. to be mastered

10. This morning there was _____ visitor to meet the boy's parents and he didn't know what to do.
    A. a unexpected   B. an unexpecting
    C. an unexpected   D. the unexpecting

11. The playwright(剧作家) and director _____ thinking of how to _____ a role/part in the play.
    A. are; do   B. are; write   C. is; create   D. is; think

12. Since each job you take _____ you advance to higher levels, you'll incorporate it into your career plan.

    A. to help   B. helping   C. helps   D. help

13. If not, you might take education that has no direct relationship with _____ you do to earn a _____.

    A. that; living   B. what; live   C. what; living   D. that; live

14. In the corporate world, a job is something _____ over to you by your boss, _____ a career is more like your personal belongings.

    A. handed; whereby   B. handed; whereas

    C. hands; whereas   D. to hand; whereas

15. You may focus solely _____ your current occupation without having any strategies _____ to anticipate changes in the job environment.

    A. in; prepared   B. on; prepared   C. on; preparing   D. in; preparing

16. Finding her car stolen, _____.

    A. a policeman was asked to help

    B. the area was searched thoroughly(彻底地,完全地)

    C. it was looked for everywhere

    D. she hurried to a policeman for help

17. —There are some mistakes in the composition.

    —If _____, please correct them.

    A. finding   B. having been found   C. found   D. find

18. _____ more attention, the trees could have grown better.

    A. To give   B. Giving   C. Given   D. Having given

19. "We can't go out in this weather." said Bob, _____ out of the window.

    A. looking   B. to look   C. looked   D. having looked

20. The purpose of new technologies is to make life easier, _____ it more difficult.

    A. not make   B. not to make   C. not making   D. do not make

Ⅱ. 交际用语:补全对话题

M: I'd like to mail this box to Hong Kong. __1__

W: Do you want to send it first class or second class?

M: __2__ And how long does it take?

W: It's a light box. First class would cost4 $8.20. I guess it will take about eight to ten days to arrive.

M: And second class?

W: Sending it second class would be cheaper, but it will arrive in a month. You'll pay $4.90 only.

M: Oh, I want it to arrive earlier than that. I'll mail it first class.

W: __3__ I need to know in order to complete the form.

M: A set of glasses. Are there any other forms I need to fill out because it's going to a foreign country?

W: Yes, one more. You have to write clearly what is in the box and the value.

M: __4__

W: You forgot to put a return address on this box. It's not a post office rule, but we usually advise people that every mail has a proper return address.

M: OK. I'll do it right now. I'll also buy ten 60-cent stamps.

W: Let's see. The box and the stamps. Your total bill comes to $14.20.

M: __5__ Have a nice day.

> A. How much is first class?
> B. What's in the box?
> C. What can I do for you?
> D. How much will it be?
> E. Thank you.
> F. Here it is.

Ⅲ. 阅读理解：判断题

There are many ways in which the memory can be improved. In fact, I believe we all have the ability to remember up to six times more than we do.

A lot of people find that visualizing information is very helpful. For example, if you are trying to remember a telephone number, imagine it written down on a piece of paper.

Remembering people's names is a problem for a lot of people. I recommend that when you are introduced to someone you concentrate on his or her first name. It probably won't offend anyone if you have to say, "What was your last name again, Sarah?" But she might be upset if you forget her first name.

Of course, regular breaks are important and it's better not to work for long periods without taking one, stopping for rest about every twenty minutes is the best.

Finally, take care of yourself physically. Avoid substances like coffee, alcohol or drugs, because they dull the mind. And don't forget your vitamins—B1 and B2 are particularly good for the memory.

1. In fact, I believe we all have the ability to remember up to six times more than we can't do.

2. A lot of people find that visualizing information is very helpless.

3. I recommend that when you are introduced to someone you should concentrate on his or her first name.

4. Of course, regular breaks are important and it's better not to work for long periods without taking one, stopping for rest about every twenty minutes is the best.

5. And don't remember your vitamins—B1 and B2 aren't particularly good for the memory.

Ⅳ. 根据括号里的中文填空

1. There are more than 3,000 companies _____ (制造品牌服装) in Shanghai.

2. _____（看到老师）entering the room, the students stood up.

3. When _____（仔细挑选）, the best careers for the future don't have to be a single career choice.

4. Changes in the economy and technology may affect jobs _____（以意想不到的方式）.

5. It's necessary to _____（掌握一两门）foreign languages.

Ⅴ. 写作

Write a letter of application to apply for your dream job.

Dear sir,

　　I am writing to ___1___（申请）the position of office clerk. I graduated from Shanghai Commercial College and my major is ___2___（商务管理）.

　　I am 21 years old and I have just left college about for three months, ___3___（其间）I have been striving to make myself proficient in shorthand and typewriting, and I ___4___（已达到,已获得）a speed of ninety words a minute respectively.

　　I believe that I can fulfill the requirements of the job.

　　Thank you ___5___（提前）for your consideration.

　　Looking forward to your reply.

Sincerely yours
×××

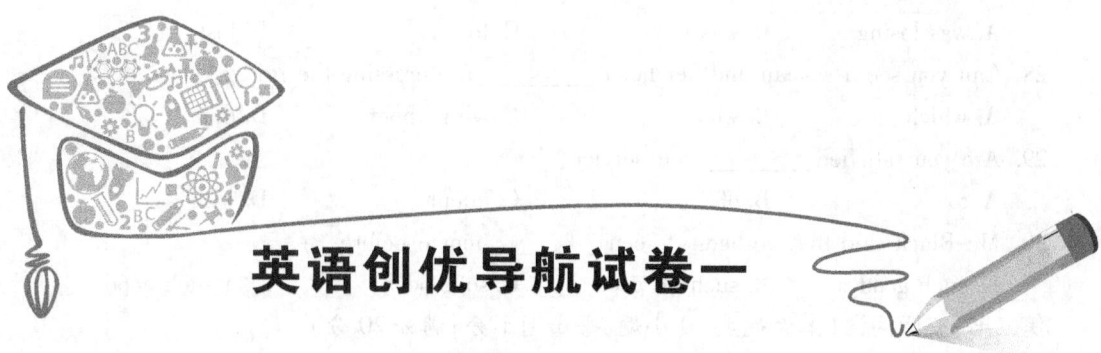

英语创优导航试卷一

第一部分 听力

(略)

第二部分 知识运用

(共三大题,每题1分,共40分)

第一节:词汇与语法(本大题共10个小题,每小题1分,共10分)

从每小题给出的A、B、C、D四个选项中选出一个符合题意的最佳选项,请将所选答案填在答题卡上。

21. Could you tell me where _____ from?
    A. she comes   B. was she   C. did she come   D. is she

22. I really don't know that the necklace is _____ 50,000,000 dollars.
    A. cost   B. paid   C. worth   D. found

23. It's said that _____ European expert will come to teach us marketing for _____ hour every week.
    A. an;a   B. an;an   C. a;an   D. a;a

24. There are three _____ doctors and five _____.
    A. woman;man nurses   B. women;men nurse
    C. women;men nurses   D. woman;men nurses

25. He, as well as I _____ interested in _____ newspapers after breakfast.
    A. am;read   B. is;to read   C. is;reading   D. am;reading

26. And me? I enjoy _____ the pop music.
    A. listening   B. to listen   C. listening to   D. to listen to

27. The credit card _____ several days ago was found yesterday evening.

A. was losing   B. was lost   C. losing   D. lost

28. Can you see a woman and her horse _____ are crossing the bridge?

     A. which   B. who   C. with whom   D. that

29. Are you satisfied _____ our service?

     A. to   B. of   C. about   D. with

30. Mr. Black said that he hadn't seen _____ movie before.

     A. such good a   B. such no good   C. so good a   D. a such good

第二节：交际用语（本大题共20小题，每小题1分；满分20分）

（一）选择

31. —Where's Jack?

     —He's gone either to Shanghai or to Beijing, but I'm not sure _____.

     A. that   B. where   C. which   D. there

32. —Dad, this is my classmate, Tom.

     —_____.

     A. Nice to see you   B. Pleased to meet you

     C. Pleased to see you   D. Nice meeting you

33. —What about having a cup of tea?

     —_____.

     A. I want it   B. Good idea   C. Help yourself   D. Me, too

34. —_____?

     —I'm Peter Snow.

     A. Where are you from   B. What are you

     C. What do you do   D. Who are you

35. —Which do you prefer, black tea or black coffee?

     —_____.

     A. I have a cup of tea   B. Yes, I like it

     C. Sure, I prefer them   D. I prefer black coffee

36. —How beautiful your clothes look!

     —_____.

     A. They aren't beautiful   B. No, thanks

     C. Yes, thank you very much   D. Thanks

37. —Please keep silent. This is a hospital!

     —_____.

     A. No problem   B. It doesn't matter

     C. OK, I will   D. All right. I won't

38. —You look sad. What's the matter with you?

     —_____.

     A. My purse's lost   B. My purse has lost

     C. What a pity   D. Lost a book

39. —Look! That boy is crying!

　　—_____.

　　A. Take care　　　　　　　　B. Let's go and see

　　C. No problem　　　　　　　D. Never mind

40. —Have you ever been to Beijing, Mr. White?

　　—_____.

　　A. Yes, never　　　　　　　　B. No, I have

　　C. Yes, go ahead　　　　　　D. No, never

(二)补全对话

A: __41__

B: It's very wonderful.

A: I think so. __42__

B: It's the worst one that I have ever heard.

A: __43__ And I also like the woman with long hair. __44__

B: Yes, __45__

```
A. She's so kind!
B. I agree with you.
C. Good idea!
D. Don't you think the music is beautiful?
E. I don't think so.
F. Do you like that film?
G. How do you like that film?
```

(三)匹配

I	II
46. 国民经济	A. Shut the Door After You
47. 随手关灯	B. Save [on] Electricity
48. 节约用电	C. Private Property
49. 私人住宅	D. Save [on] Water
50. 请勿随地吐痰	E. Switch off When Leaving
	F. National Economy
	G. No Spitting

第三节:完形填空(本大题共10小题,每小题1分,满分10分)

阅读下面短文,从各题所给的A、B、C、D四个选项中选出可填入空白处的最佳答案,并将所选答案填在答题卡上。

Food is very important for life. Without it man would die of hunger. __51__ the need for food, man also has need for house to protect him __52__ heat and cold, wind and rain.

The first man's houses were very simple. The size and kind of houses at that time were limited __53__ his building skill and also by the things for him to use. In some places, man's houses would be __54__ more than a large hole in the side of a hill, with a fire at the gate to give him light, to cook food and to keep dangerous animals away.

But in __55__ century, house building work has become an important industry. Modern science makes it possible for man to build so many large __56__ for government offices, shops, schools, hotels, hospitals, churches…

As the population of the world grows, __57__ houses of many kinds are needed.

The house with three __58__ for the average family would not be __59__ for a very rich family. The average families also want to live comfortably. So people are trying their best to improve their houses __60__ it is expensive. Different kinds of modern houses are being designed and some of them have been built up for rich families to live in, and also some for average families.

51. A. Besides   B. Except   C. Beside   D. But
52. A. of   B. from   C. to   D. away
53. A. by   B. to   C. in   D. of
54. A. anything   B. everything   C. something   D. nothing
55. A. the twenty   B. the twentieth   C. twentieth   D. twenty
56. A. buildings   B. houses   C. rooms   D. gardens
57. A. many and many   B. much and much   C. more and more   D. most and most
58. A. bedrooms   B. bathrooms   C. sitting rooms   D. classrooms
59. A. big enough   B. enough big   C. too big   D. much big
60. A. through   B. thought   C. though   D. but

第三部分　阅读理解

(共25小题,第1~4篇为选择题和判断题,每小题1分;第5篇为简答题,每小题2分;共30分)

A. 选择题

根据短文内容选择正确的答案。

Passage 1

There was once a millionaire(百万富翁) who loved money more than anything else in the world. He didn't know exactly how much money he had. So he took on a little girl to count all his money for him.

It took the little girl six days to count all the money. When she told the millionaire that he had forty-two million dollars, he was full of joy and asked, "How much do I need to pay for you," The little girl said, "Well, I work for six days, so I think you ought to pay for six days. Give me two pennies for the first day. Each day after that, just give me the amount(数额) you gave me the day before, multiplied(乘) by itself." The millionaire thought that in this way he would only have to give her a very few dollars. What a foolish little girl! So he immediately had his lawyer write up a contract(契约), fearing that the little girl changed her mind.

On the first day, the millionaire paid her two pennies and on the second day, two pennies times two is four pennies. Each day after that, he gave her the number of the pennies he had given her the day before, multiplied by itself. And by the sixth day, the millionaire had given the little girl all his money.

61. The millionaire hired the little girl to count his money because _____.
    A. he didn't know he had much money
    B. he wanted to cheat her
    C. he wanted to know how much money he had
    D. he would rather pay her than anybody else

62. The millionaire had his lawyer write up a contract because _____.
    A. he was afraid she would ask him to pay her more money than she had asked
    B. he knew how much he had to pay the girl
    C. he was afraid the girl would give up the work
    D. he liked her very much

63. According to the contract the little girl could get _____.
    A. more than 42 million dollars   B. a very few money
    C. less than 42 million dollars   D. more than 65,536 pennies

64. The millionaire was _____.
    A. greedy and clever   B. greedy but foolish
    C. rich and generous(慷慨的)   D. good at math

65. The girl who the millionaire hired _____.
    A. was not only greedy but also clever   B. wanted to get all the money
    C. had a good sense for numbers   D. needed money badly

Passage 2

In the last 500 years, nothing about people, not their clothes, ideas, or languages, has changed as much as what they eat. The original chocolate was made from the seeds of the cocoa tree(可可树) by South American Indians. The Spanish introduced it to the rest of the world during the 1500's. And although it was very expensive, it quickly became fashionable. In London, shops where chocolate drinks were served became important meeting places; some still exist today.

The potato is also from the New World. Around 1600, Spanish brought it from Peru to Europe, where it soon was widely grown. Ireland became so dependent on it that thousands of Irish people starved when the crop failed during the "Potato Famine(饥荒)" of 1845 - 1846, and thousands more were forced to leave their homeland and move to America.

There are many other foods that have traveled from South America to the Old World. But some others went in the opposite direction. Brazil is now the world's largest grower of coffee, and coffee is an important crop in Colombia and other South American countries. But it is native to Ethiopia (埃塞俄比亚), a country in Africa. It was first made into a drink by Arabs during 1400's.

According to an Arabic legend, coffee was discovered when a person named Kaldi noticed that his goats were attracted to the red berries(浆果,干果仁) on a coffee bush(灌木丛). He tried one and experienced the "wide-awake" feeling that one-third of the world's population now starts the day with.

66. According to the passage, which of the following has changed the most in the last 500 years?
   A. Clothing   B. Food   C. Ideology   D. Language
67. "Some" in the last sentence of the first paragraph refers to _____.
   A. some cocoa trees   B. some chocolate drinks
   C. some South American Indians   D. some shops
68. Thousands of Irish people starved during the "Potato Famine" because _____.
   A. they were so dependent on potatoes that they refused to eat anything else
   B. they were forced to leave their homeland and move to America
   C. the potato harvest was bad
   D. the weather conditions in Ireland were not suitable for growing potatoes.
69. Which country is the largest coffee producer?
   A. Colombia.   B. Brazil.   C. Ethiopia.   D. Egypt.
70. Which of the following statements is **NOT** true according to the passage?
   A. Coffee is native to Colombia.
   B. One-third of the world's population drinks coffee.
   C. Coffee can keep one awake.
   D. Coffee drinks were first made by Arabs.

Passage 3

What makes one person more intelligent than another? What makes one person a genius, like the brilliant Albert Einstein, and another person a fool? Are people born intelligent or stupid, or is intelligence the result of where and how you live? These are very old questions and the answers to them are still not clear.

We know, however, that just being born with a good mind is not enough. In some ways, the mind is like a leg or an arm muscle. It needs exercise. Mental exercise is a particularly important job for young children. Many child psychologists(心理学家) think that parents should play with their children more often and give them problems to think about. The children are then more likely to grow up bright and intelligent. If, on the other hand, children are left alone a great deal with nothing to do, they are more likely to become dull and unintelligent. Parents should also be careful with what they say to the young children. According to some psychologists, if parents are always telling a child that he or she is a fool or an idiot, then the child is more likely to keep doing silly and foolish things. So it is probably better for parents to say very helpful things to their children, such as "That was a very clever thing you did." or "You are such a smart child."

71. According to the passage we can guess that a genius is _____ while an idiot is _____.
   A. a normal person; a funny person

B. a strong person; a weak person

C. a highly intelligent person; a foolish or weak-minded person

D. a famous person; an ordinary person

72. A person _____ is more likely to become a genius.

A. whose parents are clever

B. often thinking about difficult problems

C. often helped by his teachers and parents

D. born with a good brain and putting it to active use

73. It is better for parents _____.

A. to praise and encourage their children more often

B. to be hard on their children

C. to leave their children alone with nothing to do

D. to give their children as much help as possible

74. Which of the following is **NOT** true according to the passage?

A. Parents play an important part in their children's growth.

B. The less you use your head, the duller you may become.

C. Intelligence is obviously the result of where and how you live.

D. What makes a person bright or stupid is still under discussion.

75. From the passage it can be seen that to say _____ things to the children is important.

A. encouragement   B. harmful   C. critical   D. professional

B. 判断题

根据短文内容判断句子的正误(正确的用"T",错误的用"F",文中未提的用"N")。

Passage 4

My interest in Chinese food started many years ago when I had my first job. I was a young reporter for *the Daily Journal* in San Francisco. Our office wasn't far from Chinatown. I usually managed to arrange my schedule so that I could go there for a good meal at least two or three times a week.

The first time I ever ate Chinese food I loved it. And since then, it just tastes better and better to me. The first thing I noticed was the fresh taste of the meat and vegetables. When I learned more about the food, I began to understand why it has the unique feature(特色).

About 5,000 years ago, China lost much of its wood because of over-population and poor management of its forests. This loss was very bad for the country, of course, but it turned very good for the food. Wood became very expensive and hard to get, so the Chinese had to find a substitute(替换物) for their valuable wood, or learn how to use it better. There wasn't any substitute available, so people found ways to economize(节约).

In order to economize in cooking, they had to use very little wood. So they started cutting their meat and vegetables into small pieces before they put them into the hot oil. That way the food cooked faster and they saved fuel(燃料). The food prepared in this way kept its fresh flavor(味道). It is the flavor that attracts people to the art of Chinese cooking.

I often wonder if the Chinese understood their solution to that ancient energy crisis(危机) as much as I do now—whenever I eat Chinese food.

76. The writer was interested in Chinese food when he was a reporter for *the Daily Journal*.

77. The first thing he noticed about Chinese food was its unique feature.

78. The reason why wood was so valuable in ancient China was that wood was very expensive.

79. The ancient Chinese were not able to find any substitute for wood about 5,000 years ago.

80. At first the Chinese cut meat and vegetables into small pieces before cooking in order to keep their fresh flavor.

C. 简答题

根据短文内容简要回答问题,每题不得超过10个单词。

Passage 5

One day in 1925, John Baird pulled an office boy into his workroom and placed him before the transmitter. The boy's face could clearly be seen on the screen a few feet away. That office boy became the first person ever to appear on the television!

Baird was educated at a technical college and the University of Glasgow. It was there that he first had the idea of transmitting pictures. His poor health prevented him from active service during the First World War. After the war, he returned to London and started again on his idea of television.

He was so poor that he accepted an offer to show his experiments in a big London store. Money from his parents allowed him to continue his work. When he had more success and transmitted a clear picture over long distances, he was offered help. Businessmen who before had refused to help now anxiously offered to share in the development of his invention. Big companies in America spent a lot of money in improving his equipment. When the BBC made the first television broadcast in 1936, American equipment was used. When it started its television service again after the Second World War, the BBC used equipment from Baird's own company.

John Baird died in 1945 and did not live to see television enter many houses in Britain.

81. Who was the first person to appear on the TV?

_____

82. When did transmitting pictures happen the earliest?

_____

83. Where did he first have the idea of transmitting pictures?

_____

84. John Baird wasn't very poor, was he?

_____

85. Why did businessmen who before had refused to help now anxiously offer to share in the development of his invention?

_____

第四部分 书面表达

(共两节,共20分)

第一节:英汉互译(共5小题,每小题2分,共10分。请将86~88题译成中文,将89~90题括号里的中文译成英文)

工科类

86. Maintenance includes testing a device and replacing the parts that are out of work.
_____

87. You shouldn't be so negative, and everyone has their strengths and weaknesses.
_____

88. You mean the problem is caused by the computer or other equipment connected?
_____

89. The job seeker bravely _____(承担)the difficult task.

90. For workers, they must _____(采取合理的预防措施)to protect their own health and safety, as well as the health and safety of others.

服务类

86. After you become a member of the website you can go to different shops and begin your online shopping.
_____

87. Your room is reserved. Please check in before 10:00 a.m.
_____

88. She not only completed the task on time but also saved a lot of money for the company.
_____

89. Great! Could you _____(推荐)me to your company?

90. The 2011 Shanghai World Expo site _____(被分成)five zones, with pavilions of over 200 countries.

第二节:应用文写作(本节共10空,每空1分,共10分)

中文提示:假如你是李哈,在湖南日报广告栏看到一家公司招聘一名英文秘书的广告,你想申请这一职位。李哈情况如下:男,22岁,1.79米,身体健康,即将毕业于上海大学文学与秘书专业,已获8级英语证书,喜欢阅读、写作、听音乐、体验恐怖,与同学相处很好。

Job-hunting Briefing(求职简介)

88 Peach Road Shanghai
June 29th

Dear Sir or Madam,

　　Today I have your advertisement in *Hunan Daily* in which you want an English secretary. I'd like to ___91___(申请)the post as an English secretary.

My name is Li Ha, ___92___ (男), 22, 1.79 meters tall and I'm in good health. I went to Shanghai University three years ago, and I am now studying here and majoring in literary language and secretary. In the meantime, I'm interested in English and I have got ___93___ (8级) English certificate already. I think I'm qualified for the position, so I want to get it and ___94___ (担任) a secretary in your company.

I can write well in English and my oral English is excellent, too. I once won ___95___ (一等奖) in an English contest ___96___ (举行) in our university. In my spare time I enjoy reading, writing and listening to music. I also like ___97___ (体验恐怖). I get on ___98___ (与……相处好) my schoolmates in our university.

If you think I am the ___99___ (正确人选), please give me a telephone call. My number is ××××-×××××××.

Yours sincerely,
___100___

英语创优导航试卷二

第一部分 听力

(略)

第二部分 知识运用

(共三大题,每题1分,共40分)

第一节:词汇与语法(本大题共10小题,每小题1分,共10分)

从每小题给出的A、B、C、D四个选项中选出一个符合题意的最佳选项,请将所选答案填在答题卡上。

21. I like animals. I have _____ cat, and _____ cat is white and black.
    A. a;a   B. a;the   C. the;an   D. the;the

22. Let me show you my new iPhone. It's really perfect. I suggest you buy _____.
    A. the one   B. one   C. it   D. that

23. —Will you show me the photo of your family?
    —OK. I'll _____ it here tomorrow.
    A. take   B. bring   C. carry   D. catch

24. The problem _____ last week is very important.
    A. was discussed   B. discussed
    C. being discussed   D. be discussed

25. You must be very tired after _____.
    A. such a long journey   B. so long journey
    C. so a long journey   D. such long journey

26. We had reserved one single room _____ a private bath for you.
    A. have   B. has   C. of   D. with

27. They have three daughters, _____ are still young.

   A. all of them   B. all of whom   C. both of which   D. and all of whom

28. I wish I _____ the exam. You don't know how I regret I didn't study hard enough.

   A. pass   B. have passed   C. had passed   D. was passed

29. You must have stayed up last night, _____?

   A. mustn't you   B. aren't you   C. didn't you   D. haven't you

30. I'm calling to see _____ you would like to have lunch with me tomorrow.

   A. if   B. unless   C. as soon as   D. when

第二节：交际用语（本大题共20小题，每小题1分，共20分）

（一）选择

31. —How's everything going?

    —Fine, thanks. How are you doing?

    —_____.

    A. I'm 16 now.   B. Yes, it is good.
    C. See you then.   D. Oh, not too bad.

32. —_____, madam?

    —Yes, I'm looking for a pen.

    A. What do you want   B. What's the matter
    C. Can I help you   D. What are you looking for

33. —May I speak to Mr. Brown?

    —_____.

    A. No, you can't   B. I'm sorry, he is out
    C. I'm Miss Gao   D. Yes, I am

34. —Would you like to have something to eat?

    —_____.

    A. No, I wouldn't   B. Help yourself
    C. Go ahead, please   D. No, thanks. I'm not hungry

35. —What's your trouble, young man?

    —_____.

    A. No, I have no trouble   B. I'm afraid I don't
    C. I've got a headache   D. Yes, I do

36. —How beautiful you are in your new dress!

    —_____.

    A. No, no just so-so   B. I am not beautiful
    C Thanks   D. Really

37. —Thank you for giving me so much advice.

    —_____.

    A. That's kind of you   B. Of course
    C. Not at all   D. Take it easy

38. —Do wait till the traffic lights are green when you cross the road.
    —_____.

    A. Sorry, I know   B. OK, I will   C. Just stop saying   D. Don't mention it

39. —I'd like to invite you to dinner this Sunday, Mr. Black.
    —_____.

    A. Oh, no, let's not   B. I'm sorry but I have other plans
    C. I'd rather stay at home   D. Oh, no, that'll be too much trouble

40. —Well, Mary, I'm sorry I have to leave.
    —_____. I hope to hear from you soon.

    A. Enjoy yourself   B. Keep in touch
    C. Don't be so sad   D. So am I

(二)补全对话

W: Good evening, sir.
A: Good evening.   41
W: Of course, sir. This way, please. (In a corner) Sit down, please. Here's the menu.
A: Sue,   42
B: A glass of orange for me, please.   43
A: I prefer beer.
W: What would you like to eat, Madam?
B: 44   Er... beef, and fried fish.
W: 45
A: Oh, yes, tomato and egg soup, please.
W: OK. Thank you.

> A. Let me see.
> B. Have you got a table for two?
> C. Can I help you?
> D. Would you like some soup?
> E. What would you like to drink?
> F. Would you like some tomatoes?
> G. What about you?

(三)匹配

46. 若已感染,清除!   A. Please Pay Here
47. 收银处   B. Staff Only
48. 撤销打印   C. Danger High Voltage
49. 当心!施工现场   D. Clean if Infected
50. 员工专用   E. No Littering
                           F. Cancel Printing
                           G. Caution Work Area

第三节:完形填空(本大题共 10 小题,每小题 1 分,共 10 分)

阅读下面短文,从各题所给的 A、B、C、D 四个选项中选出可填入空白处的最佳答案,并将所选答案填在答题卡上。

One evening I was resting in a café. I __51__ a pair of newly bought white leather shoes, which were rather expensive. Then a boy came to me.

He was in a(n) __52__ shirt, looking pale and about eleven. No sooner had I begun to speak than he opened the box in his hand and took out the tools of shoe-polishing. He bent down, took off my leather shoes, and began to shine them.

He was busy with his work __53__ a heavy rain began to pour down. People rushed to the café for protection from the rain. More and more people crowded __54__ and gradually separated the boy from me.

Hours passed, and it turned __55__ I had no shoes on my feet and I thought the boy would not __56__ my shoes, and I would have to go home on my bare feet.

When it was near midnight the __57__ ended, and there were fewer and fewer people in the café. The café was to be __58__. I had to move to the door. Just as I went to the gate, I __59__ found that a boy, looking very familiar, was sleeping at the door with his head leaning against a box and his upper body being bare. He held a package made of his shirt tightly in his arms. I shook him slightly and woke him up. He jumped up and rubbed his eyes for a while before he recognized me. Then he opened the package hurriedly gave me my leather shoes, and apologized to me shyly. I __60__ him and wrapped him with his unfit shirt, which had wrapped my leather shoes. On my way home, the image of the boy stayed in my mind.

51. A. dressed	B. wore	C. mended	D. put on
52. A. worn	B. unfit	C. small	D. dirty
53. A. when	B. after	C. before	D. since
54. A. out	B. away	C. in	D. off
55. A. dark	B. right	C. left	D. bright
56. A. shine	B. keep	C. return	D. take away
57. A. rain	B. coffee	C. wind	D. work
58. A. opened	B. locked	C. stopped	D. closed
59. A. shortly	B. surprisedly	C. sadly	D. immediately
60. A. thanked	B. forgave	C. paid	D. scolded

第三部分 阅读理解

(共 25 小题,第 1~4 篇为选择题和判断题,每小题 1 分;第 5 篇为简答题,每小题 2 分;共 30 分)

A. 选择题

根据短文内容选择正确的答案。

Passage 1

Henry often forgets things and he often gets into trouble. His friends and workmates often tell him to be careful. He agrees but he can't remember it.

A month ago the young man met his manager at the door of the office. Mr. Black called him in and said, "Go and send an important letter to Mr. Jackson. He's in Green Tree Town now. Do remember his address. I'm waiting for his answer." The young man started at once. Coming out of the train station, he didn't know where to go. He went there last year but forgot where Mr. Jackson's company was. He brought out the letter out of the bag, but he couldn't find the address. At last he remembered it was in the Band Street. He stopped an old woman and asked "Excuse me, madam. Where's the Band Street, please?"

"Go along this street and turn left at the second crossing. And that's just the street you want."

Henry thanked her and easily found the company. His manager praised him after that and he was happy. And a week later Mr. Black sent him to the company again. He stopped the same old woman and asked her the same street.

"Oh, dear!" she called out, "Are you still looking for it?"

61. Henry often gets into trouble because _____.
    A. he's too young   B. he was not good in this lessons at school
    C. he is not careful   D. he has a lot of work to do

62. The letter was very important, so _____.
    A. Henry looked after it well   B. Henry left for the town at once
    C. the manager told Henry the address   D. Henry couldn't read it

63. Henry couldn't find the right place, so _____.
    A. he began to look for the company   B. he had to call his manager
    C. he asked Mr. Jackson to meet him   D. he asked an old woman for help

64. The manager thought _____, so he praised him.
    A. Henry did as he said   B. Henry came back soon
    C. Henry became a good man   D. Henry liked to use his head

65. Which of the following is **NOT** true?
    A. Henry couldn't find the company again.
    B. Henry was still looking for the company the next week.
    C. The old woman didn't think Henry found the company.
    D. Henry met the old woman in front of the station.

Passage 2

The class teacher thought that hobbies were very important for every child. She encouraged all her pupils to have one, and sometimes arranged for their parents to come and see the work they had done as a result.

One Friday morning the teacher told the class that those of them who had a hobby could have a holiday that afternoon to get the things they had made as parts of their hobbies ready for their parents to see the following afternoon.

So on Friday afternoon, while those of the pupils who had nothing to show did their usual lessons, the lucky ones who had made something were allowed to go home, on condition that they returned before five o'clock to bring what they were going to show, and to arranged them.

When the afternoon lessons began, the teacher was surprised to see that Tommy was not there. He was the laziest boy in the class, and the teacher found it difficult to believe that he had a hobby. However, at a quarter to five, Tommy arrived with a beautiful collection of butterflies in glass cases. After his teacher had admired them and helped him to arrange them on a table in the classroom, she was surprised to see Tommy pick them up again and begin to leave.

"What are you doing, Tommy?" She asked. "Those things must remain here until tomorrow afternoon. That's when the parents are coming to see them."

"I know they are coming then," answered Tommy, " and I will bring them back tomorrow; but my big brother doesn't want them to be out of our house at night in case they are stolen."

"But what has it got to do with your big brother?" asked the teacher. "Aren't the butterflies yours?" "No," answered Tommy, "They belong to him."

"But Tommy, you are supposed to show your own hobby here, not somebody else's!" said the teacher.

"I know that," answered Tommy, "My hobby is watching my brother collecting butterflies."

66. Which students could have a holiday on the Friday afternoon according to the teacher?

   A. Those who did well in those days
   B. Those who had to get ready for the meeting
   C. Those who had a bobby
   D. Those who were ill

67. According to the passage, which of the following is **NOT** true?

   A. The pupils who had nothing to show had to stay at school as usual
   B. The pupils who had a holiday must bring something he had made himself
   C. Tom stayed at school because he was so lazy that he didn't do anything
   D. The beautiful collection of butterflies belonged to Tommy's brother.

68. What's the best title for this passage?

   A. Important Hobbies   B. Tommy's Hobby
   C. Different Hobbies   D. Hobby of Collecting Butterflies

69. The teacher _____.

   A. asked the pupils who were in her class to bring something they had made
   B. was certain that her pupils were good at making things, so she wanted to show them to the parents.
   C. invited the parents to come and see what the pupils had made
   D. allowed the pupils who had hobbies not to go to class that Friday afternoon

70. After reading the passage the readers will laugh. Why?

    A. Because Tommy was so lazy a boy.

    B. Because the teacher knew so little about Tommy.

    C. Because Tommy had made nothing at all.

    D. Because Tommy had a strange idea about hobby.

Passage 3

"Where's Papa going with the ax(斧子)?" said Fern to her mother as they were setting the table for breakfast.

"Out to the hog house(猪舍)," replied Mrs. Arable, "Some pigs were born last night."

"I don't see why he needs an ax," continued Fern, who was only eight.

"Well," said her mother, "one of the pigs is a runt(发育不全的). It's very small and weak, so your father has decided to do away with it."

"Do away with it?" shrieked(尖叫) Fern, "You mean kill it? Just because it's smaller than the others?"

"Don't yell, Fern!" she said, "Your father is right. The pig would probably die anyway."

Fern pushed a chair out of the way and ran outdoors. Soon she caught up with her father.

"Please don't kill it!" she cried. "It's unfair."

Mr. Arable stopped walking.

"Fern," he said gently, "you will have to learn to control yourself."

"Control myself?" yelled Fern, "This is a matter of life and death, and you talk about controlling myself." Tears ran down her cheeks and she took hold of the ax and tried to pull it out of her father's hand.

"Fern," said John Arable, "I know more about raising a litter of pigs than you do. It makes trouble. Now run along!"

"But it's unfair," cried Fern, "The pig couldn't help being born small, could it? If I had been very small at birth, would you have killed me?"

Mr. Arable smiled. "Certainly not," he said, looking down at his daughter with love. "But this is different. A little girl is one thing, a little runty pig is another."

"I see no difference," replied Fern, still hanging on to the ax. "This is the most terrible case I ever heard of."

A look came over John's face. He seemed almost ready to cry himself.

71. Why was Mr. Arable going to the hog house with an ax?

    A. Because some pigs were born last night.

    B. Because he wanted to repair the hog house with it.

    C. Because he was going to cut a tree.

    D. Because he was going to kill the runty pig with it.

72. The underline phrase "do away with" here means _____ in Chinese.

    A. 送走   B. 取回来   C. 收起来   D. 弄死

73. Fern was _____ when she heard her father was going to kill the runty pig.
   A. cool   B. happy
   C. surprised and angry   D. neither angry nor happy

74. Which of the following can be used to describe Fern?
   A. Warm-hearted.   B. Cruel.   C. Excited.   D. Full of love.

75. What do you guess will probably happen next?
   A. The runty pig was still killed by Mr. Arable.
   B. Mr. Arable listened to Fern's advice.
   C. The runty pig ran away itself.
   D. Fern left home with the pig.

B. 判断题

根据短文内容判断句子的正误(正确的用"T",错误的用"F",文中未提的用"N")。

Passage 4

In choosing a friend, one should be very careful. A good friend can help you study. You can have fun together and make each other happy. Sometimes you will meet fair weather friends. They will be with you as long as you have money or luck, but when you are down, they will run away. How do I know when I have found a good friend? I look for certain qualities of character, especially understanding, honesty and reliability(可靠).

Above all else, I look for understanding in a friend. A good friend tries to understand how another person is feeling. He is not quick to judge. Instead, he tries to learn from others. He puts himself in the other person's place, and he tries to think of ways to be helpful. He is also a good listener.

At the same time, however, a good friend is honest. He does not look for faults in others. He notices their good points. In short, a friend will try to understand me and accept me.

Another quality of a friend is reliability. I can always depend on(信赖) a good friend. If he tells me he will meet me somewhere at a certain time, I can be sure that he will be there. If I need a favor, he will do his best to help me. If I am in trouble, he will not run away from me.

When I meet someone who is reliable, honest, and understanding, I know I've found a friend!

76. The writer thinks understanding is the most important in choosing a friend.

77. If you have fair weather friends, they will give you all that they have when you need help.

78. Good friends need to always point out each other's mistakes.

79. This passage mainly discusses how to get along with friends.

80. The underlined phrase "In short" means "简言之" in Chinese.

C. 简答题

根据短文内容简要回答问题,每题不得超过10个单词。

Passage 5

There are many ways of putting out a fire. You may have seen people put out burning cigarettes by stepping on them. Stepping on cigarettes shuts off the air and puts out the fire.

Many fires are put out with water. Water cools the materials that are burning. It helps make the fire die out. Some of the water is changed into steam when it strikes the hot fire. The steam keeps air from the fire and helps put it out.

　　Some fires cannot be put out with water. Suppose a tank full of gasoline(汽油) is on fire. Gasoline is lighter than water. If you poured water into the tank of gasoline, the water would sink to the bottom of the tank. The gasoline would float on top of the water on the fire and flow over the edge of the tank. Then the fire would spread. Gasoline fires should be put out with sand or with chemicals of some kind, such as that used in some fire extinguishers(灭火器).

81. People often put out burning cigarettes by stepping on them. Why?
_____

82. Can all of the fires be put out with water?
_____

83. According to Paragraph 2, what will happen to the water if it is poured on the fire?
_____

84. How should gasoline fire be put out?
_____

85. Why will be water sink to the bottom of the tank when it is poured into the tank of gasoline?
_____

第四部分　书面表达

(共两节,共 20 分)

第一节:英汉互译(共 5 小题,每小题 2 分,共 10 分。请将 86~88 题译成中文,将 89~90 题括号里的中文译成英文)

理工类

86. I think the important thing is to understand your co-workers' feelings and needs.
_____

87. You should listen more and talk less on a new job.
_____

88. The most dangerous tool, I think, is the hacksaw(钢锯).
_____

89. During your work, you find the _____(安全规则) are very important and have to be strictly followed.

90. It improves productivity, and creates a safer _____(工作环境).

服务类

86. Never try to argue with your customers.
_____

87. It's known for moving talented employees quickly up the career ladder.
_____

88. You need to look into the situation and listen to the customers' opinions carefully.
_____

89. I _____(当,担任) a receptionist for three years and I'd like to have a change.

90. I'd like to _____(登记) for the flight to San Francisco.

第二节:应用文写作(本节共10空,每空1分,共10分)

中文提示:你校学生会将为来访的美国朋友举办一个晚会,要在学校广播中宣布此事,并欢迎大家参加。为使美国朋友听懂,请你用英语写一篇广播通知。要求如下:

宗旨:欢迎来访的美国朋友
组织者:学生会
时间:8月15日(星期六)晚7:30
地点:主楼顶层花园
活动内容:跳舞、唱歌、游戏、交换小礼品(请包装好,在外面写上几句祝愿词并签名)

May I have your attention, please? I have an announcement to make. ___91___ (学生会) is going to hold a party on ___92___ (星期六晚上), to ___93___ (欢迎朋友们) from the United States. The party ___94___ (将举行) in the roof garden of the Main Building. It will begin at 7:30 p.m. There will be music, ___95___ (舞蹈), singing, games and ___96___ (交换礼品). Will everybody please bring along a small gift for this purpose. Remember to ___97___ (把礼物包好), ___98___ (签名) and write a few words of ___99___ (美好祝愿).

Don't forget: 7:30, Saturday evening, roof garden, Main Building. There's sure to be a lot of fun. Everybody ___100___ (受欢迎的).

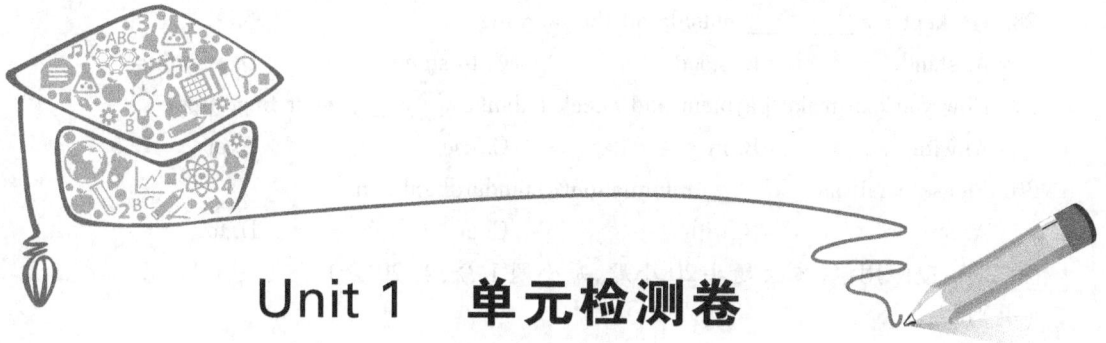

Unit 1 单元检测卷

第一部分 听力

(略)

第二部分 知识运用

(共三大题,每题1分,共40分)

第一节:词汇与语法(本大题共10小题,每小题1分,共10分)

从每小题给出的 A、B、C、D 四个选项中选出一个符合题意的最佳选项,请将所选答案填在答题卡上。

21. _____ this festival families get together and have a big dinner.
  A. In   B. On   C. At   D. /

22. It sounds _____ but I prefer _____ at home.
  A. interesting;stay   B. interested;to stay
  C. interesting;to stay   D. interested;staying

23. Everyone had dressed up _____ me because I had no new clothes.
  A. beside   B. besides   C. but for   D. except

24. I hate _____ stories in public.
  A. saying   B. telling   C. speaking   D. talking

25. On Christmas Day his friends _____ at his house.
  A. came   B. got   C. reached   D. arrived

26. My car _____ on the way home.
  A. broke up   B. broke into   C. broke down   D. broke out

27. My boss asked me to cash a check but I don't know _____ to do it.
  A. what   B. how   C. where   D. when

28. He kept me _____ outside all the morning.
    A. stand　　　　B. stood　　　　C. to stand　　　　D. standing
29. Now you can make payment and check balance _____ your fingertips.
    A. with　　　　B. in　　　　C. use　　　　D. at
30. Please email us _____ information@ standardbank. cn.
    A. on　　　　B. with　　　　C. at　　　　D. for

第二节：交际用语(本大题共20小题，每小题1分，共20分)

(一)选择

31. —How is everything with you?
    —_____.
    A. Good morning　　　　B. Glad to see you, too
    C. Fine, thank you　　　　D. How good it is
32. —How is your new boss?
    —_____.
    A. He is a doctor　　B. He is over thirties　　C. He is quite well　　D. He is John
33. —Show me your passport, please.
    —_____.
    A. OK, here it is　　B. Sure, here you are　　C. Thank you　　D. Both A and B
34. —You are late again for class.
    —_____.
    A. It doesn't matter　　　　B. I'm terribly sorry
    C. It's not my fault　　　　D. I don't think so
35. —Sally, you should not talk during the class.
    —_____ I need a ruler.
    A. I'm sorry, but　　B. No, I didn't talk.　　C. OK,　　D. Thank you,
36. —Would you like another bottle of beer?
    —_____.
    A. I won't　　B. I'm sorry　　C. Excuse me　　D. No, thanks
37. —May I have that pair of compasses, please?
    —Yes, _____.
    A. here they are　　B. here are you　　C. it is here　　D. they are here
38. —Could I borrow a book from you?
    —OK, _____.
    A. here is it　　B. you are here　　C. here you are　　D. it's here
39. —Can you do me a favor, Mr. Black?
    —Certainly. _____
    A. Hold on, please.　　B. It doesn't matter.　　C. What is it?　　D. Not at all.
40. —May I look at your new camera?
    —_____.

A. Certainly　　　B. No, you can　　　C. Yes, you can't　　　D. You're welcome

(二)补全对话

A: Hello, may I speak to Mr. Green?
B: Speaking.
A: ___41___ This is Liu Wei from the Traveling Agency.
B: Good evening, Mr. Liu.
A: I wish to tell you that a visit to Zhangjiajie has been arranged. ___42___
B: Certainly, I've been looking forward to it. ___43___
A: Tomorrow morning at 7:30. ___44___ Please try to be ready before that time.
B: I will. Thank you. Is that all?
A: ___45___ Good-bye.

> A. Yes, that's all.
> B. Good evening, Mr. Green.
> C. We'll gather at the gate of the hotel at 7:20.
> D. I wonder if you'd like to go.
> E. What time are we leaving?
> F. Anything do you want to know?
> G. Oh.

(三)匹配

I	II
46. 不准张贴	A. Pull
47. 削价销售	B. No Smoking
48. 保持安静	C. On Sale
49. 禁止U形转弯	D. No Bills
50. 闲人免入	E. No U Turn
	F. No Admittance
	G. Silence

第三节:完形填空(本大题共10小题,每小题1分,共10分)

阅读下面短文,从各题所给的A、B、C、D四个选项中选出可填入空白处的最佳答案,并将所选答案填在答题卡上。

My hobby is playing tennis. My father taught me ___51___ to play it when I was six years old. He ___52___ me every time for the first year. But then, on my ___53___ birthday, I won for the first time. Now I am always the winner between us.

It takes about a day to learn the rules. ___54___ if you want to be good, you have to practice for years. You don't need much to play tennis—just a pair of tennis bats and someone to play with. Tennis sets ___55___ be cheap, or quite expensive. My neighbor collects all kinds of tennis sets as a hobby, but I ___56___ to play.

There is a tennis club in our school. We meet every week to play with each other. I am the best 57 in the club, and the captain(队长) of the school tennis team. This year we 58 the All American School's Championship(锦标赛). I had to go up on the stage(舞台) in front of the whole school to collect the prize(奖品).

I'm saving up my pocket money to buy some tennis 59 . It's very useful for 60 the skill. I'm sure I'll make more progress.

51. A. how	B. where	C. why	D. what
52. A. fought	B. lost	C. beat	D. hit
53. A. fourth	B. tenth	C. seventh	D. eighth
54. A. And	B. Yet	C. So	D. But
55. A. will	B. can	C. must	D. should
56. A. prefer	B. hope	C. want	D. try
57. A. player	B. fan	C. learner	D. leader
58. A. received	B. won	C. owned	D. lost
59. A. dictionary	B. books	C. bags	D. games
60. A. developing	B. changing	C. making	D. playing

第三部分 阅读理解

(共25小题,第1~4篇为选择题和判断题,每小题1分;第5篇为简答题,每小题2分;共30分)

A. 选择题

根据短文内容选择正确的答案。

Passage 1

A young man and an old man were waiting for a bus at a station. They sat next to each other.

"What's that in your bag?" asked the young man, pointing to a big bag beside the old man.

"Gold, nothing but gold," answered the old man.

"What?" the young man said to himself in surprise. "So much gold? My God! How do I wish to be able to get so much gold!" Then he thought about how to get the bag.

The old man looked tired and sleepy and it was clear that he could hardly keep his eyes open.

"Are you sleepy, sir?" asked the young man. "Then you'd better lie down on the chair and have a good rest. Don't worry about the bus. I'll wake you up in time."

"It's very kind of you, young man." the old man said and lay down. Soon he fell asleep.

The young man took the big bag gently. But when he was going to run away, he found a corner of his woolen coat was under the old man's body. Several times he tried to pull it out, but he failed. At last he took off his coat and went away with the bag.

The young man ran out of the station as fast as possible. When he reached a place where he thought the old man couldn't find him, he stopped and quickly opened the bag.

He didn't think there was nothing but a lot of small stones in it. He hurried to the station at once. But when he got there, the old man had left.

61. At first the young man _____ at the station.
    A. wanted to help the old man
    B. waited for a bus with the old man
    C. did his best to get the gold
    D. wanted to know what was in the bag

62. The young man was surprised when _____ .
    A. he heard there was so much gold in the bag
    B. the old man opened his bag
    C. he saw so much gold in the bag
    D. the old man looked tired and sleepy

63. The young man did his best to get the bag because he thought _____ .
    A. it was big enough to hold his woolen coat
    B. he wanted to put some presents into it
    C. it was full of gold
    D. it was too heavy for the old man to carry

64. The young man took off his coat because _____ .
    A. the weather was hot and he didn't need it
    B. the gold was much more important than his coat
    C. he was afraid the old man would catch him
    D. the old man was too tired and he wouldn't wake him up

65. At the end of the story _____ .
    A. the young man got nothing
    B. the old man lost his coat
    C. the young man got a bag full of stones but lost his coat
    D. the young man got a lot of gold

Passage 2

One day, an old farmer was walking along a road with his son Ben. The father said, "Look! There's a horseshoe. Pick it up and put it in your bag." Ben said slowly, "It isn't worth the trouble, Daddy." His father said nothing but he picked it up himself. When they got to a nearby town, they had a rest. There the farmer sold the horseshoe and bought some cherries(樱桃) with a few pennies.

The father and the son continued their way. The sun was very strong in the sky. They couldn't have a rest because there wasn't a house or even a tree. Ben felt too thirsty to walk on. At this time, his father dropped a cherry on the ground and Ben picked it up quickly and ate it. After a while, his father dropped another cherry, his son picked it up and put it into his mouth again.

And so they went on. The old farmer dropped the cherries and the son picked them up. When Ben had eaten up all the cherries, his father said to him, "My dear son, if you had bent down early to pick up that horseshoe, you wouldn't bend so many times for the cherries. Always remember the lesson:if a person does not worry about the little things,he cannot do the great things."

66. Who picked up the horseshoe at last?
   A. The son.   B. The father.
   C. Both the father and the son.   D. Neither the father nor the son.
67. When the son refused to pick up the horseshoe, the father _____.
   A. beat the son   B. said nothing
   C. felt very happy   D. became very angry
68. The farmer bought _____ with the money after he sold the horseshoe.
   A. some bread   B. some water   C. some cherries   D. some pennies
69. The father dropped the cherries one by one, because _____.
   A. he wanted to teach his son a lesson   B. he wanted his son to do more exercise
   C. he wanted his son to eat them all   D. he wanted to laugh at his son
70. From the story, we can learn that _____.
   A. cherries are so delicious that most of us like to eat them
   B. a horseshoe is so expensive that it can bring us a lot of money
   C. if we want to eat cherries, we must pick up a horseshoe
   D. if we don't worry about the little things, we cannot do the great things

Passage 3

People who can't tell all colors apart are said to be color blind. Most color-blind people can see yellows and blues, but confuse(混淆) reds and greens. It's very rare for a person to be blind to all colors, but they may see everything in shades of black, white and gray.

It is interesting to note that many color-blind people don't even realize that they are color-blind, they don't know the colors they are seeing and naming are not the actual colors that people with normal vision(正常的视觉) can see. This can be particularly dangerous when a color-blind person is passing by a traffic light. Color blindness is thought to be inherited(遗传), and although doctors have devised tests to decide color blindness, there is no cure or treatment for it.

71. A color-blind person _____.
   A. can't see any colors
   B. is only blind to some colors
   C. can only see yellows and blues
   D. sees everything in shades of black, white and gray
72. The writer says in this passage that _____.
   A. most people are color blind
   B. color-blind people can't see anything
   C. most color-blind people know they're color blind
   D. not many color-blind people know they're color blind
73. It's dangerous for a color-blind person to pass by a traffic light, because _____.
   A. he can't see the cars
   B. he is blind to reds and greens

C. the greens he is seeing must be red

D. the police don't let a color-blind person pass by

74. Which of the following is **TRUE**?

A. If one always makes his eyes too tired, he will become color blind.

B. Doctors now have managed to cure color blindness.

C. The color-blind people's parents are probably color blind.

D. Now people still don't begin to find what causes color blind.

75. If you're a color-blind person,_____.

A. you should be more careful when you are passing by a traffic light

B. you ought to go to see a doctor at once for some treatment

C. you'd better wear a pair of glasses

D. the color you see mustn't be the actual ones

B. 判断题

根据短文内容判断句子的正误(正确的用"T",错误的用"F",文中未提的用"N")。

Passage 4

Sports and games make our bodies strong, prevent us from getting too fat, and keep us healthy. But these are not their only use. They give us valuable practice in making eyes, brain and muscles work together. In tennis, our eyes see the ball coming, judge its speed and direction and pass this information onto the brain. The brain then has to decide what to do, and to send its orders to the muscles of the arms, legs and so on, so that the ball is met and hit back where it ought to go. All this must happen with very great speed, and only those who have had a lot of practice at tennis can carry out these events successfully.

Sports and games are also very useful for character(性格) training. In their lessons at school boys and girls may learn about such good qualities as unselfishness, courage, discipline(纪律) and love of their country; but what is learned in books cannot have the same deep effect(影响) on a child's character as what is learned by experience(体验). The ordinary day-school cannot give much practical training in living, because most of the pupils' time is spent in classes, studying lessons. So it is what the pupils do in their spare time that really prepares them to take their place in society as citizens when they grow up. If each of them learns to work with his team and not for himself on the football field, he will later find it natural to work for the good of his country instead of only for his own benefit.

76. When we play tennis we have to use, first, our eyes, then the brain and finally the muscles.

77. What is most important to a football team is its team work.

78. By character training, the author means that sports and games can help a child get along well with others, work for his country not only for himself and be a good citizen in society.

79. According to the author, a child's character can be most deeply influenced by what he learns in books.

80. What the students do in their free time isn't important.

C. 简答题

根据短文内容简要回答问题，每题不得超过 10 个单词。

Passage 5

Trouble at the Supermarket

Every Friday morning Mrs. Bell goes to the supermarket and gets the groceries(杂货) for the next week. Last Friday, as usual, she drove to the supermarket. She found a parking(停车) space outside the supermarket. She parked and locked the door.

She went into the supermarket and got a trolley(手推车). She went to the fruit section(部门) first. And there she got some apples and oranges. Then she went to the meat counter and got some steak. She wanted some wine because she was giving a dinner party that evening. She started walking towards the wines and spirits section(酒及饮料区).

At the wines and spirits section she met her neighbor, Mrs. Young. Mrs. Young's three-year-old daughter, Lily, was with her. As she was too heavy to carry, Mrs. Young let her sit in the trolley. The two women started talking. Mrs. Bell told Mrs. Young about the dinner party.

Lily wasn't interested in their conversation(会话). So she began to examine the bottles on the shelves(货架). They were much more interesting. She picked up a bottle of whisky(威士忌). Neither of the women noticed.

After Lily had looked at the bottle for a few seconds, she got bored. She couldn't open the bottle, so she put it in Mrs. Bell's shopping bag which was hanging from the handle(把柄,把手) of the trolley.

Mrs. Bell found a nice bottle of red wine and put it in her trolley. She went to the checkout and joined the queue. The store detective(侦探) was standing near the checkout. He saw the bottle of whisky in Mrs. Bell's bag. Mrs. Bell paid all the things in her trolley and walked towards the exit(出口).

She was just going out when the shop detective stopped her and asked why she hadn't paid for the whisky. Mrs. Bell was astonished(惊讶的). She explained(解释) that she didn't know anything about the bottle of whisky. The store detective didn't believe her and asked Mrs. Bell to go with him to the manager's office.

81. What does Mrs. Bell do every Friday?

_____

82. To which sections of the supermarket did Mrs. Bell go?

_____

83. Why was Lily put in the trolley?

_____

84. What did Lily do while her mother was talking with Mrs. Bell?

_____

85. Did Mrs. Bell know she didn't pay for the whisky?

_____

第四部分 书面表达

(共两节,共20分)

第一节:英汉互译(共5小题,每小题2分,共10分。请将86~88题译成中文,将89~90题括号里的中文译成英文)

86. You can imagine how I felt when I saw that everyone had dressed up except me.

_____

87. That's not a big deal.

_____

88. Mr. Hall drank a lot that night and did not wake up until the middle of the next day.

_____

89. It sounds interesting but I _____(更愿意) stay at home.

90. I hate telling stories _____(在公共场合).

第二节:应用文写作(本节共10空,每空1分,共10分)

中文提示:王林写信给张华,告诉张华,他与朋友 Johnny 及其家人一起度过了复活节。在复活节当天他们一起准备了复活节彩蛋。当蛋准备好时,Johnny 的父母把蛋藏在花园里,然后王林和 Johnny 一起找蛋。他们玩得很开心。最后他们找到了所有蛋。Johnny 父母给了他们巧克力作为奖励。王林和 Johnny 分享了巧克力。

Dear   91   ,

_____92_____(你好吗)? I ____93____(度过) Easter with my American friend Johnny and his family.

On the Easter Day I prepared the Easter eggs with them. When the eggs were ____94____(准备好), Johnny's parents hid the eggs in the garden. After that, Johnny and I ____95____(寻找) the eggs and we ____96____(玩得开心). ____97____(最后), we ____98____(找到) all the eggs and his parents gave us chocolates ____99____(作为) a prize. I ____100____(分享) the chocolates with him.

Yours
Wang Lin

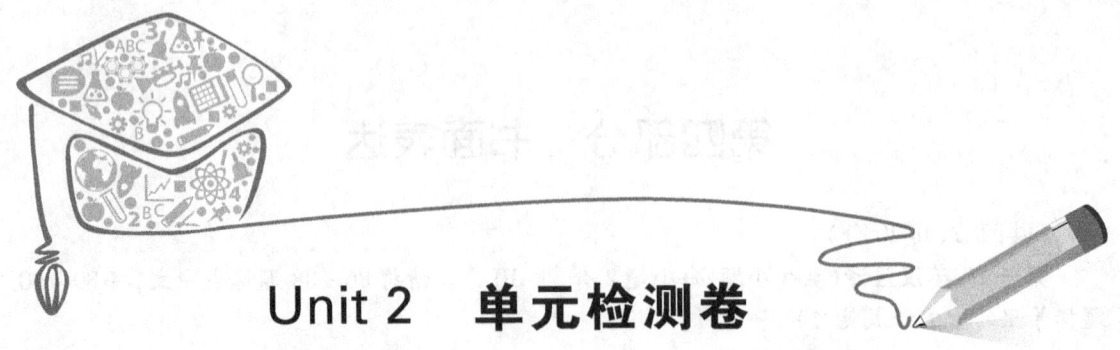

Unit 2 单元检测卷

第一部分 听力

(略)

第二部分 知识运用

(共三大题,每题1分,共40分)

第一节:词汇与语法(本大题共10小题,每小题1分,共10分)

从每小题给出的A、B、C、D四个选项中选出一个符合题意的最佳选项,请将所选答案填在答题卡上。

21. Make a brochure to introduce your service _____ the customers.
    A. for   B. to   C. with   D. of

22. You need to fill in a form and deposit _____ least 10 yuan.
    A. at   B. by   C. in   D. about

23. The exchange rate today is 1 US dollar _____ 6.8 RMB.
    A. with   B. of   C. by   D. to

24. Please _____ your name here.
    A. write to   B. leave   C. sign   D. note

25. Now you can do your banking and _____ your bills anytime anywhere.
    A. put   B. change   C. give   D. pay

26. Bank _____ phone or fax is convenient and easy.
    A. on   B. by   C. with   D. use

27. Some students learn business skills _____ operating their own companies.
    A. by   B. on   C. through   D. with

28. The bank was opened _____ the school campus for one hour two days a week.
    A. in   B. among   C. between   D. on
29. They trained them to do all the different kinds _____ bank jobs.
    A. to   B. of   C. in   D. for
30. They also learned _____ ask for a job.
    A. how to   B. what to   C. when to   D. where to

第二节：交际用语(本大题共20小题，每小题1分，共20分)

(一)选择

31. —Which season do you prefer, spring or autumn?
    —_____.
    A. I think so   B. I prefer spring
    C. Yes, I like spring   D. The autumn is too dry

32. —Let's chat online.
    —_____.
    A. Not at all   B. Thank you   C. Good luck   D. Good idea

33. —Would you like to help me?
    —_____.
    A. With pleasure   B. Right   C. That's OK   D. No, I'm busy

34. —Do you mind if I sit here?
    —_____.
    A. No, not at all B. Yes, sit here   C. No, you can't   D. Yes, of course

35. —Could you please tell me _____?
    —It's next to the post office.
    A. where is the supermarket   B. where the supermarket is
    C. where was the supermarket   D. where the supermarket was

36. —May I borrow your car, John?
    —_____. Here you are.
    A. Yes, you may   B. Oh, no   C. No problem   D. Certainly not

37. —Would you mind my smoking here?
    —_____.
    A. I'm afraid you'd better not   B. Yes, you may
    C. I don't know   D. No, you wouldn't

38. —How are you getting on with your school?
    —_____.
    A. That's right   B. Yes, thanks   C. That's great   D. Just fine

39. —Would you like to come to the party?
    —_____.
    A. No, I don't like   B. Quite well
    C. Yes, I'd love to   D. Sure, that's right

40. —_____?
   —I enjoy it very much.
   A. What's the novel like
   B. What's the novel about
   C. How much did it cost
   D. How did you like the novel

(二)补全对话

Daniel: Oh, Li Ming. You look worried. ___41___

Li Ming: Yeah, Daniel. We are going to have an exam next week. But I don't think I'm well ready for it.

Daniel: What subject is it?

Li Ming: ___42___ The main problem is not the knowledge but the language.

Daniel: You mean you can't understand the knowledge of science well because of the language?

Li Ming: Yes. Each time I finish a science class, I feel so tired.

Daniel: I see. I think that you should use your dictionary more often. When you read the science textbook, and you'll understand it better.

Li Ming: ___43___ But what shall I do with my exam?

Daniel: Don't worry. ___44___ I am good at science. We can go over science together.

Li Ming: ___45___

Daniel: You are welcome. There is nothing to worry about now. Let's start this afternoon.

A. Thanks a lot.
B. Let me help you.
C. Is there any problem?
D. What's he doing now?
E. You are welcome.
F. Maybe you are right.
G. Science.

(三)匹配

I	II
46. 此处撕开	A. Insert Here
47. 招聘	B. Toll Free
48. 禁止鸣笛	C. Ticket Office
49. 不准超车	D. No Honking
50. 免费通行	E. Hands Wanted
	F. Do not Pass
	G. Split Here

第三节:完形填空(本大题共10小题,每小题1分,共10分)

阅读下面短文,从各题所给的 A、B、C、D 四个选项中选出可填入空白处的最佳答案,并将所选答案填在答题卡上。

Bedtime stories are one of the delights of early childhood. But according to Dr. Julie Spreadbury from Queensland University, parents should not ___51___ up reading to their children ___52___ they enter primary school. She says listening to, reading and discussing the stories help children's ___53___.

"My ___54___ indicates that once children can read themselves, most parents stop reading ___55___ them," Dr. Spreadbury says.

"___56___ may be at the end of Year 1, which is far too ___57___."

Dr. Spreadbury says ___58___ reading not only gives children a good start at school, but brings parents and their children closer.

"This makes it ___59___ for them to open up and talk to parents about things that are worrying them, or things they are ___60___ in their everyday life."

51. A. speed   B. keep   C. give   D. hold
52. A. after   B. until   C. if   D. unless
53. A. thinking   B. comprehension   C. relaxation   D. development
54. A. theory   B. research   C. story   D. decision
55. A. about   B. from   C. to   D. through
56. A. Some   B. Most   C. They   D. That
57. A. difficult   B. early   C. much   D. informed
58. A. daily   B. health   C. fast   D. bedtime
59. A. easier   B. funnier   C. rarer   D. cleaner
60. A. reading   B. promising   C. celebrating   D. receiving

第三部分　阅读理解

(共 25 小题,第 1~4 篇为选择题和判断题,每小题 1 分;第 5 篇为简答题,每小题 2 分;共 30 分)

A. 选择题

根据短文内容选择正确的答案。

Passage 1

Mr. Black and Mr. White were two very famous artists in the city. Their drawings were also very popular in the city. But they tried to see who could draw the best picture.

One day they asked an old man to be the judge. Mr. Black drew an apple tree. He put his picture in the field. Soon the birds came and tried to eat the apples. The old man saw it and said, "You have certainly won. Mr. White can not draw so good a picture."

They went to Mr. White's house. There were nothing but red beautiful curtains on the wall. The old man asked, "Where is your picture, Mr. White?" He said, "Lift the curtains, and you will find my picture." The old man tried to lift the curtains but found that they were drawn there. They were in

Mr. White's picture. The old man said, "Birds thought the apples were real. Men thought the curtains were real. So Mr. White won. His picture is the better one."

61. The judge thought Mr. Black's picture was good because _____ .
    A. it was in the field   B. it was a tree
    C. the birds liked it   D. the birds thought it was a real tree
62. Mr. White's drawn _____ .
    A. an apple tree   B. curtains   C. nothing   D. a window
63. Mr. Black drew _____ .
    A. an apple tree   B. the best picture   C. birds   D. a field
64. Mr. White won because the picture looked real to _____ .
    A. the judge   B. the birds   C. the children   D. the women
65. Which of the following is **TRUE**?
    A. The birds came and ate the apples up.
    B. The two pictures were not very good.
    C. The old man said Mr. White's picture was the better one at last.
    D. The curtains on the wall were real ones.

Passage 2

The airport in Boswell is twenty-one miles from the city. The banks and business offices are in the center of the city. Read these notes from the diary of Mr. Reg Simpson, March 2008.

15 MON Group of 35 Australian students visiting Boswell _____ want cheap holiday.

16 TUE Mr. and Mrs. J. Grant arriving from Sydney-leaving early on the 18th by air.

17 WED Mr. Nagahima, Tokyo, arriving for two days, business trip.

18 THUR 65 German students need two days in a cheap hotel.

19 FRI

20 SAT Mr. and Mrs. Johnson, from New York City, arriving by air.

21 SUN

22 MON Mr. and Mrs. F. Ray, small inexpensive(便宜的) hotel needed for two days.

66. Mr. Reg Simpson is probably _____ .
    A. a headmaster   B. a travel manager   C. a traveler   D. an engineer
67. Mr. Nagahima is from _____ .
    A. Australia   B. Japan   C. America   D. Germany
68. Mr, and Mrs. J. Grant will leave Boswell on _____ .
    A. Tuesday   B. Wednesday   C. Thursday   D. Friday
69. How many travelers will Mr. Reg Simpson meet in just over a week?
    A. 107   B. 65   C. 35   D. 131
70. Where does Mr. Reg Simpson work according to the passage?
    A. New York.   B. Tokyo.   C. The Airport.   D. The center of city.

Passage 3

"Hello" became popular as a greeting with the invention(发明) of the telephone. It is said that Alexander Graham Bell, the inventor(发明者) of the telephone, was the first person to use "hello" in a telephone conversation. For the first several years that telephones were used, the opening phrase in a conversation was usually, "Are you there?" Perhaps this was because it was difficult for the two parties(双方) to hear each other and the phones weren't completely reliable (可靠的). "Hello" quickly became a popular greeting and was also used in everyday speech.

Many different words have been used over time to attract(吸引) a distant(远处的) person's attention(注意力). "Hello" has had many variations(变化) throughout the history of the English language. It may have originated(起源) as a variation of the familiar "ahoy" that sailors(水手) used to hail ships. One early form was probably "hallow", sometimes called the "sailor's hail(招呼)". In the sixteenth century, a common form was "halloo" or "hallo." Later, there were many variations, such as "hillo" "hilloa" "holla" "holloa" "hullo" and "hollo." Hunters(猎人) often used these words, because their sounds traveled well when they were shouted. Most calling words and greetings had an echoic(回声的) origin, because they were meant to travel long distances(距离) across water or hills.

71. This passage is about _____.
    A. talking on the telephone   B. ways of greeting people
    C. shouting messages   D. spelling mistakes

72. When sailors greeted another ship they shouted "_____!"
    A. Hi   B. Hello   C. Ahoy   D. Hallow

73. We can understand from this passage that _____.
    A. the telephone has caused many changes
    B. some words in common use today were derived from similar words used long ago
    C. Alexander Graham Bell was a great man
    D. Hunters had very loud voices

74. Echoic means _____.
    A. sounding like an echo   B. music
    C. empty   D. sick

75. By whom was the word "hello" used first according to the passage?
    A. Mr. Bell.   B. Mr. Ring.   C. Mr. Smith.   D. Mr. Alexander.

B. 判断题

根据短文内容判断句子的正误(正确的用"T",错误的用"F",文中未提的用"N")。

Passage 4

At Harton College, there are many rules. Fifteen-year-old boy Bob Sanders often breaks these rules.

The boys must return to school by 6 o'clock. One afternoon Bob walked to the town. He looked at the shops and then went to the cinema. After the cinema, it was 8 o'clock. He walked back to Harton College as fast as possible.

When he arrived, the main entrance was locked. He looked up at the window of his dormitory. It was on the third floor. He couldn't climb up the wall very easily. Then he saw another open window on the ground floor. It was the window of the headmaster's study, and no one was there. He quickly climbed and jumped into the room. Just then he heard a noise. Then someone turned on a light in the corridor(走廊). Bob had to hide under the sofa. One minute later, Mr. Mason, the headmaster, came in. He turned on the light and then he sat down on the sofa and began to read a book.

Bob lay under the sofa as quietly as possible. He looked at the headmaster's shoes and socks for nearly an hour.

Finally, the headmaster closed his book and walked towards the door.

"Thank Heavens, he didn't find me under the sofa!" thought Bob.

Then Mr. Mason stopped and spoke towards the sofa. "Would you turn off the light when you leave?" He said and left the study.

76. Bob is 16 years old.

77. The boys must return to school by 6 o'clock.

78. Bob ate a lot that afternoon.

79. Bob hid himself under the sofa for about one hour.

80. Mr. Mason didn't find Bob under the sofa.

C. 简答题

根据短文内容简要回答问题,每题不得超过10个单词。

Passage 5

I started my school life at six. At first the school for me, a boy, meant play, play and more play instead of sitting in the classroom and learning something. However, I changed the way I used to behave at school with the help of my teachers. I tried my best to do well in my schoolwork and follow the school rules.

Growing and learning were great fun. Every year we had different kinds of school trips. Not only could we learn things from them, but also we were given many projects as homework. It helped us know more. At the same time, we made many friends. In Grade 8, I won prizes in drawing and English speech competitions. When I was in Grade 9, I realized that I should give all my attention to studies because I had to take the exams for senior schools.

Whenever I think of my school life, I feel very happy and I think in everybody's school life there are many ups and downs that influence his future life. School is a place where all of us learn to care and share. "School" is not just a place, but a large building made up of rules, knowledge and love. I think in everybody's success, school plays a key role. I can describe my school in "Three Ss." They are: Small, Sweet and Simple. My school was the best, is the best and will always be the best.

81. When did the writer start to go to school?

82. Who helped him change the way he used to behave at school?

83. Why does he think the school trips were useful?

_____

84. Why did he give all his attention to his studies in Grade 9?

_____

85. What do the "Three Ss" stand for?

_____

第四部分 书面表达

(共两节,共20分)

第一节:英汉互译(共5小题,每小题2分,共10分。请将86~88题译成中文,将89~90题括号里的中文译成英文)

86. You can use our Auto Banks to draw cash, make deposits or to recharge your airtime.

_____

87. Making payments and checking balances are now at your fingertips.

_____

88. Our Internet banking users have easy access to this service.

_____

89. Sorry for _____(让您久等了).

90. Would you please _____(出示你的护照).

第二节:应用文写作(本节共10空,每空1分,共10分)

中文提示:请你以顾客办公室的身份写一个通知。内容是:为了省去来银行排队等候的麻烦,将为顾客提供自助银行服务,它可随时随地帮助办理银行业务。下面是简单服务介绍。银行一共提供4种自助服务,它们是自动银行、手机银行业务、网络银行业务和电话银行业务。因为他们可随时随地让你办理银行业务,很容易,方便使用。如果你想更进一步地了解这些服务,请发电子邮件到银行,电子邮箱是:information@standardbank.cn。

_____91_____

____92____(为了)save your trouble of coming to the bank and ____93____(排队等候), We are offering ____94____(自助服务)banking for you. It will help you to do your banking ____95____(随时随地).

The ____96____(以下)is a brief introduction of the service:

There are all together ____97____(4种)self-service banking offered in our bank. They are Auto Banks, Cell phone banking, Internet banking and Telephone banking. They are convenient and easy to use because they can make you ____98____(办理银行业务)anytime anywhere. If you want to ____99____(更多了解)the services, send emails to our bank. The email address is ____100____.

Customer Service Office

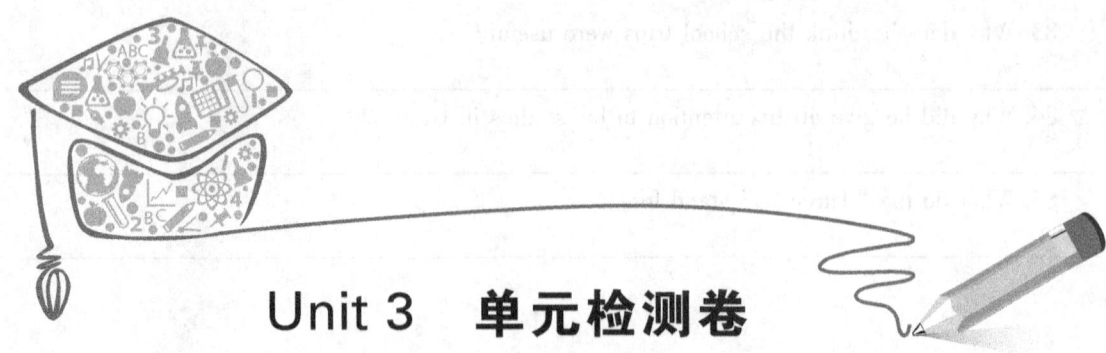

Unit 3 单元检测卷

第一部分 听力

(略)

第二部分 知识运用

(共三大题,每题1分,共40分)

第一节:词汇与语法(本大题共10个小题,每小题1分,共10分)

从每小题给出的A、B、C、D四个选项中选出一项符合题意的最佳选项,请将所选答案填在答题卡上。

21. We have courses _____ computer programming.
    A. about   B. on   C. of   D. in

22. It impressed me that many Australian students earn their tuition fees _____ part-time employment.
    A. by   B. besides   C. with   D. on

23. I don't know what other difficulties I will have, but I will never _____ .
    A. give out   B. give up   C. keep up   D. give off

24. Will you do the _____ kind of part-time jobs as Zhang Lin did?
    A. such   B. so   C. same   D. as

25. _____ I want to learn is something new about computer programming.
    A. How   B. When   C. What   D. That

26. It is uncertain _____ the sports meeting will be held in our school.
    A. where   B. when   C. what   D. that

27. The question was _____ we should take the children to the theater or leave them at home.

A. how　　　　B. however　　　　C. if　　　　　　D. whether
28. _____ no one is against it, let's carry out our plan.
　　A. Why　　　　B. That　　　　　C. As　　　　　　D. As for
29. I got up early _____ I could catch the first bus.
　　A. in order that　B. because　　　C. for　　　　　　D. so as to
30. Look! The couple _____ in formal clothes.
　　A. put on　　　B. is wearing　　　C. have on　　　　D. are dressing

第二节:交际用语(本大题共20小题,每小题1分,共20分)
(一)选择
31. —Excuse me, sir. Could you please tell me the way to the nearest bank?
　　—_____.
　　A. That's right　B. You're right　C. Of course　　　D. Good idea
32. —We are going to make a trip. How about tomorrow?
　　—_____.
　　A. Sorry, I am afraid not　　　　　B. Yes, it is
　　C. Yes, we do　　　　　　　　　D. Sorry, I'm not
33. —Would you like to come to our party?
　　—_____.
　　A. Yes, I like　　B. Yes, I do　　　C. Yes, I'd like　　D. Yes, I'd like to
34. —Mike, you'd better not do it again.
　　—_____.
　　A. Yes, I do　　B. No, I won't　　C. No, I'm not　　D. Yes, I can
35. —Let me carry it for you.
　　—_____.
　　A. I have no idea　　　　　　　　B. No, thank you
　　C. You're welcome　　　　　　　D. I'm afraid not
36. —Hello, 88776655. Who's that?
　　—_____.
　　A. I don't know you　　　　　　　B. I'm Jim
　　C. This is Jim　　　　　　　　　D. That's Jim
37. —How long may I keep the book?
　　—_____.
　　A. That's over there　　　　　　　B. It's a nice book
　　C. Sorry, you can't　　　　　　　D. Half a month
38. —Could you look after my pet cat?
　　—_____.
　　A. You're welcome　　　　　　　B. With pleasure
　　C. Yes, it is　　　　　　　　　　D. Yes, here you are
39. —Would you please lend me your camera?

—_____, but you'll have to buy some films yourself.

  A. No problem   B. Don't worry   C. I'm sorry   D. Never mind

40. —My watch doesn't work. _____?

  —It's half past eleven.

  A. What is it   B. What's your watch

  C. How about your watch   D. What time is it by your watch

(二)补全对话

A:Excuse me. Could you please tell me where the doctor's office is?

B:Sure. It's on the fifth floor. Just take the elevator.

A:Mm. First I need to buy a book. ___41___

B:Yes, you can find Xinhua Bookstore on the third floor.

A: ___42___

B:There is a bank on the first floor. It's over there.

A:Good. ___43___

B:Yes, there's a drug store on the fourth floor. ___44___

A:Thank you. ___45___

B:You're welcome.

> A. You can take the elevator.
> B. Do you know where I can buy some aspirin(阿司匹林)?
> C. Is there a bookstore here?
> D. It's very kind of you.
> E. Where is the bookstore?
> F. I also need to exchange some money.
> G. That's right.

(三)匹配

46. 请别打扰   A. No Camera!

47. 注册免费邮箱   B. Caution! Wet Floor!

48. 游客止步   C. Don't Disturb!

49. 轻拿轻放   D. Sign up for Free E-mail.

50. 不要乱扔垃圾   E. Handle with Care!

            F. No Visitors!

            G. No Littering!

第三节:完形填空(本大题共10小题,每小题1分,共10分)

阅读下面短文,从各题所给的 A、B、C、D 四个选项中选出可填入空白处的最佳答案,并将所选答案填在答题卡上。

  Once a little a boy was traveling with his father on a train. ___51___ was new to the little boy, so he put his head out of the window of the train and wanted to ___52___ so many things. "Ted, don't put your head out of the window," the father said. ___53___ the little boy did not stop   54   out of the window again, he took the boy's hat at once, and put it   55   him. "There now!" said the father.

    The little boy lost his hat and began to   56   . His father said to him, "I have told you not to put your head out of the window. The   57   will take the hat away. Don't cry. I will ask the hat to come back again." Suddenly the father said, "come back." He showed him the hat behind his back, the boy was very   58   .

    The boy sat with no words for a while. "How did my father   59   the hat to come back?" the boy thought, "I will see it once again." The boy suddenly picked up his father's hat and   60   out of the window, and he said, "Please ask your hat to come back now, Father."

( )51. A. Anything   B. Something   C. Everything   D. Nothing
( )52. A. see   B. find   C. visit   D. look
( )53. A. As   B. And   C. Even   D. But
( )54. A. to look   B. looking   C. to make   D. making
( )55. A. near   B. before   C. under   D. behind
( )56. A. cry   B. smile   C. speak   D. shout
( )57. A. sun   B. wind   C. cloud   D. rain
( )58. A. surprised   B. trouble   C. happily   D. sad
( )59. A. want   B. make   C. let   D. ask
( )60. A. threw   B. dropped   C. felt   D. put

第三部分　阅读理解

（共 25 小题，第 1~4 篇为选择题和判断题，每小题 1 分；第 5 篇为简答题，每小题 2 分；共 30 分）

A. 选择题

根据短文内容选择正确的答案。

Passage 1

    As you know, the great American writer Jack London was often in need of money when he began to write his books. He worked very hard but it did not help him.

    Once he promised a New York magazine to write a story for it, but he was busy at that time and could not keep his promise. The leader of the magazine wrote letters to Jack London several times asking him to send the story. At last he went to the hotel where Jack London stayed and left him a note.

    "Dear Jack London, if I don't get the story within twenty-four hours, I'll come up to your room and kick you downstairs, and I always keep my promise."

    Jack London read the note and answered, "Dear Dick, if I could do my work with my feet like you, I would keep my promise, too."

61. Jack London was a great _____.
    A. English writer   B. American president
    C. American author   D. English poet
62. Jack London promised a New York magazine to _____ for it.
    A. write a story   B. write a poem
    C. draw a picture   D. take a photo
63. Jack London was _____ when he began to write his books.
    A. very rich   B. very bad   C. not well   D. very poor
64. The leader of the magazine went to the hotel and _____.
    A. kicked him downstairs   B. left him a note
    C. gave him a present   D. gave him money
65. Jack London answered that he couldn't _____ because he was not writing with his feet.
    A. keep his promise   B. keep healthy
    C. break his promise   D. promise in himself

Passage 2

Football is the most popular game in England. One has only to go to one of the important matches to see this.

One of the most surprising things about football in England to a stranger is the great knowledge of the game which even the smallest boy seems to have. He can tell you the names of the players in the most of important teams. He has photographs of them and knows the results of large numbers of matches.

Most schools in England take football seriously—much more seriously than nearly other European schools, where lessons are all important, and games, left for private arrangements. In England, it is believed that education is not only a matter of filling a boy's mind with facts in a classroom; education also means character training; and one of the best ways of training character is by means of games, especially team games, where a boy has a lesson to work with others for his team, instead of working selfishly for himself alone. The school therefore arranges games and matches for its pupils. Football is a good team game. It is a good exercise for the body; it needs a skill and a quick brain; it is popular and it is cheap. And as a result, it is the schools' favorite game in winter.

66. The smallest boy in England seems to have _____.
    A. the greatest team of football
    B. a large number of football
    C. the most photographs of football players
    D. a great knowledge of football
67. According to the information given in this passage, the smallest boy in England may **NOT** know _____.
    A. the names of the players in most important teams
    B. the results of a number of important matches

C. the faces of important players

D. the places where important matches were held

68. Lessons are all important and games are left for private arrangements in _____ .

   A. most British schools   B. most Japanese schools

   C. most European schools   D. most American schools

69. Football in England is believed to be _____ .

   A. a private arrangement   B. a way of character training

   C. a favorite game for small boys   D. a serious match

70. Why do most schools in England take football seriously?

   A. Because football is a good team game.

   B. Because football is a good exercise for the body.

   C. Because football is a cheap game in winter.

   D. Because football is a quick skill in the brain.

Passage 3

Nowadays more and more people care about the exploitation(开采)of the natural <u>resources</u>, such as oil. Though there're many kinds of resources, with the fast increase of population and the appearance of many more factories, the more we use, the fewer there will be left for the future. Oil is getting less and less year after year. It's said that oil can last for only 50 years, and natural gas perhaps will last about 38 years.

Oil can be used in many ways and it's difficult to imagine what the modern world will be like without oil. But oil isn't easy to find and get out of the earth. Men must study the rocks. When they think the rocks in a certain place may have oil, a metal tower is built. A machine in the tower cuts a hole down into the ground. At the same time, a steel pipe is pushed down to stop the sides from falling in and to keep out water. At last if the men are right, usually the oil rushes up the sides with great strength by the pressure(压力)of the gas in the top of the rock, and it rushes high into the air. If the oil catches a light, there will be a terrible fire. So a kind of cover is fixed on the top of the pipe, and the oil can run out through taps.

If we make a well near the middle of the oil field, we can also get gas. Such gas is sent through pipes to towns far away and used in houses and factories like coal gas.

Today oil is under pressure as never before. The price of oil keeps rising all the time. In many countries, the governments encourage people to save oil as much as possible.

71. The underlined word "resources" in Paragraph 1 means _____ .

   A. 现象   B. 资源   C. 商品   D. 资料

72. Which is the right order of the exploitation of oil?

   ①Push down a steel pipe   ②Study the rocks

   ③Build a metal tower   ④Oil rushes up

   A. ②③④①   B. ②①③④   C. ②③①④   D. ①②③④

73. Which of the following can be **TRUE** according to the passage?

   A. Coal gas can't be used in houses and factories.

B. Oil is very important in the modern world.

C. Many governments encourage people to use oil as much as possible.

D. Gas can get through a hole to towns.

74. According to the passage, we can learn about that the oil and gas is _____ .
    A. used up   B. very important   C. useless   D. more and more

75. The best title for the passage is "_____."
    A. The Development of Oil   B. The Use of Oil
    C. The Price of Oil   D. The Exploitation of Oil

B. 判断题

根据短文内容判断句子的正误(正确的用"T",错误的用"F",文中未提的用"N")。

Passage 4

John is a paperboy. He delivers(投递) newspapers to different houses in his street every day. He has about 80 customers(客户). Half of his customers only take the newspapers in weekdays and about half of them take the newspapers on weekdays and Sundays. Two of John's customers only take the newspaper on Sundays.

John has to get up at 4:30 every morning. It takes longer to deliver the newspapers on Sundays. The Sunday newspapers are twice as heavy as those on weekdays.

John is saving his money to buy a new bicycle. He is also saving money for college. He has saved 600 dollars.

76. John sells newspapers every day.

77. He sends out about 80 pieces of newspaper in his street every day.

78. John is saving his money to buy a new car.

79. Not all his customers take their newspapers on weekends.

80. He gets up at 4:30 p.m. every day.

C. 简答题

根据短文内容简要回答问题,每题不得超过10个单词。

Passage 5

In New York City some bike riders have formed a group called Bike for a Better City. For several years this group has been trying to get the city government to help bike riders. For example, they want the city to have special lanes(车道) for bicycle only on some of the main streets. Bike for a Better City feels that if there were special lanes, more people would use bikes.

But not everyone thinks it is a good idea. Taxi drivers don't like the idea. They say it would slow traffic down. Some store owners on the main streets don't like the idea either. They say that if there is less traffic, they will have less business. And most people live too far from downtown to travel by bike.

The city government wants to keep everyone happy. On weekends, the Central Park, the largest open space in New York, is closed to cars, and the roads may then be used by bikes only. But Bike for a Better City says that this is not enough, and it keeps fighting to get bicycle lanes downtown.

81. Who formed the group Bike for a Better City?
_____

82. Why does Bike for a Better City want special lanes for bicycles?
_____

83. Why don't taxi drivers like the idea proposed by Bike for a Better City?
_____

84. What does more traffic mean to some store owners?
_____

85. On weekends, can people drive cars in the Central Park in New York?
_____

第四部分　书面表达

(共两节,共20分)

第一节:英汉互译(共5小题,每小题2分,共10分。请将86~88题译成中文,将89~90题括号里的中文译成英文)

86. You can find our homepage on the Internet and fill in the application form online.
_____

87. It impressed me that many Australian students earn their tuition fees through part-time employment.
_____

88. I do not need financial help from my parents any more.
_____

89. The teaching materials in our school always _____ (与……同步) the latest development.

90. How do I _____ (报名)?

第二节:应用文写作(本节共10空,每空1分,共10分)

中文提示:你参加了一所培训学校的国际英语口语培训。这是一个为期3个月的周末培训。在这个活动中,你不仅与来自不同国家的学生交流,而且在不同地方工作并练习英语。3个月之后,你获得了A级英语口语证书,圆满完成了这次培训。

I ___91___ (参加了) an international English speaking ___92___ (课程) in a ___93___ (培训学校) this term. It was a ___94___ (3个月的) weekend program. During the program, I ___95___ (不仅) communicated with the students from different countries, ___96___ (而且) worked in ___97___ (各种地方) to practice my English. After three months, I ___98___ (完成了) the program ___99___ (以……/拥有) a certificate for ___100___ (英语口语).

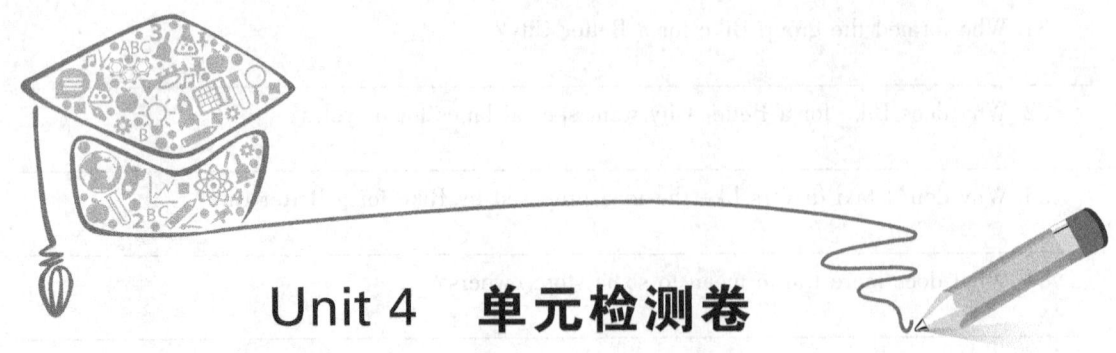

Unit 4 单元检测卷

第一部分 听力

(略)

第二部分 知识运用

(共三大题,每题1分,共40分)

第一节:词汇与语法(本大题共10小题,每小题1分,共10分)
从每小题给出的A,B,C,D四个选项中选出一项符合题意的最佳选项,请将所选答案填在答题卡上。

21. _____ we have been partners _____ so long, we will pay for your loss.
  A. Because;in   B. When;for   C. Since;for   D. For;since

22. Please decide on a solution _____ the problem.
  A. of   B. for   C. about   D. to

23. We started very early _____ we can arrive there on time.
  A. for   B. in order to   C. so that   D. as for

24. You can't enter the room, _____ you are not the member of our company.
  A. for   B. to   C. with   D. since

25. The population(人口) will reduce _____ 20% by the end of this year.
  A. in   B. till   C. by   D. at

26. You can get the goods _____ a lower price.
  A. to   B. till   C. by   D. at

27. Don't _____ your watch when you are taking the shower.
  A. dress   B. be putting on   C. wear   D. in

28. When the customer complains _____ you, you should work out a solution.
  A. to   B. with   C. at   D. for

29. I am not satisfied _____ your service.

    A. at   B. with   C. about   D. in

30. I attended the English evening _____ I could improve my speaking.

    A. as long as   B. as soon as   C. so that   D. in case

第二节:交际用语(本大题共20小题,每小题1分,共20分)

(一)选择

31. —Excuse me. Are there any jobs for waiters?

    —_____.

    A. Yes, the position has been filled
    B. Of course, no such jobs are available at present
    C. You are not the sort of person we need
    D. Sorry, no such jobs are available now

32. —John's mother is seriously ill and she will be in hospital for a week.

    —_____.

    A. I'm glad to hear that   B. Is that so? That's nice
    C. Really? God bless me   D. I'm so sorry to hear that

33. —Do you have the time on you?

    —_____.

    A. Sorry, my watch is very nice   B. Yes, my watch works well
    C. Oh? My watch keeps good time   D. Sorry, my watch doesn't work well

34. —What's wrong with you, young boy?

    —_____.

    A. I've got a toothache   B. Fine, thank you
    C. Oh dear, you are so kind   D. My pleasure

35. —May I speak to Mr. Liu, please?

    —_____. Would you like to leave a message?

    A. No, you can't   B. I'm afraid he isn't in
    C. I'm afraid so   D. I think he is in

36. —_____?

    —She is medium build and she has short hair.

    A. What is she   B. What does she do
    C. What does she like   D. What does she look like

37. —Look, John's fallen asleep.

    —_____.

    A. How lazy he is!
    B. What's he doing now?
    C. Why didn't you wake him up?
    D. Oh, he must have stayed up too late last night.

38. —Why not play table tennis with us?

    —_____.

A. It doesn't matter B. That's right
C. I like it D. OK, I'd love to

39. —Shall I book some seats for the play?
    —_____. The theater won't be full this evening.
    A. Yes, you may B. No, you mustn't
    C. No, you needn't D. I'd rather not

40. —What was the date yesterday?
    —_____.
    A. It was Monday B. It was a fine day
    C. It was June 5th D. It was October the 1st

(二)补全对话

A: Good afternoon, sir. ___41___

B: Yes, I'd like to send this letter registered to Guangzhou.

A: ___42___ Ah, it's all right now. It needs 2 yuan, please.

B: All right. ___43___

A: OK, here is your change. ___44___ Now well, here is your receipt.

B: Thank you.

A: ___45___

A. You are welcome.
B. What can I do for you?
C. Please wait for a while again.
D. How much is it?
E. Just a minute.
F. Here's 5 yuan.
G. With pleasure.

(三)匹配

I	II
46. 高压危险	A. On Sale
47. 更改图标	B. Cancel Printing
48. 取消打印	C. Danger High Voltage
49. 减价销售	D. Move the Cursor to…
50. 将光标移到……	E. No Pedestrians
	F. Disk Drive
	G. Change Icon

第三节:完形填空(本大题共10小题,每小题1分,共10分)

阅读下面短文,从各题所给的 A、B、C、D 四个选项中选出可填入空白处的最佳答案,并将所选答案填在答题卡上。

Being lame(瘸的), I didn't dare to walk in front of my classmates. I was afraid that I might be ___51___ at. In those days I was very sad to see others walking ___52___.

One day, a few students came up to me and asked me to go outside. I was really ___53___. They encouraged me with a(n) ___54___ smile and ___55___ me in my wheelchair(轮椅) from place to place. I was ___56___ to them for giving me a chance to see the ___57___ of our lovely school with my own eyes.

After that we often read, played and talked together. My friends are always ___58___ to help me. It made me ___59___ I am disabled(残疾的).

Once they asked me, "What is the most beautiful thing in our school?" Without hesitation(犹豫) I said, "It is the ___60___."

51. A. laughed	B. smiled	C. stared	D. looked
52. A. quickly	B. slowly	C. happily	D. shyly
53. A. brave	B. sad	C. hurt	D. excited
54. A. honest	B. friendly	C. luckily	D. handsome
55 A. pushed	B. placed	C. drew	D. pulled
56 A. satisfied	B. sorry	C. pleased	D. grateful
57. A. signs	B. sights	C. buildings	D. students
58. A. ready	B. smart	C. wise	D. unwilling
59. A. forget	B. remember	C. imagine	D. think
60. A. teachers	B. schoolyard	C. classmates	D. friendship

第三部分 阅读理解

(共25小题,第1~4篇为选择题和判断题,每小题1分;第5篇为简答题,每小题2分;共30分)

A. 选择题
根据短文内容选择正确的答案。

Passage 1

1.
The London Home,
a center for people with AIDS.
The London Home gives love and care, but money is always needed.
111/117 Bute Road, London
Tel:0171 - 792 1200

2.
Do you want to join our group at our weekly meetings and help to make our world safer and cleaner?
Can you spare a few hours a week to hand out information brochures(手册)?
WORLD WATCHERS
Needs you!

Write to *The Information Office*
PO BOX 379 GD30 6QA

3.

At Solutions we teach people how to help themselves. In parts of Africa and India we have helped the poor a lot. Now they have hope for a better life.

Solutions

Finding solutions(解决办法) to help the poor. Call 0044 – 173 654 2427

61. World Watchers is a center for _____ .
    A. searching information   B. protecting the environment
    C. finding solutions   D. helping people with themselves

62. With the help of _____ , people can learn how to help themselves.
    A. Solutions   B. The London Home
    C. World Watchers   D. The Information Office

63. If a person with AIDS wants to get help, he can _____ .
    A. go to the Information Office   B. call 0040 – 173 654 2427
    C. post to PO BOX 379 GD30 6QA   D. write to 111/117 Bute Road, London

64. If you are a member of World Watchers, you should hand out information brochures _____ .
    A. for a few hours a day   B. for a few hours a week
    C. for a few days a week   D. every day

65. The three passages are _____ .
    A. notices   B. advertisements   C. help wanted   D. posters

Passage 2

Every day we go to school and listen to the teacher, and the teacher will ask us some questions. Sometimes, the classmates will ask your opinions of the work of the class. When you are telling others in the class what you have found out about these topics, remember that they must be able to hear what you are saying. You are not taking part in a family conversation or having a chat with friends—you are in a slightly unnatural situation where a large group of people will remain silent, waiting to hear what you have to say. You must speak so that they can hear you—loudly enough and clearly enough but without trying to shout or appearing to force yourself.

Remember, too, that it is the same if you are called to an interview whether it is with a professor of your school or a government official who might meet you. The person you are seeing will try to put you at your ease(轻松), but the situation is somewhat(有点儿) different from that of an ordinary conversation. You must take special care that you can be heard.

66. When you speak to the class, you should speak _____ .
    A. as loudly as possible   B. in a low voice
    C. loudly   D. forcefully

67. Usually, when you speak to your family or have a chat with your friends, you can be _____ .
    A. nervous   B. excited   C. at ease   D. sensitive

68. If you are having a conversation with an official, the most important thing for you is _____.

    A. to show your ability   B. to be very gentle

    C. to make sure that you can be heard   D. to put the official at ease

69. The main idea of the passage is that we must _____.

    A. use different ways at different situations

    B. speak loudly

    C. keep silent at any time

    D. talk with the class

70. Which is the best title of the passage?

    A. When do you speak?   B. Whom do you speak to?

    C. Where do you speak?   D. Why do you speak?

Passage 3

Smoking, which may be a pleasure for some people, is a serious reason of discomfort for their fellows. Medical scientists have expressed their concern about the effect of smoking on the health not only of those who smoke, but also of those who do not. In fact, nonsmokers who take in the air polluted by tobacco smoke suffer more than the smokers themselves.

A great number of students have joined in an effort to persuade the university to forbid smoking in classrooms. I believe they are completely right in their aim. However, I think it more important to achieve(使……成功) this by calling on the smokers to use good judgment and to show concern for others.

Smoking is not allowed in theaters, cinemas, and other public places, therefore, smoking must be forbidden in our classrooms.

71. What is the students' aim?

    A. To express their discomfort.   B. To enjoy smoking.

    C. To forbid smoking in classrooms.   D. To suffer from smoking.

72. The writer of the article is likely to be _____.

    A. a medical doctor   B. a government official

    C. a university student   D. a smoker

73. According to the passage, people who don't smoke _____ when taking in the air polluted by tobacco smoke.

    A. suffer less than smokers   B. suffer more than smokers

    C. suffer as much as the smokers   D. don't suffer at all

74. The writer thinks it important for smokers to _____.

    A. show concern for others

    B. forbid others to smoke

    C. show concern for their own health

    D. know the effect of smoking on their health

75. The passage suggests that _____.

    A. many students have joined in smokers

B. many students have stopped smoking
   C. most students are smoking in classrooms
   D. many students have been smoking in classrooms

B. 判断题

根据短文内容判断句子的正误(正确的用"T",错误的用"F",文中未提的用"N")。

Passage 4

Waves are beautiful to look at, but they can destroy ships at sea, as well as houses and buildings near the shore. What causes waves? Most waves are caused by winds blowing over the surface of the water. The sun heats the earth, causing the air to rise and the winds to blow. The winds blow across the seas, pushing little waves into bigger and bigger ones.

The size of a wave depends on how strong the wind is, how long it blows, and how large the body of water is. In a small bay, big waves will never build up. But at sea the wind can build up giant and powerful waves.

A rule says that the height of a wave (in meters) will usually be no more than one-tenth of the wind's speed (in kilometers). In other words, when the wind is blowing at 120 kilometers per hour, the giant waves are much higher. In 1933 the United States Navy reported the largest measured wave in history. It rose in the Pacific Ocean to a height of thirty-four meters.

76. One can guess the height of a wave by knowing how fast the wind is blowing.

77. The largest measured wave in history was in the Indian Ocean.

78. When the wind is blowing at 80 kilometers per hour, the height of most waves will be about 8 meters.

79. Air rises when the sun heats the earth.

80. The best title for this passage is "Beautiful Waves."

C. 简答题

根据短文内容简要回答问题,每题不得超过10个单词。

Passage 5

A woman saw three old men sitting in her front yard. She said, "I don't think I know you, but you must be hungry. Please come in and have something to eat."

"We don't go into a house together," they replied.

"Why is that?" she wondered.

One of the old men explained, "His name is Wealth, this is Success, and I am Love. Now go in and discuss with your husband which one of us you want in your home."

The woman discussed with her husband, but they had different opinions. Then the daughter made a suggestion, "Would it be better to invite Love? Our home will then be filled with love!"

"Let's take our daughter's advice." said the father.

So the woman went out and asked Love to come in. Love got up and started walking toward the house. The other two also followed him. Surprised, the lady asked Wealth and Success, "I only invited Love. Why are you coming in?"

The old men replied together, "If you had invited Wealth or Success, the other two of us would have stayed out, but since you invited Love. Wherever HE goes, we go with him. Wherever there is Love, there is also Wealth and Success!"

81. What did the woman do when she saw three old men sitting in her front yard?
_____

82. Why didn't the three old men go into the house together when they received the invitation?
_____

83. Whose advice did the couple take?
_____

84. As a result, who went into the house?
_____

85. Which is the most important for people according to the passage?
_____

第四部分　书面表达

(共两节,共20分)

第一节:英汉互译(共5小题,每小题2分,共10分。请将86~88题译成中文,将89~90题括号里的中文译成英文)

86. The cameras are badly damaged.
_____

87. There is something wrong with the alarm of my watch.
_____

88. Would you please show me your receipt so that I can take down some details?
_____

89. I am very _____(感到失望)its quality.

90. We'll get this watch exchanged for you _____(立刻).

第二节:应用文写作(本节共10空,每空1分,共10分)

中文提示:Carl Thomas 7月13日订购了一批照相机,货到后检查发现有5台照相机被严重损坏,很明显是由于包装不好造成的,所以不能以正常价格销售,故提议对方给10%的折扣,如果不行,只能退换。希望能理解,对损坏的货物进行补偿。

Dear Sir,

　　We are writing to ___91___(通知,告知)you that the cameras we ordered ___92___(在7月13日)arrived in unsatisfactory condition. After ___93___(检查),we found that 5 cameras ___94___(被严重损坏),obviously ___95___(由于)the poor packing. ___96___(因此,所以),we cannot sell them ___97___(以正常价格). We suggest that you give us a ___98___(10%的折扣)。If you cannot accept,I'm afraid we shall have to return them for ___99___(替换)。Hope you understand that we expect compensation for our damaged goods.

　　　　　　　　　　　　　　　　　　　　　　　　　___100___
　　　　　　　　　　　　　　　　　　　　　　　　　Carl Thomas

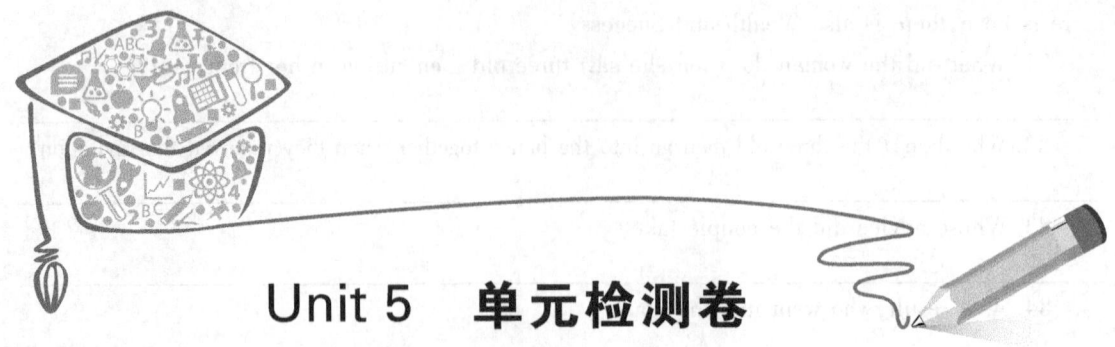

Unit 5 单元检测卷

第一部分 听力

(略)

第二部分 知识运用

(共三大题,每题1分,共40分)

第一节:词汇与语法(本大题共10小题,每小题1分,共10分)

从每小题给出的A、B、C、D四个选项中选出一项符合题意的最佳选项,请将所选答案填在答题卡上。

21. We'll _____ groups to complete the tasks.
　　A. divide into　　B. separate into　　C. be divided into　　D. be separated into

22. The students _____ a two-week social practice program this summer.
　　A. joined　　B. take part in　　C. attended　　D. participated in

23. They also _____ pre-sales works.
　　A. joined　　B. joined us in　　C. took part　　D. attended in

24. They were divided into three teams to sell the bags. One of teams sold bags to Holpe, one of..., while _____ team signed Pepsi onto their customer list.
　　A. the other　　B. other　　C. another　　D. the others

25. This is the third time that the school _____ such social practice.
　　A. organizes　　B. organized　　C. has organized　　D. is organizing

26. He said _____.
　　A. that I am a teacher　　B. I was a teacher
　　C. that he is a teacher　　D. he was a teacher

27. He asked _____.
　　A. how am I getting along　　B. how are you getting along

C. how I was getting along   D. how was I getting along

28. He _____ me _____ the window.
   A. said to; to close   B. told to; closing
   C. asked; to close   D. said to; please close

29. He _____ me _____ that again.
   A. said to; not to do   B. said to; don't do
   C. told; don't do   D. told; not to do

30. Would you mind _____ something about your work experience?
   A. speak   B. talking   C. to tell   D. saying

第二节：交际用语（本大题共 20 小题，每小题 1 分，共 20 分）

（一）选择

31. —I'd like to invite you to our weekend party.
    —_____.
   A. No at all, thanks   B. That's too much trouble for you
   C. It's my pleasure   D. Thank you and I'll be glad to

32. —Excuse me, Professor Smith. Can you spare me a few minutes?
    —_____.
   A. What's on   B. What's up   C. What's wrong   D. What's more

33. —Hi, Mary. I enjoyed myself so much at your party yesterday.
    —_____.
   A. Oh, that's kind of you   B. Congratulations
   C. It's my pleasure   D. Oh, I'm glad to hear that

34. —Lost and Found Office. _____?
    —I wonder if you have a camera of Canon.
   A. What's that   B. Who's that   C. Can I help you   D. Is there anything

35. —Johnny!
    —_____, sir?
    —Come and help me hand out the papers.
   A. Right   B. What   C. Yes   D. Pardon you

36. —Thank you for your help.
    —_____.
   A. No way   B. Don't mention it   C. No trouble at all   D. It depends

37. —Do you think I could borrow your bike?
    —_____.
   A. Yes, help yourself   B. Yes, go on to do it
   C. Take your time   D. How come

38. —Would you like some more tea?
    —_____, please.
   A. No more   B. Just a little   C. Yes, I would   D. I've had enough

39. —Hi, haven't seen you for years! You look fine!

—_____. You look well, too

    A. Great   B. Thanks   C. Oh, no   D. Not at all

40. —Shall we meet at 6:00 or 7:00?

    —_____.

    A. Any time is OK   B. At any time

    C. Yes, at 6:00   D. Well, either time will do

(二)补全对话

M: May I help you?

W: Yes, I'm looking for a skirt for my daughter. __41__

M: That's $50.

W: Oh, that's a little too expensive.

M: __42__ We sell a lot of these.

W: Yes, it is nice. __43__

M: __44__

W: No, that's all, thank you.

M: Is that cash charge?

W: Charge. __45__ But I don't have any card with me.

M: That's all right. Your name?

W: Mrs. Emily K. Ball.

M: Your address?

W: 1717 Main Street.

> A. I think I'll take it.
> B. I have an account here.
> C. How much does the red one cost, please?
> D. Here is the card.
> E. Will there be anything else?
> F. Here's a nice white one for $35.
> G. How much is the white skirt?

(三)匹配

I	II
46. 保持干燥	A. Visitors Please Register
47. 问询处	B. Instructions
48. 推	C. Keep in Dark Place
49. 来宾登记	D. Keep Dry
50. 说明	E. Information
	F. Push
	G. Pull

第三节:完形填空(本大题共10小题,每小题1分,共10分)

阅读下面短文,从各题所给的 A、B、C、D 四个选项中选出可填入空白处的最佳答案,并

将所选答案填在答题卡上。

Have you ever had to decide whether to go shopping or stay at home and watch TV on a weekend? Now you ___51___ do both at the same time. Home shopping television networks have become a way for many people to shop without ever having to leave their homes.

Some shoppers are ___52___ of department stores and supermarkets fighting the crowds, waiting in long lines, and sometimes hope of finding anything they want to buy. They'd rather sit quietly at home in front of the TV set and ___53___ a friendly announcer describe a product ___54___ a model shows it. And they can ___55___ around the clock, buying something simply by making a phone call.

Department stores and even mail-order companies are ___56___ to join in the success of home shopping. Large department stores are busy setting up their own TV channels to encourage TV shopping in the future. ___57___ can ask questions about products and places orders all through their TV sets.

Will shopping by television finally take the place of shopping in stores? Some industry managers think so. ___58___ many people find shopping at a real store a great enjoyment. And for many shoppers, it is still important to ___59___ or try on dresses they want to buy. That's ___60___ specialists say that in the future, home shopping will exist together with store shopping but will never entirely replace.

51. A. must	B. should	C. shall	D. can
52. A. proud	B. fond	C. tired	D. purpose
53. A. see	B. watch	C. let	D. notice
54. A. until	B. since	C. if	D. while
55. A. shop	B. wait	C. turn	D. deliver
56. A. nervous	B. lucky	C. equal	D. eager
57. A. Guests	B. Assistants	C. Managers	D. Customers
58. A. Then	B. Yet	C. Because	D. Therefore
59. A. design	B. make	C. wear	D. touch
60. A. how	B. why	C. what	D. when

第三部分 阅读理解

(共25小题,第1~4篇为选择题和判断题,每小题1分;第5篇为简答题,每小题2分;共30分)

A. 选择题
根据短文内容选择正确的答案。

Passage 1

Every town in the United States has a post office. Some are very small, and you may also find them in the corner of a shop. Others are larger buildings. They are open on weekdays and on

Saturday mornings. From Monday to Friday they are usually open from 8:30 to 4:30. If you know how much the postage is for your letter, you can buy stamps at any window. In some post offices you can buy stamps by machines. Stamps are sold many different prices, from one cent to many dollars. If you are not sure how much postage is for your letter, you may ask the man or the woman in the post office for help. He or she will give you the stamps you need. If you are sending your letter far away, you should use airmail envelops. Remember that postage will be more expensive for a letter to be sent outside the country.

At a post office you can also buy postcards. A postcard is cheaper than a letter. Usually the price of postage for a postcard is about half that of a letter. The postcards that you buy at a post office don't have pictures. However, also they are not to be sent outside the country.

Letters are an easy and cheap way to keep in touch with people in many different countries.

61. The passage tells us that we can find _____ easily in the United States of America.
    A. post offices   B. large buildings   C. small shops   D. different banks
62. The post offices in the United States are open _____ at weekdays.
    A. seven hours a day   B. six hours a day
    C. five hours a day   D. eight hours a day
63. If you are not sure how much postage is for your letter, you can _____ .
    A. go and buy some stamps from the machine in the post offices and a cheap postcard instead of your letter
    B. get in touch with somebody you know in the post office
    C. ask the man or the woman in the post office for help
    D. ask the policeman in the shops for help
64. The price of postage for _____ is more expensive.
    A. a beautiful postcard   B. a letter written on envelop
    C. a letter by airmail   D. a postcard with picture
65. The passage tells us something about _____ in the U.S.A.
    A. the post   B. the postage   C. letters   D. postcards

Passage 2

Many children use the Internet to get useful knowledge and information, and to relax in their free time but some of them are not using it in a good way. Here are some rules to make sure you are safe and have fun on the Internet.

Make rules for Internet use with your parents. For example, when you can go online, for how long and what activities you can do online.

Don't give your password to anyone else and never give out the following information: your real name, home address, age, school, phone number or personal information.

Check with your parents before giving out a credit card number.

Never send a photo of yourself to someone in e-mail unless your parents say it's OK.

Check with your parents before going into a chat room. Different chat rooms have different rules and attract different kinds of people. You and your parents will want to make sure it's a right place for you.

Never agree to meet someone you met on the Internet without your parents' permission. Never meet anyone you met online alone.

Always remember that people online may not be who they say they are. Treat everyone online as if they were strangers.

If something you see or read online makes you uncomfortable, leave the site, tell a parent or teacher right away.

Treat other people as you'd like to be treated. Never use bad language.

Remember—not everything you read on the Internet is true.

66. The writer tells children to _____.
    A. send their own photos to him
    B. make rules for Internet use with parents
    C. believe everything they read on the Internet
    D. give out their personal information
67. It's good for children to _____ on the Internet.
    A. give password to others
    B. get useful knowledge and information
    C. give out a credit card number
    D. go into a chat room as they'd like to
68. What shouldn't be done when you are online?
    A. Using bad language.
    B. Sending messages and e-mails.
    C. Leaving the site if you feel uncomfortable.
    D. Treating everyone online as strangers.
69. If your parents don't agree, never _____.
    A. read anything on the Internet
    B. relax in your free time
    C. have a face-to-face meeting with anyone you met online
    D. treat other people as you'd like to be treated
70. What's the best title for this passage?
    A. How to Use Computers   B. Surfing on the Internet
    C. Information on the Internet   D. Internet Safety Rules

Passage 3

FOR SALE

Rose Cottage

$115,000

Built in 1780,

2 bedrooms, a bathroom, a living room, a kitchen, a beautiful garden, 20 meters long,

50 meters from the sea, 2 kilometers from the shops and town center

Seaview

$135,000

Built in 1927,

3 bedrooms, a living room, 2 dining rooms, a kitchen,

50 meters from the sea, 1 kilometers from the shops and town center

Park House

$95,000

Built in 1975,

3 bedrooms, a living room, a bathroom, a kitchen, a breakfast room, a big garage, a small garden, 8 meters long,

1.5 kilometers from the sea, 50 meters from the town center, next to a park

71. Park House is _____ cheaper than Seaview.

  A. four thousand dollars   B. fourteen thousand dollars

  C. forty thousand dollars   D. four million dollars

72. Rose Cottage was built _____ .

  A. in the eighteenth century   B. in the seventeenth century

  C. three hundred years ago   D. in the sixteenth century

73. Which of the following is **TRUE**?

  A. Park House is smaller than Rose Cottage.

  B. Park House is the nearest to the town center.

  C. Seaview has got a garage.

  D. Park House has got a bigger garden than Rose Cottage.

74. The Greens want to buy a house with three bedrooms, a bathroom, a living room, a kitchen and a garage, not far away from the sea and the center of the town, for less than one hundred thousand dollars. Which one do they choose?

  A. Rose Cottage.   B. Seaview.

  C. Park House.   D. None of the above.

75. If the Greens have sixty-seven thousand dollars and they can save one thousand and two hundred dollars a month. How many years can they pay off the debts?

  A. Two.   B. Three.

  C. Four.   D. Five.

B. 判断题

根据短文内容判断句子的正误(正确的用"T",错误的用"F",文中未提的用"N")。

Passage 4

  Pop music is the name for various forms of popular, commercial (商业的) music. It "originated" in the United States and spread through the whole world during the 1950s and 1960s. It is widely liked by the young people. The best known early form of pop music was "rock & roll." Pop music has taken the place of native music in many parts of the world. It has caused the number of people for Jazz to become much smaller than in the 1950s and earlier, and it has now begun to rule musical stage productions. It is a big industry. Much pop music is without artistic value, but the work of some pop singers like the Beatles, Bob Dylan, and some groups like Pink Floyd and Crosby, Stills and Nash, is on a higher musical level. And there is still great interest in it today. Pop music concerts and festivals are held all over the world.

76. Jazz belongs to pop music.
77. Pop music began in America and spread through the whole world in the 1960s.
78. Pop music has replaced native music in many parts of the world.
79. Not all the pop music is without artistic value.
80. The passage says pop music has now begun to rule music stage productions.

C. 简答题

根据短文内容简要回答问题,每题不得超过 10 个单词。

Passage 5

An explosion on Thursday killed one and injured 21 in a busy street in Tongren, Southwest China's Guizhou Province.

The bomb was hidden in a rubbish bin in the city's commercial hub(商业中心), where lots of shops and restaurants are concentrated.

The ear-splitting blast was heard around 12:50 p.m., said a local newspaper, cutting witnesses. The power of the blast shattered(使粉碎) nearby shop windows and ripped the stainless (不生锈的) steel rubbish can to pieces.

One passer-by, identified(确认) only as Zhang, said she was shocked by the noise and saw a lot of pedestrians lying on the ground when she got to the scene.

Thirteen of the injured were taken to a local hospital after the explosion. A doctor there said five were in serious condition but already out of danger after emergency treatment. The others were just slightly hurt.

"The cause of the explosion is still under investigation," said an officer with the Tongren police, but he refused to speculate as to the cause.

81. How many people were injured by the explosion on Thursday?

82. Where was the bomb hidden?

83. When was the ear-splitting blast heard?

84. What did the power of the blast shatter and rip into pieces?

85. What did one passer-by see when she got to the scene?

第四部分 书面表达

（共两节，共20分）

第一节：英汉互译（共5小题，每小题2分，共10分。请将86~88题译成中文,将89~90题括号里的中文译成英文）

86. Attention, everyone. We are to start working right now.
_____

87. They told their son that the earth goes round the sun.
_____

88. Mr. Zhang said we should be divided into at least 3 groups.
_____

89. Changsha Vocational School students _____ (参加了) a two-week social practice program this summer.

90. Some of us are going to _____ (当、做、成为) packagers on the assembly line.

第二节：应用文写作（本节共10空,每空1分,共10分）

中文提示：假如你是空中乘务员，现在请提醒乘客飞机马上起飞，请乘客坐好、系上安全带、保证座椅背直立、收好托盘及随行物品,最后不要抽烟。

Good morning ___91___（女士们,先生们）

Welcome ___92___（乘坐）China Airlines flight.

We will ___93___（起飞）immediately. First, please ___94___（坐好）. ___95___（系好）your seat belt, and then ___96___（确保）your seat back is ___97___（直立）. After that make sure your tray table is closed and your carry-on are securely stowed. ___98___（最后）, this is a ___99___（无烟的）flight; please do not smoke on board.

We hope you ___100___（旅途愉快）! Thank you!

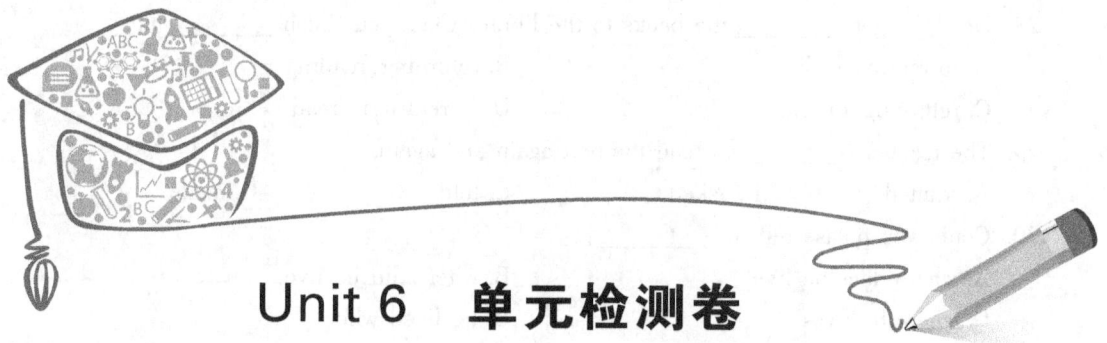

Unit 6 单元检测卷

第一部分 听力

(略)

第二部分 知识运用

(共三大题,每题1分,共40分)

第一节:词汇与语法(本大题共10小题,每小题1分,共10分)

从每小题给出的 A、B、C、D 四个选项中选出一项符合题意的最佳选项,请将所选答案填在答题卡上。

21. Would you mind _____ the window? It is so hot now.
    A. open   B. to open   C. opening   D. opened

22. Your application letter _____ you are hardworking, outgoing and cooperative.
    A. reads   B. says   C. tells   D. writes

23. You can know the result _____ about one week.
    A. on   B. in   C. for   D. /

24. Since my graduation, I have _____ as a secretary.
    A. been work   B. work   C. working   D. been working

25. The job is the only one _____ I am looking for.
    A. which   B. that   C. what   D. whom

26. After your graduation, you will _____ qualified for this job.
    A. can   B. could be   C. be able to   D. be able to be

27. May you _____ !
    A. success   B. succeed   C. successful   D. succession

28. Don't forget _____ the books to the library when you finish _____ it.
    A. to return; reading　　　　　　　B. returning; reading
    C. returning; to read　　　　　　　D. to return; to read

29. The teacher _____ us read the text again and again.
    A. wanted　　　B. asked　　　C. told　　　D. made

30. Could you please tell me _____?
    A. where does he live　　　　　　B. where did he live
    C. where he lives　　　　　　　　D. he lived where

第二节：交际用语(本大题共 20 小题，每小题 1 分，共 20 分)

(一)选择

31. —Excuse me, can you tell me where the nearest bank is, please?
    —_____ Oh, yes! It's past the post office, next to a big market.
    A. Oh, I beg your pardon?　　　　B. Mm, let me think.
    C. You're welcome.　　　　　　　D. What do you mean?

32. —How do you feel the lecture by Mr. Black?
    —_____.
    A. By bike　　　　　　　　　　　B. Very boring
    C. In the conference hall　　　　　D. With the help of Mrs. Black

33. —How are things with you?
    —_____.
    A. Things are good　　　　　　　B. Ask yourself first
    C. Yes, I'm fine with the things　　D. Not too bad, thank you

34. —May I take your order now?
    —_____.
    A. Yes, we obey orders　　　　　　B. No, I don't like any order
    C. Yes, I'd like a dish of chicken　 D. No, I am in trouble now

35. —Can I speak to Miss White, please?
    —_____.
    A. Who are you?　　B. Are you Jack?　　C. I am Miss White.　　D. Speaking.

36. —Jack, I am sorry I used your MP4 when you were away yesterday.
    —_____.
    A. It's a pleasure　　B. With pleasure　　C. That's all right　　D. You're so kind

37. —I am entering the final of the high jump race.
    —_____!
    A. Congratulations　　B. Enjoy yourself　　C. Wonderful　　D. Good luck

38. —Waiter. Check please.
    —This time is on me.
    —_____
    A. All right, if you insist.　　　　　B. Oh, no, let me.

C. Then why not?   D. It's my pleasure.

39. —Shall we go to the zoo right away?
    —_____.
    A. It's your opinion   B. It's all up to you
    C. I don't mind   D. It's your decision

40. —Good morning. May I help you?
    —Morning. I am just looking around.
    —_____
    A. It's up to you.   B. Thanks for coming to see me.
    C. Take your time then.   D. How are you feeling today?

(二)补全对话

W: Good morning, sir? ___41___

M: Yes, I'd like to post this package to Beijing.

W: How would you like to send it?

M: ___42___

W: What does it contain?

M: I enclosed some photos in it.

W: Put it on the scale, please. ___43___ You'll have to pay extra.

M: ___44___

W: It'll be $2.25.

M: How long does it take?

W: About three days. ___45___

M: Thank you.

W: Not at all.

```
A. Express, please.
B. Here is your receipt.
C. What's the postage for it?
D. Can I help you?
E. It's a bit too heavy.
F. Would you like it registered?
G. Please show me your ID card.
```

(三)匹配

I	II
46. 紧急求救信号	A. Exit
47. 此处撕开	B. Entrance
48. 禁止鸣喇叭	C. Split Here
49. 出口	D. No Honking
50. 此处插入	E. EMS

F. SOS

G. Insert Here

第三节:完形填空(本大题共 10 小题,每小题 1 分,共 10 分)

阅读下面短文,从各题所给的 A、B、C、D 四个选项中选出可填入空白处的最佳答案,并将所选答案填在答题卡上。

My life, as it really is, is always filled with sadness and little joy. However, no matter what happens, I can always face ___51___ bravely.

In July, last year, I couldn't believe the news that I was allowed to enter the only key high school in my hometown. Then I rushed to my home and told my parents. But my father didn't seem as excited as I was. He just kept smoking without saying a word and my mother put her head down and couldn't help ___52___.

What I saw didn't make me ___53___. I knew very well what my family was like. My mum had been in bed for two years because of her disease. I knew my family lived a ___54___ life and couldn't afford my tuition fee. I felt so upset at the moment but I could say ___55___ to my parents.

I decided to help my father with his work to support my family instead of ___56___ my study.

___57___ my surprise, things completely changed just three days before the beginning of the new term. My head teacher who had taught me for three years came to my family with some money, which had been ___58___ by my schoolmates. He encouraged me, "Always have a dream."

At the same time, my father also earned some extra money ___59___ he could afford part of my tuition fee.

I knew I was such a lucky dog and decided to study harder in return. With tears in my eyes, I stepped into the key high school that I had dreamed of.

I have been studying hard since I entered the high school. Whenever I meet difficulties, I always ___60___ my teacher and schoolmates, and I can always get enough courage to go on. Because I have a college dream and must work hard for it no matter how hard life it is. Just as a philosopher's(哲学家) saying goes, "When one door shuts, another opens in life."

51. A. them	B. they	C. those	D. it
52. A. smiling	B. to smile	C. crying	D. to cry
53. A. surprising	B. surprised	C. to surprise	D. surprise
54. A. strange	B. happy	C. pleasant	D. hard
55. A. something	B. anything	C. nothing	D. everything
56. A. stopping	B. continuing	C. enjoying	D. starting
57. A. To	B. In	C. At	D. On
58. A. raised	B. spent	C. planned	D. made
59. A. so that	B. even though	C. what if	D. but
60. A. dream of	B. thank for	C. hear of	D. think of

第三部分 阅读理解

(共 25 小题,第 1~4 篇为选择题和判断题,每小题 1 分;第 5 篇为简答题,每小题 2 分;共 30 分)

A. 选择题

根据短文内容选择正确的答案。

Passage 1

We often use gestures to express our feelings, but the problem is that gestures can be understood in different ways.

It is true that a smile means the same thing in any language. So does laughter or crying. Fear is another emotion that is shown in much the same way all over the world. In Chinese and in English literatures, a phrase like "he went pale and began to tremble" suggests that the man either is very afraid or has just got a very big shock. However, "he opened his eyes wide" is used to suggest anger in Chinese whereas in English it means surprise. In Chinese, surprise can be described in a phrase like "they stretched out their tongues!" But "Stretching out your tongue" in English is an insulting gesture or expresses strong dislike.

Even in the same culture, people differ in their abilities to understand and express feelings. Experiments in America have shown that women are usually better than men at recognizing fear, anger, love and happiness on people's faces. Other studies show that older people usually find it easier to recognize or understand body language than younger people do.

61. Which of the following is **TRUE** according to the passage?

    A. We can easily understand what people's gestures mean.

    B. Words can be better understood by older people.

    C. Gestures can be understood by most people but words are not.

    D. It is difficult to tell what people's gestures really mean sometimes.

62. People's facial expressions may be misunderstood in different cultures because _____.

    A. people of different sexes may understand a gesture differently

    B. people speaking different languages have different facial expressions

    C. people of different ages may have different interpretations(解释,理解,说明)

    D. people from different cultures have different meanings about some facial expressions

63. From the passage, we can conclude that _____.

    A. gestures can be used to express feelings

    B. gestures can be more effectively used than words to express feelings

    C. words are often more difficult to understand than gestures

    D. gestures are used as frequently as words to express feelings

64. In the same culture, people _____.

A. hardly ever fail to understand each other's ideas and feelings

B. are equally intelligent even if they have different backgrounds

C. almost all have the same understanding of the same thing

D. may have different abilities to understand and express feelings

65. The best title for this passage can be "_____."
    A. Gestures
    B. Feelings
    C. Gestures and Feelings
    D. Culture and Understanding

Passage 2

Who will stage the games?

Preparing for the Olympics Games is a huge undertaking. Just like the athletes, the host city spends years getting ready for the event. Before deciding which city will host the Olympic Games, the International Olympic Committee(IOC) has to examine bids from all over the world. Bidding for the games begins about ten years in advance. Without preparing a very strong bid(投标), a city will not win the competition to host the games. Beijing was chosen for the 2008 games from other four bidders—Osaka, Pairs, Toronto and Istanbul.

Why does it take so long to prepare?

Building the infrastructure(基础设施) costs huge amount of money. Holding the World Cup in 2002 in Japan and Korea, for example, meant that ten new stadiums had to be built, as well as many hotels and an improved transport system. In Beijing, after winning the bid the government began major construction projects——the extension of the underground, the improvement of the airport and the building of new motorways. Each host city must also build an Olympic village for the athletes. By planting trees and creating parks, the city becomes more attractive for tourists.

Why do countries want to host the Olympic Games?

Hosting the games has a major effect on the economy and brings international prestige to the country. Thousands and thousands of visitors come to the games and the host cities are permanently improved.

66. Bidding for the Olympic Games usually starts _____ before the games are really held.
    A. two years   B. eight years   C. one year   D. ten years

67. Beijing was one of the _____ bidders for the 2008 games.
    A. four   B. five   C. then   D. three

68. The World Cup in 2002 was held in _____.
    A. Japan   B. Korea   C. China   D. A and B

69. What construction projects did Beijing start after winning the bid?
    A. The extension of the underground.
    B. The improvement of the airport.
    C. The building of new motorways.
    D. All of the above.

70. Why do countries want to host the Olympic Games?
    A. Because it has a major effect on the economy.
    B. Because it brings international prestige to the country.

C. Because the host cities are permanently improved.

D. All of the above.

Passage 3

In 1909 an English newspaper offered $1,000 to the first man to fly across the English Channel in an aeroplane. Today, modern jets can cross it in minutes. But at that time it still seemed a good distance. The race to win the money soon became a race between two men. Both were very colorful.

One was Louis Bleriot. He owned a factory in France that made motor car lamps. He was already well known as a pilot(飞行员) because he had had accidents several times. Some people laughed at him. One man said, "He may not be the first to fly across the English Channel but he will certainly be the first to die in an accident!" But Bleriot was really a good and brave pilot. He also had many good ideas about aeroplane design.

The other man was Hubert Latham. He was half French and half English. He took up flying when his doctors told him he had only a year to live. "Oh, well," he said, "if I'm going to die soon, I think I shall have a dangerous and interesting life now." Latham was the first to try the flight across the Channel. Ten kilometers from the French coast, his plane had some trouble. It fell down into the water and began to sink under the water. A boat reached Latham just in time. He was sitting calmly on the wing and was coolly lighting a cigarette(香烟).

Bleriot took off six days later. He flew into some very bad weather and very low cloud. He somehow got to the English side and landed in a farmer's field. When he did so, a customs(海关) officer rushed up to his plane. Planes have changed since then, but customs officers have not. "Have you anything to declare?" the officer demanded.

71. The story took place _____.

    A. in the early 20th century   B. in the 19th century

    C. right after World War One   D. at a time not mentioned in the passage

72. Bleriot was well known as a pilot because _____.

    A. he was unusually brave

    B. he was quite rich

    C. he had many good ideas about aeroplane

    D. he had had a few accidents

73. The flight for Bleriot was _____.

    A. a sad one   B. a dangerous one   C. his first one   D. an easy one

74. Why did Hubert Latham want to fly across the Channel?

    A. He thought he could manage it easily.

    B. He wanted to be the first one to cross the Channel.

    C. He knew he only had a year to live.

    D. He had always been interested in flying.

75. Which of the following is **NOT** true?

    A. Latham became a pilot on the doctor's advice.

B. Latham was told he could live another year.

C. Latham's plane had some trouble.

D. Latham was saved by a boat when his plane was sinking.

B. 判断题

根据短文内容判断句子的正误(正确的用"T",错误的用"F",文中未提的用"N")。

Passage 4

A Frenchman came to London to study English. He lived at his English friend's home. He worked hard at his lessons. Every morning he did some reading by the window before he went to class.

His friend, Grant, liked to keep birds. Every day, early in the morning he took his birds out of the room. Sometimes he hung his cage(笼)on a tree in his garden or sometimes on his window upstairs.

One morning when he took out his birdcage and tried to hang it on the window upstairs, the cage suddenly fell off his hand. He couldn't catch it. So he shouted,"Look out!" As soon as he heard the shout, the Frenchman put his head out of the window and tried to look at what was happening. The cage was just in time to hit him on the head! From then on the Frenchman knew what the English "Look out!" really meant.

76. The Frenchman worked in London.

77. Every day the Frenchman did some reading after he went to class.

78. Sometimes Grant hung his cage on a tree or sometimes on his window upstairs.

79. One day the Frenchman tried to hang his cage on the window upstairs but the cage fell off his hand.

80. The Frenchman wanted to look at what was happening.

C. 简答题

根据短文内容简要回答问题,每题不得超过10个单词。

Passage 5

When you take a walk in any of the cities in the west, you often see a lot of people walking dogs. It is still true that a dog is the most useful and faithful animal in the world, but the reason why people keep a dog has changed. In the old days people used to train dogs to protect themselves against attacks by other beasts. And later they came to realize that a dog was not only a useful protection but willing to obey its master. For example, when people took them for hunting, the dogs wouldn't eat what was caught without permission. But now people in the city need not protect themselves against attacks by animals. So why do they keep dogs, then? Some people keep dogs to protect themselves from robbery. But the most important reason is for companionship. For a child, a dog is his best friend when he has no friends to play with. For young couples, a dog is their child when they have no children. For old couples, a dog is also their children when their children have grown up. So the main reason why people keep dogs has changed from protection to friendship.

81. What do you often see when you take a walk in any of the cities in the west?

82. Why did people use to keep dogs in the old days?

83. What is a dog for a child when he has no friends to play with?
_____

84. What is the most important reason why people keep dogs?
_____

85. The main reason for keeping dogs has changed from friendship to protection, hasn't it?
_____

第四部分　书面表达

(共两节,共20分)

第一节:英汉互译(共5小题,每小题2分,共10分。请将86~88题译成中文,将89~90题括号里的中文译成英文)

86. I'm calling to apply for the marketing position that your company advertised in yesterday's newspaper.
_____

87. I'm afraid I can't make it.
_____

88. Would you mind saying something about your work experience?
_____

89. I can work overtime and _____ (与……相处融洽) others.

90. I believe that I am quite _____ (能胜任) for it.

第二节:应用文写作(本节共10空,每空1分,共10分)

中文提示:请以周艳的身份,根据提示写一封求职信。

Dear Sir or Madam,

　　I want to ___91___ (申请) the position that you advertised in yesterday's ___92___ (湖南日报)。

　　I'm ___93___ (19岁). I'm ___94___ (容易相处并工作努力). During my school years, I ___95___ (一直学习努力) and gained much knowledge and many skills. And I once ___96___ (担任) a secretary in a company. In July this year, I'll ___97___ (从……毕业) Zhangjiajie Vocational School. So, I ___98___ (正在找) a job. And the job your company offered ___99___ (十分适合) for me. I'm sure that I'm the best person for the job.

　　I would ___100___ (感激) it if you can give me a personal interview. I'm available at anytime.

　　Looking forward to your reply.

　　With many thanks,

Zhou Yan

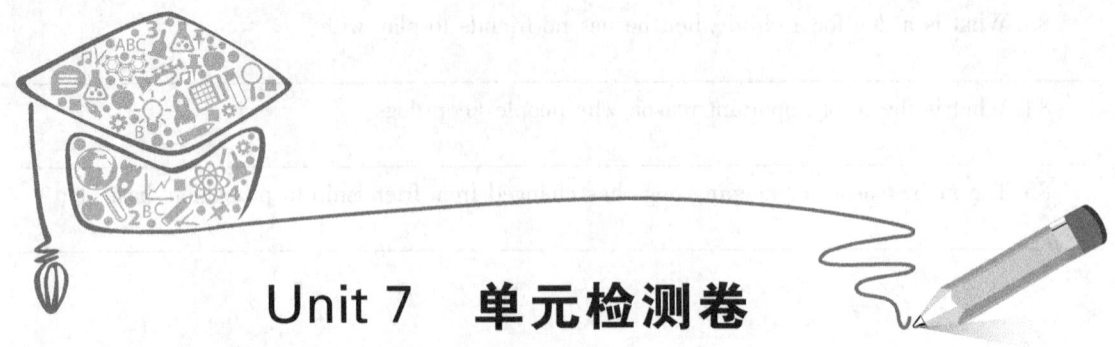

Unit 7 单元检测卷

第一部分 听力

(略)

第二部分 知识运用

(共三大题,每题1分,共40分)

第一节:词汇与语法(本大题共10小题,每小题1分,共10分)

从每小题给出的A、B、C、D四个选项中选出一项符合题意的最佳选项,请将所选答案填在答题卡上。

21. It is _____ box that no one can move it.
    A. such heavy   B. so heavy   C. so a heavy   D. so heavy a

22. She dresses like that _____ everyone will notice her.
    A. when   B. so that   C. in order to   D. after

23. After living in Paris for 40 years he returned to the small town _____ he grew up as a child.
    A. which   B. that   C. where   D. when

24. The boy always boasts(自夸) of his learning, _____, of course made the others unhappy.
    A. who   B. that   C. which   D. what

25. The train _____ she was traveling was late.
    A. which   B. where   C. on which   D. on that

26. They talked for about an hour of things and persons _____ they remembered.
    A. which   B. who   C. that   D. what

27. —How far is the school from your house?

—It is _____ walk.

　　A. two hour　　　B. two hours　　　C. two-hours　　　D. two-hour

28. —Thank you for your help.

　　—_____.

　　A. Sorry to hear that　　　　　　B. With pleasure

　　C. It's my pleasure　　　　　　　D. It doesn't matter

29. I used to _____ up late, but now I get used to _____ up early now.

　　A. get; get　　　B. getting; getting　　　C. get; getting　　　D. getting; get

30. _____ English, we also learn Chinese, mathematic and history.

　　A. Expect　　　B. Beside　　　C. Besides　　　D. But

第二节:交际用语(本大题共20小题,每小题1分,共20分)

(一)选择

31. —How are you doing, Betty?

　　—_____

　　A. How are you doing?　　　　　B. How do you do?

　　C. That's very good.　　　　　　D. Fine. Thanks.

32. —Hi, Lucy, I'd like to introduce my friend, Bob to you.

　　—_____

　　A. How do you do?　　　　　　　B. Nice to see you.

　　C. Yes, please.　　　　　　　　　D. Go ahead, please.

33. —I'm going to London next week, Bob.

　　—_____.

　　A. I'm going there, either　　　　B. Sure, you can go

　　C. Have a good journey　　　　　D. Go slowly

34. —May I use your dictionary?

　　—_____.

　　A. Yes, you are sure　　　　　　B. Here we are

　　C. Yes, here you are　　　　　　D. You're welcome

35. —I'm awfully sorry. I didn't mean to hurt you.

　　—_____.

　　A. You really hurt me　　　　　　B. You're welcome

　　C. Never mind, I'm all right　　　D. That's all

36. —_____?

　　—It's very nice of you, but I have to see my mother in hospital.

　　A. What can I do for you

　　B. Excuse me. Can you give me a hand

　　C. May I ask you a question

　　D. Would you like to have dinner with me tonight

37. —Do you mind going to the cinema?

—_____

　　A. Yes, let's go.　　　　　　　　　B. No, we can't go.
　　C. OK, why not?　　　　　　　　　D. No, why not?

38. —_____

　　—No, I don't like the music very much.

　　A. How do you like the film?
　　B. Do you like the film?
　　C. What do you think of the film?
　　D. I think it is a good film.

39. —What is your favorite festival?

　　—_____.

　　A. Mid-autumn Day　　　　　　　B. I don't like Christmas Day
　　C. Children's Day is very near　　D. No, I don't like it at all

40. —_____

　　—Glad to hear you on the phone, Peter.

　　A. Hello! This is Peter speaking.　B. I'm Peter.
　　C. Is that Tom speaking?　　　　D. Who is that speaking?

(二)补全对话

A: Hello, what can I do for you?
B: Hello, ___41___
A: ___42___
B: Fruit salad. And some drinks, please. ___43___
A: We have orange juice, apple juice and tea. ___44___
B: What is it?
A: It's hot milk with sugar and chocolate. It tastes good.
B: Well, I will have a try. ___45___
A: They are 35 yuan.
B: All right. Here's the money.
A: Well, here's your change.
B: Thanks. Bye.

　　　A. How much is it?
　　　B. I'd like a beef hamburger and salad.
　　　C. What drinks do you have?
　　　D. What drinks would you like?
　　　E. How much are they?
　　　F. What kind of salad would you like?
　　　G. And we have a new kind of hot chocolate.

(三)匹配

I	II
46. 新货上市	A. Airman First Class
47. 一等兵	B. New Arrival
48. 智能词汇处理器	C. Use No Hooks
49. 勿用钩子	D. Scan All Files
50. 详细说明	E. Intelligent Word Processor
	F. No Fishing
	G. Detailed Guide

第三节:完形填空(本大题共10小题,每小题1分,共10分)

阅读下面短文,从各题所给的A、B、C、D四个选项中选出可填入空白处的最佳答案,并将所选答案填在答题卡上。

When Dave was eighteen, he bought a secondhand car for 200 yuan so that he could travel to and from work more ___51___ than by bus. It worked quite well for a few years, but then it got so old, and it was costing him ___52___ much in repairs that he decided to ___53___ it.

He asked among his friends to see if anyone was particularly ___54___ to buy a cheap car, but they all knew that it was falling to pieces, so ___55___ of them had any desire to buy it. Dave's friend Sam saw that he was ___56___ when they met one evening, and said, "What's ___57___, Dave?"

Dave told him, and Sam answered, "Well, what about advertising it on the paper? You may ___58___ more for it that way than the cost of the advertisement!" Thinking that Sam's ___59___ was sensible(合理的), he put an advertisement on an evening paper, which read "For sale:small car, ___60___ very little petrol, only two owners. Bargain at 50 yuan."

For two days after the advertisement first appeared, there was no answer. But then on Saturday evening he had an inquiry(询问). A man rang up and said he would like to see him about the car. "All right," Dave said, feeling happy. He asked the man whether ten o'clock the next morning would be suitable or not. "Fine," the man said, "and I'll bring my wife. We intend to go for a ride to test it."

51. A. directly   B. safely   C. properly   D. easily
52. A. so   B. such   C. very   D. too
53. A. keep   B. repair   C. sell   D. throw
54. A. anxious   B. lucky   C. ashamed   D. generous
55. A. some   B. neither   C. none   D. most
56. A. delighted   B. unhappy   C. calm   D. astonished
57. A. on   B. up   C. it   D. that
58. A. learn   B. miss   C. get   D. find
59. A. message   B. advice   C. request   D. description
60. A. uses   B. loses   C. has   D. spends

第三部分　阅读理解

（共 25 小题，第 1~4 篇为选择题和判断题，每小题 1 分；第 5 篇为简答题，每小题 2 分；共 30 分）

A. 选择题

根据短文内容选择正确的答案。

Passage 1

Early one morning, more than a hundred years ago, an American inventor called Elias Howe finally fell asleep. He had been working all night on the design of a sewing machine but he had run into a very difficult problem: It seemed impossible to get the thread to run smoothly around the needle.

Though he was tired, Howe slept badly. He turned and turned. Then he had a dream. He dreamed that he had been caught by terrible savages whose king wanted to kill him and eat him unless he could build a perfect sewing machine. When he tried to do so, Howe <u>ran into</u> the same problem as before. The thread kept getting caught around the needle. The king flew into the cage and ordered his soldiers to kill Howe. They came up towards him with their spears raised. But suddenly the inventor noticed something. There was a hole in the tip of each spear. The inventor awoke from the dream, realizing that he had just found the answer to the problem. Instead of trying to get the thread to run around the needle, he should make it run through a small hole in the center of needle. This was the simple idea that finally made Howe design and build the first really practiced sewing machine.

Elias Howe was not the only one in finding the answer to his problem in this way.

Thomas Edison, the inventor of the electric light, said his best ideas came into him in dreams. So did the great physicist Albert Einstein. Charlotte Bronte also drew in her dreams in writing *Jane Eyre*.

To know the value of dreams, you have to understand what happens when you are asleep. Even then, a part of your mind is still working. This unconscious（无意识的）, but still active part understands your experiences and goes to work on the problems you have had during the day. It stores all sorts of information that you may have forgotten or never have really noticed. It is only when you fall asleep that this part of the brain can send messages to the part you use when you are awake. However, the unconscious part acts in a special way. It uses strange images which the conscious part may not understand at first. This is why dreams are sometimes called "secret messages to ourselves."

61. According to the passage, Elias Howe was _____.

　　A. the first person we know of who solved problems in his sleep

　　B. much more hard-working than other inventors

C. the first person to design a sewing machine that really worked

D. the only person at the time who knew the value of dreams

62. The problem Howe was trying to solve was _____.

    A. what kind of thread to use

    B. how to design a needle which would not break

    C. where to put the needle

    D. how to prevent the thread from getting caught around the needle

63. Thomas Edison is spoken of because _____.

    A. he also tried to invent a sewing machine

    B. he got some of his ideas from dreams

    C. he was one of Howe's best friends

    D. he also had difficulty in falling asleep

64. Dreams are sometimes called "secret messages to ourselves" because _____.

    A. strange images are used to communicate ideas

    B. images which have no meaning are used

    C. we can never understand the real meaning

    D. only specially trained people can understand them

65. What did the underlined phrase "ran into" mean?

    A. met with   B. did exercise   C. walked quickly   D. went through

Passage 2

Language learning begins with listening. Children are greatly different in the amount of listening they do before they start speaking, and later starters are often long listeners. Most children will "obey" spoken instructions some time before they can speak, though the word "obey" is hardly accurate as a description of the eager and delighted cooperation usually shown by the child. Before they can speak, many children will also ask questions by gesture and by making questioning noises.

Any attempt to study the development from the noises babies make to their first spoken words leads to considerable difficulties. It is agreed that they enjoy making noises, and that during the first few months one or two noises sort themselves as particularly expressive as delight, pain, friendliness, and so on. But since these can't be said to show the baby's intention to communicate, they can hardly be regarded as early forms of language. It is agreed, too, that from about three months they play with sounds for enjoyment, and that by six months they are able to add new words to their store. This self-imitation(模仿) leads on to deliberate(有意的) imitation of sounds made or words spoken to them by other people. The problem then arises as to the point at which one can say that these imitations can be considered as speech.

It is a problem that we need to get out teeth into(专注于;认真处理). The meaning of a word depends on what a particular person means by it in a particular situation and it is clear that what a child means by a word will change as he gains more experience of the world. Thus the use at seven months of "mama" as a greeting for his mother cannot be dismissed as a meaningless sound simply because he also uses it at other times for his father, his dog, or anything else he likes. Playful and meaningless imitation of what other people say continues after the child has begun to speak for himself. I doubt, however whether anything is gained when parents take advantage of this ability in an attempt to teach new sounds.

66. Before children start speaking _____.

    A. they need equal amount of listening

    B. they need different amounts of listening

    C. they are all eager to cooperate with the adults by obeying spoken instructions

    D. they can't understand and obey the adult's oral instructions.

67. Children who start speaking late _____.

    A. may have problems with their listening

    B. probably do not hear enough language spoken around them

    C. usually pay close attention to what they hear

    D. often take a long time in learning to listen properly

68. A baby's first noises are _____.

    A. an expression of his moods and feelings

    B. an early form of language

    C. a sign that he means to tell you something

    D. an imitation of the speech of adults

69. The problem of deciding at what point a baby's imitations can be considered as speech _____.

    A. is important because words have different meanings for different people

    B. is not especially important because the changeover takes place gradually

    C. is one that should be properly understood because the meaning of words changes with age

    D. is one that should be completely ignored(忽略) because children's use of words is often meaningless

70. The speaker implies _____.

    A. parents can never hope to teach their children new sounds

    B. children no longer imitate people after they begin to speak

    C. children who are good at imitating learn new words more quickly

    D. even after they have learned to speak, children still enjoy imitating

Passage 3

What is the sky? Where is it? How high is it? What lies above the sky? I am sure that you have asked these questions. They are very difficult to answer, aren't they?

If someone asked you, "What color is the sky?" I expect that you would answer: "Blue." I am afraid that you would be wrong. The sky has no color. When we see blue, we are looking a blue sunlight. The sunlight is shinning on little bits of dust in the air.

Is the sky full of air? I am sure that you have asked this question, too. We know that there is air around the world. We could not breathe without air. Airplanes could not fly without air. They need air to lift their wings. Airplane cannot fly very high because as they are higher, the air gets thinner. If we go far enough away from the earth, we find there is no air.

Perhaps we can answer some of our questions now. What is the sky? Nothing. Where is it? It is all around the world. The sky is space. In this space there is nothing except the sun, the moon, and all the stars.

Scientists (men who study science) have always wanted to know more about the other world in space. They have looked at them through telescopes and in this way they have found out a great deal. They know many facts about the moon, for example. They know how big it is and how far it is away. But they wanted to know more about it. The only way to find out more was to send men to the moon. Then they would know all about it.

The moon is about 384,000 kilometers away from the earth. An airplane cannot fly to the moon because the air reaches only 240 kilometers. Then there is no air. But there is something that can fly even there is no air. This is a rocket.

I am sure that you are asking: "How does a rocket fly?" If you want to know, get a balloon and then blow it up, until it is quite big. Do not tie up the neck of the balloon. Let go! The balloon will fly off through the air very quickly. The air inside the balloon tries to get out. It rushes out through the neck of the balloon and this pushes the balloon through the air. It does not need wings like an airplane.

This is how a rocket works. It is not made of rubber like a balloon, of course; it is made of metal. The metal must not be heavy but it must be very strong. There is a gas inside the rocket which is made very hot. When it rushes out of the end of the rocket, the rocket is pushed up into the air.

Rockets can fly far out into space. Rockets, with men inside them, have already reached the moon and other places in space. Several rockets, without men inside them, have been sent to the world much farther away. One day rockets may be able to go anywhere in space.

71. The sky is _____ .

 A. blue   B. grey   C. white   D. colorless

72. An airplane cannot fly _____ .

 A. where the air is thick   B. where the air is thin
 C. 240 kilometers high   D. more than 240 kilometers high

73. A rocket is made of _____ .

 A. rubber   B. strong, heavy mental
 C. strong, light metal   D. steel

74. A rocket is pushed along by _____ .

 A. air   B. steam
 C. fire   D. hot gas rushing out from the end of it

75. Men have flown _____ .

 A. to the moon and other spaces in rockets
 B. to the sun in rockets

C. to the moon

D. to anywhere in space in rockets

B. 判断题

根据短文内容判断句子的正误(正确的用"T",错误的用"F",文中未提的用"N")。

Passage 4

Laptop computers are popular all over the world. People use them on trains and airplanes, in airports and hotels. These laptops connect people to their workplace. In the United States today, laptops also connect students to their classrooms.

Westlake College in Virginia will start a laptop computer program that allows students to do schoolwork anywhere they want. Within five years, each of the 1,500 students at the college will receive a laptop. The laptops are part of a $10 million computer program at Westlake, a 110-year-old college. The students with laptops will also have access to the Internet. In addition, they will be able to use e-mail to "speak" with their teachers, their classmates, and their families. However, the most important part of the laptop program is that students will be able to use computers without going to computer labs. They can work with it at home, in a fast food restaurant or under the trees—anywhere at all!

Because of the many changes in computer technology, laptop use in higher education, such as colleges and universities, is workable. As laptops become more powerful, they become more similar to desktop computers. In addition, the portable computers can connect students to not only the Internet, but also libraries and other resources. State higher-education officials are studying how laptops can help students. State officials are also testing laptop programs at other universities, too.

At Westlake College, more than 80 percent of the staff use computers. The laptops will allow all teachers to use computers in their lessons. As one Westlake teacher said, "Here we are in the middle of Virginia and we're giving students a window on the world. They can see everything and do everything."

76. The main purpose of the laptop program is to give each student a laptop to use for their schoolwork.

77. At Westlake College all teachers use computers.

78. "A window on the world" in the last paragraph means that students can get information from around the world.

79. The most important part of the laptop program is that students will not be able to use computers without going to computer labs.

80. Because of the development in computer technology, laptop use in higher education is workable.

C. 简答题

根据短文内容简要回答问题,每题不得超过10个单词。

Passage 5

According to the Center for Disease Control and Prevention(CDC)(疾病控制预防中心), if you don't often wash your hands, you can pick up viruses(病菌) from many places and make yourself ill. You're at risk every time you touch your eyes, nose or mouth. In fact, one of the most common ways people catch cold is by rubbing their noses or their eyes when there are cold viruses on their hands. If you don't often wash your hands, especially when you're sick, you may spread the viruses directly to others. You should wash your hands in the following situations:

After using the bathroom.

After blowing your nose of coughing.

Before eating, serving or preparing food.

After touching pets or other animals.

After visiting anyone who is sick.

When your hands are dirty.

There's a right way to wash your hands. Follow these simple steps to keep your hands clean.

Use warm water (not cold or hot).

Wash for 15 seconds.

Rinse(冲洗) well under warm running water and dry them with a clean towel.

81. According to the passage, what must we do before having a meal, after using the bathroom and visiting a sick people, etc. ?

___

82. What water shall we use to wash our hands?

___

83. How long is needed to wash your hands?

___

84. Is one of the most common ways that people catch cold by rubbing their noses or their eyes when there are cold viruses on their hands?

___

85. What will happen if you don't often wash your hands?

___

第四部分　书面表达

(共两节,共20分)

第一节:英汉互译(共5小题,每小题2分,共10分。请将86~88题译成中文,将89~90题括号里的中文译成英文)

86. There is a hospital opposite to our community.

___

87. Let me show you the way.

___

88. Although I haven't got used to the new life here, I really enjoy some of the differences

between my new neighborhood and that in China.

89. _____(据说)students involved in service projects help themselves as well as their communities.

90. Students _____(被要求)to do some kind of community service as part of their studies.

第二节:应用文写作(本节共10空,每空1分,共10分)

中文提示:根据括号里所提供的中文,完成下列填空,使短文完整。

I live in a ____91____(现代化的社区)Jinbi Huayuan. I like a lot of things about my neighborhood. First, I like the places. ____92____(有)a swimming pool where I can ____93____(玩得开心)in summer. Near the pool is the community center. Many ____94____(已退休的)people enjoy chatting, playing chess, singing and dancing there. There is also a café which offers good service and delicious food ____95____(以公正的价格). My family often goes there when my parents have no time to cook. The place ____96____(我最喜欢的)is the small but beautiful park where I can ____97____(锻炼身体). ____98____(第二), I also like the people here because they are friendly and ____99____(愿意)to help others. The only thing I dislike is that the community is so ____100____(离……近)the railway that the noise sometimes makes it difficult for me to go fall asleep.

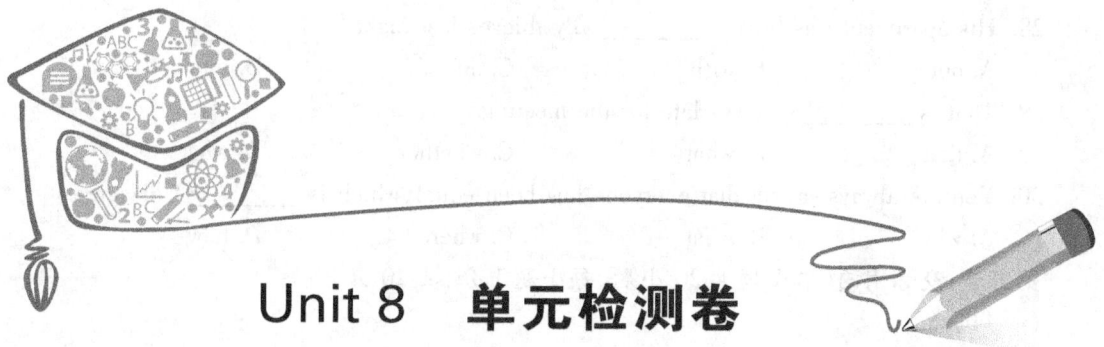

Unit 8 单元检测卷

第一部分 听力

(略)

第二部分 知识运用

(共三大题,每题1分,共40分)

第一节:词汇与语法(本大题共10小题,每小题1分,共10分)

从每小题给出的A、B、C、D四个选项中选出一项符合题意的最佳选项,请将所选答案填在答题卡上。

21. It's necessary for themselves _____ their communities.
     A. also   B. too   C. either   D. as well as

22. I have _____ confidence to get the job.
     A. no   B. not   C. none   D. nothing

23. What's _____ in the cinema tonight?
     A. in   B. on   C. about   D. of

24. Spring is coming, and it gets _____ .
     A. warm and warm   B. warmer and warmer
     C. more and more warmer   D. much warm

25. Remember _____ use your mobile phone while _____ .
     A. not;drive   B. not to;driving   C. no;drive   D. not;driving

26. Don't _____ noise in class.
     A. make   B. to make   C. hear   D. speak

27. John runs _____ than Jack.
     A. fast   B. fastest   C. more fast   D. much faster

28. His apartment was broken _____ by thieves last night.
   A. out B. with C. off D. into
29. That's _____ she was late for the meeting.
   A. that B. what C. whether D. why
30. You are always saying that everyone has been equal, which is _____ I disagree.
   A. why B. what C. where D. how

第二节：交际用语（本大题共 20 小题，每小题 1 分，共 20 分）

（一）选择

31. —Good morning, Mike.
   —_____ I don't think I know you.
   A. I'm sure but B. I'm sorry, but
   C. I'm sorry so D. Excuse me
32. —Have a good summer holiday.
   —_____.
   A. I'm afraid I don't B. OK. Let's have a good time
   C. All right, I will D. Thanks, and you too
33. —My brother fell off his bike and hurt himself when he was riding.
   —_____.
   A. It doesn't matter B. I'm sorry to hear that
   C. Don't worry D. He should be more careful
34. —Would you mind if I played the violin here?
   —_____.
   A. No, you won't B. No, do as you please
   C. Yes, I don't mind D. Yes, do as you please
35. —Will you make me a kite?
   —_____.
   A. I'm glad B. I'll be glad that
   C. I'm going to glad D. I'll be glad to
36. —_____?
   —Sure, it's 65250786.
   A. What's your telephone number B. Can I have your telephone number
   C. Can I help you D. Can you make your telephone number
37. —I have an appointment with Mr. Black. My name is John Brown.
   —Ah, yes, your appointment is at 4:15. _____, please, Mr. Brown?
   A. Wait a minute B. May you wait
   C. Can you wait a minute D. Take it easy
38. —Hello, Mr. Black!
   —_____
   A. Hi! Thank you. B. How do you do?

C. Hello! You must be tired.   D. Hello, Mrs. Smith!

39. —Hi, Susan, this is Mr. Li.
    —_____, Mr. Li
    A. Glad to meet you   B. Thank you
    C. How are you   D. Welcome home

40. —Hello, Kate! Fancy meeting you here! Working again, are you?
    —Yes, I have _____ because I want to pass the exams.
    A. must do   B. no other way   C. get to   D. on way

(二)补全对话

A: Hey, Jim. Get up quickly!
B: It's only six o'clock. Let's sleep for another hour.
A: ___41___
B: Ah, how could it be? It's only November!
A: Let's go out and have a look.
B: Wait a minute. You always cheat me.
A: Isn't it wonderful? Look at the snow, so beautiful.
B: ___42___
A: ___43___
B: Yeah, sometime it can be several inches thick. What's the weather like in your hometown?
A: ___44___
B: Does it often rain there?
A: ___45___

> A. I think there will be a snow.
> B. Yes, it does, especially in spring.
> C. It's snowing outside.
> D. Do you have snow in your city?
> E. My goodness! It's really snowing.
> F. You mean winter? Very nice. It isn't so cold and seldom snows.
> G. What's the weather like?

(三)匹配

I   II
46. 谢绝入内   A. Protect Public Property
47. 不准张贴   B. Drinking Water
48. 节约用水   C. No Through Road
49. 此处插入   D. No Admittance
50. 请爱护公共财产   E. No Bills
                           F. Save on Water
                           G. Insert Here

第三节:完形填空(本大题共 10 小题,每小题 1 分,共 10 分)

阅读下面短文,从各题所给的 A、B、C、D 四个选项中选出可填入空白处的最佳答案,并将所选答案填在答题卡上。

The hall was crowded. I had never seen it so full all my thirty years. The professor, __51__ was on a raised platform(演讲台), got up very slowly from his chair. There was a sudden shout of cheers and applause(热烈鼓掌), which __52__ several minutes. Finally one of the five men on the platform raised first one hand, and then both hands before the noise died __53__.

"I don't think I need to introduce Professor Evans," he said. There was a great cheer __54__ this. "He isn't unknown to you." Another shout of cheers followed, and the man sat down. The professor, a short fat man, smiled and looked at the audience. He wore __55__ glasses. He seemed nervous because he cleared his voice twice. He put a hand into one of the side pockets of his jacket. His glasses became __56__ heavier and the hall was completely silent as he stood looking at his audience. It was an __57__ hot in the hall and there was little air. I was sitting near the platform and I __58__ hear the loud tick of the clock on the wall. Surprisingly, the professor very quickly turned his back to us, and __59__ to the men on the platform. He thought he couldn't be heard by the audience, but everyone in the first five __60__ could hear the words, "I've lost my notes."

51. A. he	B. that	C. whom	D. who
52. A. passed	B. kept	C. lasted	D. remained
53. A. of	B. down	C. from	D. out
54. A. at	B. of	C. about	D. with
55. A. low	B. high	C. deep	D. thick
56. A. more	B. less	C. very	D. even
57. A. uninteresting	B. uncomfortable	C. incomplete	D. inspiriting
58. A. clearly	B. hardly	C. exactly	D. carefully
59. A. called	B. cried	C. shouted	D. whispered
60. A. rows	B. benches	C. places	D. groups

第三部分 阅读理解

(共 25 小题,第 1~4 篇为选择题和判断题,每小题 1 分;第 5 篇为简答题,每小题 2 分;共 30 分)

A. 选择题

根据短文内容选择正确的答案。

Passage 1

The first satellite went into orbit(轨道) on 4th October 1957. Its name was Sputnik. Sputnik is the Russian word for satellite. In the satellite there was a small radio. People on the earth heard its "bleep, bleep" on their radios and televisions. Sputnik traveled round the earth every 96 minutes. It was in space for 92 days and it fell back to the earth on 4th January 1958.

Russia's second satellite, Sputnik 2, went into orbit on 3rd November 1957. It carried a dog Laika. Laika couldn't come back to the earth. She died in orbit.

America sent up her first satellite on January 31st 1958. The first astronaut and the first woman astronaut were Russian, Yuri Gagarin made one orbit of the earth on 12th April 1961. Gagarin died in a plane crash in 1968. Valentina Tereshkova went into orbit on 16th June 1963. A Russian rocket took the first satellite to the moon, too. Luna 2 crashed on the moon in September 1959. But then on 20th July 1969 the men landed on the moon. They weren't Russian. They were the American astronauts, Neil Armstrong and Buzz Aldrin. On 12th April 1981 America sent up the space shuttle (航天飞机), Columbia. Now the space shuttle regularly carries satellites into orbit.

61. An animal was carried into space for the first time by _____.
    A. the satellite Sputnik   B. Sputnik 2
    C. the first astronaut   D. the space shuttle

62. The first satellite to the moon carried _____.
    A. one astronauts   B. two astronauts
    C. two astronauts and a dog   D. no astronauts

63. The first astronaut into orbit was _____.
    A. Laika   B. Neil Armstrong
    C. Valentina Tereshkova   D. Yuri Gagarin

64. America sent up her first satellite _____.
    A. over three months after Russia did it   B. over three months before Russia did it
    C. over three years after Russia did it   D. over three years before Russia did it

65. From the passage we can see that in the first ten years of the race for outer space, _____.
    A. many countries took part
    B. quite a few countries were at the same level
    C. Russia took the leading position
    D. America was first in the world

Passage 2

Most people want to work, but it has become more difficult in today's world to find work for everyday. The economics (经济) of the world need to grow by 11% each year just to keep the old jobs for people. Often this is not possible, and so more people are without work. Some people have no jobs now because new machines can do the work of many people in a shorter time. Also, machines do not ask for more money and longer holidays. In all of countries in the world machines are taking work from people, not only in factories, but also on the farms. One machine can often do the work of 40 people. About 95,000 people are moving to the cities a day to look for jobs, but only 70% of them can find jobs.

66. Which of the following is **TRUE** according to the passage?

A. It was easier for people to find work before than today.

B. It was more difficult for people to find work before than today.

C. It was not possible for people to find work not long ago.

D. Today people find work as difficult as before.

67. If the economies of the world grow by 11% each year _____.

    A. 11% of people will have jobs too

    B. 89% of the people will have jobs

    C. people can have the same number of jobs as before

    D. people will have no jobs

68. One machine can do as much work as _____.

    A. 40 people   B. 11% of the people in the world

    C. 95,000 people   D. 70% of the people

69. How many people are moving to the cities a day to look for jobs?

    A. About 11% of the people in the world.   B. About 95,000 people.

    C. More than 95,000 people.   D. 70% of the people.

70. Which of the following is **NOT** true according to the passage?

    A. Machines are taking jobs instead of people not only in factories but also on the farms.

    B. Machines need more money and longer holidays.

    C. Most people want to have jobs.

    D. Now more people are without work.

Passage 3

Working Wives

Last week, we published an article about modern marriage. A recent survey(调查) showed that in England 51 percent of married women go out to work. People were asked what they thought of "working wives." The result were as follows:

	Men	Women
In favor(赞成)	15%	80%
Against	10%	20%
Don't know	20%	0%

We asked readers to write down and tell us their opinions.

Here are some of the hundreds of letters we received.

I'm a (woman) photographer. I make plenty of money, travel a lot, and meet a lot of people. I enjoy my work, and would hate to stay at home. I would never marry a man who wanted me to give up my work.

Ms. Jobs O'Leary

Hampstead

At present there are over 1,000,000 unemployed men in Britain. If a woman gets a job, she puts one more man out of work. Perhaps that man has a wife and twelve children to support. Let women stay at home where they belong.

Ted Stubbs
Southend

I am the mother of twelve children. When I go to work, my husband looks after the children. He is very good with the children and enjoys staying at home with them. And enjoy my job as a bus driver.

Mrs. E. Boot
Battersea

We are twin sisters, who both got married recently. One of us (Doreen) kept her job. The other (Doris) gave up her job. But Doris gets bored (厌烦) staying at home, and Doreen gets bored going out to work. So now Doreen works for a week, while Doris stays at home. Then Doris does Doreen's job for a week, while Doreen stays at home. At work, they never know if it's Doris who's working today!

Doris and Doreen Bean
Hendon

71. Last week we published an article about _____.
    A. marriage nowadays   B. working women
    C. working wives   D. a strange marriage

72. The woman photographer would not marry a man who _____.
    A. has less money than her   B. likes staying at home
    C. is not very gentle   D. wants her to stay at home

73. Ted Stubbs thought that women going out to work _____.
    A. would make men lose chances for work
    B. would be better than men
    C. would weaken the right of the husband at home
    D. would be meaningless

74. When the bus driver goes to work, _____.
    A. her children take care of themselves
    B. a nurse looks after her children instead her
    C. her husband looks after the children
    D. she has to have everything ready for the children

75. _____ likes to stay at home.
    A. Ms. Jobs O'Leary   B. Ted Stutbbs
    C. Doris   D. Doreen

B. 判断题

根据短文内容判断句子的正误(正确的用"T",错误的用"F",文中未提的用"N")。

Passage 4

A grown-up person has ten or eleven pints(品脱)of blood inside his or her body. We can lose a pint of blood without feeling anything, but if we lose a great deal of blood, we feel weak and cold. Our face becomes pale. We may die.

This is what often happens when somebody is hurt in an accident, or a soldier is wounded in a battle. Many people used to die in this way. But nowadays they can be taken to hospital and given more blood. Almost at once they feel better. Their faces are no longer pale. They do not die.

Where does this blood come from? People who are healthy give some blood so that it can be used in this way. Every three months they go to a place where blood is collected. A special kind of needle is put into the arm. It does not hurt. The blood runs through the needle and through a rubber tube into a bottle. A pint of blood is taken in this way. After that the person who has given the blood drinks a cup of tea or coffee. He sits down for a few minutes. Then he feels quite well and goes off. Three months later he comes back and gives another pint.

A person who gives blood in his way feels happy. He knows that his blood will be used to save someone's life. Perhaps one day he himself will need blood too, when he is old.

76. The underlined word "pale" is closest in meaning to with little color in the face.

77. A person who has lost much blood has to go to see a doctor at once.

78. The healthy people feel terrible after they give some blood to others.

79. The passage tells us it'll be safe if you give a pint of blood to others.

80. One person can give blood when he is old enough and strong enough.

C. 简答题

根据短文内容简要回答问题,每题不得超过10个单词。

Passage 5

Oscar Film Themes Symphony Concert

Film highlights accompanied by live performances of movie theme music by the China Opera and Dance Drama Theater Symphony Orchestra, which recorded the music for many films. Familiar tunes will come from such flicks as *Titanic*, *Jurassic Park* and *Waterloo Bridge*.

Where: Nationality Cultural Place Theater

When: March 8, 7:30 p.m.

Admission: 80-380 yuan

Tel: 65287674 ext 508

Fantastic View All the Way

The mountains in this area are not very high, but the vistas are excellent. This walk is gentle and very interesting, going through valleys, over passes, along a ridge and through a few little tranquil(安静的) villages that are located in amazing places. Many sites along the walk offer panoramic view of the surrounding mountains.

Where: Pinggu, northeast of Beijing

When: March 9, meet 8:30 a.m. outside Starbucks at Lido Hotel, or 9 a.m. at Capital Paradise front gate, return 5 p.m.

Admission: adults 150 yuan, children 100 yuan

E-mail: fjhikers@yahoo.com.uk.

Spring Greetings

Paintings in bold colors in traditional Chinese style by young artist Tian Xifeng are displayed to welcome the spring. Tian is a student of famous bird-flower painting artist Wang Qing. He has won several prizes at various national painting exhibitions and developed a style emphasizing vivid close-ups of natural scenes.

Where: Melodic Gallery, 14 Jianwai Dajie, opposite Friendship Store

When: till March 31, 9 a.m. − 5 p.m.

Admission: free

Tel: 65188123

Cala, My Dog

Directed by Lu Xuechang, starring Ge You. The story is about a middle-aged working man, known as Lao Er, whose chief source of stability(稳定) and comfort in life is his dog, Cala. One day, when his wife is out walking Cala, a policeman confiscates(没收) the unregistered canine (犬,犬科动物). As Lao Er endeavors(努力) to recover his dog, the difficult circumstances(境况) of his life are revealed(展示). Chinese with English subtitle(字幕).

Where: Dongchuang Theater, 3 Xinzhongjie, Dongzhimenwai

When: March 13 and 20, 8:30 p.m.

Admission: 20 yuan

Tel: 64169253

81. If you are a music lover, where can you go on Women's Day?

_____

82. How much will you have to pay if you and your parents went to enjoy Fantastic View All the Way?

_____

83. What is shown at the exhibition held in Melodic Gallery?

_____

84. Which number should you dial in order to book a ticket for a film?

_____

85. What is the film *Cala, My Dog* mainly about?

_____

第四部分　书面表达

(共两节,共20分)

第一节:英汉互译(共5小题,每小题2分,共10分。请将86~88题译成中文,将89~90题括号里的中文译成英文)

86. In my opinion, speeding is perhaps the main cause of car accidents.

87. There are more and more cars on the road today.

88. Never drive when you are sleepy and remember not to use your mobile phone while driving.

89. You should _____ (注意) the traffic lights.

90. Don't talk on your cell phone or look _____ (心不在焉) when walking toward your building after dark.

第二节:应用文写作(本节共10空,每空1分,共10分)

中文提示:根据空格中的中文提示完成下面的日记。

____91____ (7月15日) Friday　　　　　　　　　　　　　____92____ (雨天)

Today we held ____93____ (一场英语竞赛) in the school auditorium. It was about ____94____ (怎样学好英语). I also ____95____ (做了演讲). My topic was "____96____ (最好的方法) to Learn English." I did a good job.

When the English competition ____97____ (完成), an American teacher read an English poem for us. Then he ____98____ (教) us an American folk song. We all ____99____ (认为) we learned a lot ____100____ (从) the English competition.

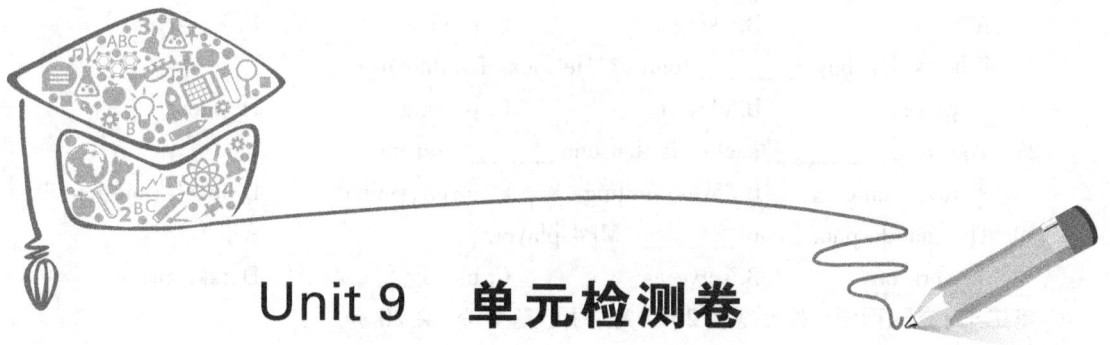

Unit 9 单元检测卷

第一部分 听力

(略)

第二部分 知识运用

(共三大题,每题1分,共40分)

第一节:词汇与语法(本大题共10小题,每小题1分,共10分)

从每小题给出的A、B、C、D四个选项中选出一项符合题意的最佳选项,请将所选答案填在答题卡上。

21. The fashion fair in Shanghai is going to _____ from 1 to 5, November.
    A. hold   B. be held   C. holding   D. held

22. I heard the organizers also _____ a trade fair and a job fair there last year.
    A. hold   B. was held   C. had been held   D. held

23. The China International Fashion Fair is an international trade event _____ every summer.
    A. takes place   B. took place   C. taking place   D. taken place

24. The 70 leading designers lead the latest fashion trends, _____ in clothing, _____ in jewelry and shoes.
    A. not only...but   B. neither...nor   C. either...or   D. whether...or

25. More and more exhibitors _____ the large market in the near future.
    A. will use up   B. make use to   C. will be used to   D. used to

26. He rushed into the _____ house immediately and looked for the old man in the fire.
    A. burn   B. being burning   C. burning   D. burned

27. The piano _____ at the concert is made in France.

A. uses　　　　B. using　　　　C. used　　　　D. is used

28. Who is that boy _____ tennis? He looks familiar to me.

　　A. plays　　　B. played　　　C. playing　　　D. play

29. The most _____ teacher is that one _____ at me.

　　A. love;smile　　B. loves;smiling　　C. loved;smiled　　D. lovely;smiling

30. The mobile phone can _____ MP4 player.

　　A. work on　　B. serve as　　C. use as　　D. take place

第二节：交际用语(本大题共20小题,每小题1分,共20分)

(一)选择

31. —I'll be away on a business trip. Would you mind looking after my cat?
　　—No problem. _____.

　　A. I've no time　　B. I'd rather not　　C. I'd like it　　D. I'd be happy to

32. —Can I go and have a look at it?
　　—Yes, of course. _____.

　　A. After me　　B. Come this way　　C. You may look　　D. This direction

33. —_____ do you want?
　　—Half a kilo, please.

　　A. How many apples　　　　B. What apples
　　C. What kind of apples　　　D. What other

34. —I'm sorry to say that I can't come to your party tonight.
　　—_____? Haven't we agreed on?

　　A. What is it　　　　　　　B. What is it now
　　C. What has happened　　　D. What do you think

35. —Would you like to come to the cinema with me, Frank?
　　—_____ I have to do my homework.

　　A. OK, I think.　　　　　　B. Excellent, I'm afraid.
　　C. Very sorry.　　　　　　 D. Oh, out of pity!

36. —I'm glad to have met you. Drop in sometime.
　　—_____

　　A. Thank you.　　　　　　　　B. Give me a call, will you?
　　C. Me too and I certainly will.　D. Me too and take care.

37. —Please allow me to introduce Mr. Smith, director of the department to you.
　　—_____(久仰大名)

　　A. I haven't seen you before.　　B. I've heard so much about you.
　　C. Haven't we met before?　　　D. How do you do?

38. —It's nice to see you in New York. How's your family?
　　—_____. My wife asked me to say hello to you.

　　A. They are fine　　B. It's very well　　C. That's all right　　D. They are good

39. —I can't see words on the backboard.

—Perhaps you need _____.
　　A. to be examined your eyes　　　　B. to have your sight tested
　　C. to have your sight testing　　　　D. your eyes to be examined
40. —My whole body feels weak and I've got a headache.
　　—_____?
　　A. How long ago did you get this　　B. How long have you been like this
　　C. How soon have you got it　　　　D. How soon have you liked this

(二)补全对话

A：Would you like another piece of chicken?
B：Yes, please. It's delicious. ___41___
A：Oh, no. It's from Kentucky Fried Chicken. ___42___
B：Well, just one, please. ___43___ You bought them at Kentucky Fried Chicken too, didn't you?
A：___44___ Let me give you some more chicken. There's plenty more.
B：No thanks. I'm full. I'd like a cup of tea, please.
A：OK. ___45___
B：Thank you. What a delicious supper!

```
A. Here you are.
B. Well, it's delicious too!
C. Yes, I did.
D. Give you.
E. Did you cook it yourself?
F. How about some sandwiches?
G. Yes, I do.
```

(三)匹配

I	II
46. 单击此处	A. To Make a Copy of the File, Click Copy
47. 复制文件,点击复制	B. Check Your File Format
48. 输入当前密码	C. Enter Current Password
49. 检查文件格式	D. Select Background
50. 注册免费邮箱	E. Click Here
	F. Make Sure the Disk is not Write-protected
	G. Sign up for Free E-mail

第三节：完形填空（本大题共 10 小题，每小题 1 分，共 10 分）

阅读下面短文，从各题所给的 A、B、C、D 四个选项中选出可填入空白处的最佳答案，并将所选答案填在答题卡上。

　　Ms. Evans had just gone into the kitchen ___51___ the afternoon tea when she saw a mouse ___52___ around on the kitchen floor. She was frightened and jumped onto the table. As soon as the mouse disappeared, she jumped down ___53___ the table, rushed out of the kitchen, pulled on her coat, ran out of the house and got on a bus ___54___ was going into the town. There she hurried into a shop and bought a large mouse-trap. She intended to put an end to this mouse as quickly as possible.

When she got home ___55___ the trap, she realized that she had forgotten to buy any cheese to put in it. It was too late to buy any because now all the shops were closed. She wondered ___56___.

___57___ she had a clever idea. She took a pair of scissors and cut a picture of a piece of cheese out of a magazine. Then she put the picture in the trap ___58___ a piece of cheese.

The next morning, Ms. Evans came down to the kitchen and went straight away to the place ___59___ she had put the trap. She wanted to see ___60___ her plan had worked. The picture of cheese had gone and in its place was a picture of a mouse.

51. A. to make	B. to do	C. to become	D. to be
52. A. ran	B. runs	C. running	D. to run
53. A. on	B. at	C. under	D. from
54. A. what	B. which	C. while	D. when
55. A. in	B. on	C. from	D. with
56. A. what to do	B. to do what	C. doing what	D. what of doing
57. A. By the end	B. To the end	C. In the end	D. At the end
58. A. instead of	B. including	C. instead	D. with
59. A. which	B. what	C. when	D. where
60. A. which	B. if	C. why	D. when

第三部分 阅读理解

(共 25 小题,第 1~4 篇为选择题和判断题,每小题 1 分;第 5 篇为简答题,每小题 2 分;共 30 分)

A. 选择题

根据短文内容选择正确的答案。

Passage 1

Come to Austria!

Soll is a village in the mountains in western Austria. And the Post Hotel is clean and expensive. It is opened by a local(当地的)family. From the hotel you can see the whole village, the forests and the mountains. Temperatures in summer are usually 20 ℃ – 25 ℃ in the daytime, but much cooler by evening.

Enjoy Thailand!

When you visit Bangkok in Thailand, don't miss the early morning river boat trip to the floating market just outside the city. There you will find many kinds of fruits and vegetables. And you can pay for them when you sit in your boat. Don't forget your hat: the sun can be strong and it may be as hot as 40 ℃ at noon!

Visit Hawaii!

Maybe the most beautiful place in Hawaii is Kauai. You can visit its long, sandy beaches in the south and west of the island, and mountains and forests in the north, but don't be surprised if it rains in the center of the island. Daytime temperatures there are usually around 24 ℃ to 26 ℃ by the sea, and only a little cooler by late evening.

61. The advertisements above are about _____.
    A. shopping　　　B. food　　　C. travel　　　D. hotels
62. If you go to Bangkok, you can _____.
    A. climb up the mountains
    B. enjoy the scenery of the forests
    C. live in the Post Hotel
    D. buy fruits while sitting in your boat
63. _____ is one better way to prevent the strong sunshine in Bangkok.
    A. Going to the sandy beaches
    B. Wearing a hat
    C. Climbing up the mountains
    D. Staying in the forests
64. Which place will you choose if you want to visit both mountains and beaches?
    A. Soll in Austria.
    B. Bangkok in Thailand.
    C. The floating market.
    D. Kauai in Hawaii.
65. According to the advertisements, we know that _____.
    A. the hottest travel place is Soll
    B. maybe it often rains in the center of Kauai
    C. the floating market is in the middle of Bangkok
    D. the Post Hotel in Austria is clean but the price is low

Passage 2

Have you ever tried to draw a straight line, only to find it turns out all wrong? Or, wanted to show yourself off at a party and the song you'd practiced so many times suddenly becomes more difficult?

I've had both these experiences. As a senior school student, I have to take many exams. Each time I enter one, thinking "I can't fail this time", I get a low mark.

But don't be surprise. It's not because we don't try or make enough preparations or take it seriously. On the contrary, it is because we give it too much attention. It is thinking "I must" makes us taste the terrible flavor of failure.

We often say to our friends "Don't be too hard on yourself." But, when we set our own goals, we may not listen to our own advice.

But, we are making our path to success increasingly difficult.

So why not throw away this crazy pursuit to get the best? Just face the problem lying before you with a calm mind, enjoy the hard work and you will succeed.

In my opinion, keeping a calm state of mind is a skill for life. For people who want to succeed, realizing this is a very important lesson.

So next time when you're trying to draw a straight line or put on a performance, tell yourself, "If I can just do it better than last time, it's a success."

<u>Keep a calm state of mind, and you will be happy whether you succeed or fail.</u>

66. Which of the following is an idea the writer is trying to get across?

    A. You don't need to practice so many times to sing a song well.

    B. We don't always have to follow our own advice.

    C. We should not force ourselves to do well in exam.

    D. To draw a straight line needs a lot of skills.

67. What the writer tells us not to be surprised at is that _____.

    A. people fail though they've tried hard

    B. people may succeed though they don't try

    C. straight lines are not really straight

    D. everybody should taste the flavor of failure

68. Which of the following is the correct order in which the article is organized?

    ①suggestions to try success   ②cause of failure   ③examples of failure

    A. ①②③   B. ②①③   C. ③①②   D. ③②①

69. The underlined paragraph mainly tells us _____.

    A. why we make our path to success difficult

    B. how to keep a calm state of mind

    C. how important it is to be calm

    D. why some people are successful in life

70. Which of the following can be a proper title for the article?

    A. Calm People Wine Success   B. Hope for the Best, Plan for the Worst

    C. Failure Is the Mother of Success   D. Hard Work Leads to Success

Passage 3

Mr. Brown had an umbrella shop in a small town. There he sold all kinds of umbrellas. Sometimes people also brought him broken umbrellas, and then he took them to a big shop in London where they are repaired. Several days later, Mr. Brown went there and got them back.

A few weeks ago, Mr. Brown went to London by train. He forgot to take an umbrella with him that day. Sitting in front of him there was a man with an umbrella standing by the seat. When the train arrived in London, Mr. Brown and the man stood up. In a hurry, Mr. Brown was stopped by a man. "That's my umbrella!" said the man angrily. Mr. Brown said sorry and gave it back to him.

Then Mr. Brown went to the big shop. The people there had got his six umbrellas ready. After a close look at them, he said, "You've repaired them very well."

In the afternoon he went to the station and got into the train again. The same man was in the same seat. He looked at Mr. Brown and his umbrella. "You've had a nice day!" he said.

71. What did Mr. Brown sell?
    A. Cloth.　　　　B. Picture.　　　　C. Umbrellas.　　　　D. Papers.
72. Mr. Brown went to London by _____.
    A. train　　　　B. car　　　　C. bike　　　　D. plane
73. Why did the man say "You're had a nice day"?
    A. Because the man thought Mr. Brown had a nice day.
    B. Because the man was angry.
    C. Because the man wanted to laugh at him.
    D. Because the man wanted to wish Mr. Brown.
74. The people there had got his _____ umbrellas ready.
    A. four　　　　B. five　　　　C. six　　　　D. seven
75. Why was Mr. Brown stopped by a man when he wanted to get off the train?
    A. Because Mr. Brown knocked into the man.
    B. Because Mr. Brown took the wrong umbrella.
    C. Because Mr. Brown stole the mans umbrella.
    D. Because Mr. Brown stole some money.

B. 判断题

根据短文内容判断句子的正误(正确的用"T",错误的用"F",文中未提的用"N")。

Passage 4

Recently Dr. Cleiman has proved that everyone has a daily energy cycle(能量循环). During the hours when you labor through your work, you may say that you are "hot." That is true. The time of day when you feel most energetic(full of energy) is when you cycle of body temperature is at its peak(top). For some people the peak comes during the forenoon. For others it comes in the afternoon or evening. No one has discovered why this is so.

Much family quarrelling ends when husbands and wives realize what this energy cycle means and which cycle each member of the family has.

You cannot change your cycle, but you can learn to make your life fit it better. Habits can help, Dr. Cleiman believes. If your energy cycle is low in the morning but you have an important job early in the day, rise before your usual hour, and then you will work better at your low point.

Get off to a slow start which saves your energy. Get up with a lazy yawn(呵欠) and stretch(伸腰). Sit on the edge of bed before putting your feet on the floor. Avoid the troublesome searching for clean clothes by laying them out the night before.

76. Dr. Cleiman did not explain in the passage how people can make their life fit their cycle.
77. Husbands and wives have different cycles of energy so many husbands and wives quarrel with each other.
78. According to the passage, one should get up earlier if he wants to work better at his low point in the morning.
79. Sitting for a while before getting out of bed can save your energy in the morning.
80. If you know your cycle, you can change it to fit your life.

C. 简答题

根据短文内容简要回答问题，每题不得超过 10 个单词。

Passage 5

No one really knows when or where the first kite flew in the wind. However, most scientists think that the Chinese had kites about 2,000 years ago. Some Europeans who visited the East brought the first kites to the West. They probably brought the brightly colored kites home to their children as gifts.

Kite flying has always been a very important sport in Asia. In China there used to be great holiday each year on the ninth day of the ninth month. It was called the Festival of Ascending on High. Thousands of people, young and old, flew their kites on the day. Kites of different shapes and size filled the sky. There were kites that looked like lions and tigers, and there were kites that looked like fish and birds.

In Japan there is Kite Day, which is still held each year on May 5th. All day long, kites that look like fish are flown from roof tops. They are flown in order to remember a brave Japanese boy, who once saved a group of fishermen by killing a man-eating fish.

Kite fighting is the most popular kite sport in India. There are kite makers who spend their lives making fighter kites. The kite line has two parts. One part is the common string. It is usually white. The other part is a brightly colored cutting string. The cutting string is covered with glass. In kite fighting, a kite flier tries to make the cutting string of his kite across another flier's white string. When the white string is cut, the loser's kite flies away.

Kites are not only for fun. They have been very useful throughout history. Ben Franklin's famous kite experiment proved that lighting is really electricity. And people have used kites to learn more about weather.

The most common kites flown in the United States are the Eddy and box kites. The Eddy kite was brought to the States by a man named William Eddy. In fact, it really came from Asia. Most children fly the Eddy kite. It looks like a diamond. And it has two crossed sticks in back. The box kite was invented by a man in the early 1890's.

Kites had their place in the past and still do in the present. And if you have never flown a kite, you ought to. Then you will better understand why people have been flying kites for the past 2,000 years-and probably always will.

81. When did the Chinese have kites?

_____

82. Who brought the first kites to the West?

_____

83. What did people do on the Festival of Ascending on High in China?

_____

84. What did the kites in the sky look like?

_____

85. What day is May 5th in Japan?
_____

第四部分　书面表达

（共两节，共20分）

第一节：英汉互译（共5小题，每小题2分，共10分。请将86~88题译成中文，将89~90题括号里的中文译成英文）

86. Packed with gracefully designed women's fashion, visitors will leave the show full of inspired design ideas.
_____

87. The fair has become one of the largest fashion events in the Asia-Pacific region.
_____

88. May I know the arrangement of the fashion fair?
_____

89. The fashion fair is certain to bring more and more exhibitors to _____（利用）the large market.

90. There will be press conferences and _____（关于时装潮流的演讲）.

第二节：应用文写作（本节共10空，每空1分，共10分）

中文提示：假定你是高三(5)班的班长，学校决定对全体学生进行一次体检，请你在黑板上用英语给本班同学写一个通知，通知说明以下几点：

1. 体检时间：2017年5月16日下午；
2. 体检地点：长沙市第四人民医院；
3. 集合地点和时间：校门口，下午1:30；
4. 学校安排班车接送，本班学生坐2号班车；
5. 据报道，明天有雨，别忘了带雨伞。

_____91_____

Students in ____92____（高三(5)班），

Our headmaster has decided that every student in our school will go and ____93____（进行一次身体检查）at Changsha No. 4 People's Hospital on the afternoon of ____94____（2017年5月16日）. Our school will arrange ____95____（几台公共汽车）to take us there. The bus number of our class is No. 2. Please ____96____（集合）at the gate of our school ____97____（在一点半）. Please do come ____98____（按时）. One more thing, ____99____（据报道）it is going to rain tomorrow. ____100____（不要忘记带）an umbrella with you.

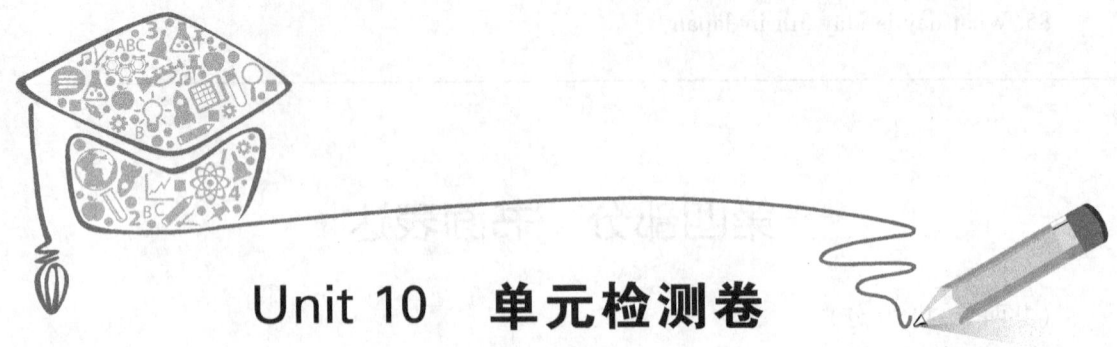

Unit 10 单元检测卷

第一部分 听力

（略）

第二部分 知识运用

(共三大题,每题1分,共40分)

第一节:词汇与语法(本大题共10小题,每小题1分,共10分)
从每小题给出的 A、B、C、D 四个选项中选出一项符合题意的最佳选项,请将所选答案填在答题卡上。

21. _____ I've studied math, and I have a good attitude, my application was accepted.
  A. For   B. As   C. In case   D. Though

22. I'm _____ of my job and considering a change.
  A. fond   B. sick   C. crazy   D. interested

23. I always have to work late at night, and the company keeps me _____ in the office.
  A. work   B. to work   C. working   D. worked

24. _____ that dream for so long, you surely will make it.
  A. Have   B. Had   C. Having   D. To have

25. The best careers for the future are those _____ will reward you with long term joy and fulfillment.
  A. which   B. that   C. what   D. who

26. Then you will _____ look for other jobs.
  A. no longer   B. not more   C. not any longer   D. not any more

27. You will achieve much more and will be highly _____.
  A. satisfy   B. satisfaction   C. satisfying   D. satisfied

28. When carefully _____, the best careers for the future don't have to be a single career choice.
   A. choose B. to choose C. choosing D. chosen

29. Now _____ the importance of computers in daily life and work, almost every employer wants people with computer skills.
   A. realize B. to realize C. realizing D. realized

30. _____ mastering skills necessary for a new career, you'll find both work and financial satisfaction along your career journey.
   A. Unless B. Now that C. Once D. In case

第二节：交际用语（本大题共20小题，每小题1分，共20分）

（一）选择

31. —Could you play basketball with me?
   —_____, and I must finish my homework first.
   A. I don't think so B. I'm afraid not
   C. That's a good idea D. Yes, do please

32. —I'll be away on a business trip. Would you mind looking after my cat?
   —Not at all. _____.
   A. I've no time B. I'd rather not C. I'd like it D. I'd be happy to

33. —May I take your order now?
   —_____.
   A. No, my affairs are in order B. Yes, soldiers must obey orders
   C. Yes, I'd like a dish of chicken D. No, I don't have a choice of meat

34. —There's going to be a film tonight, isn't there?
   —_____.
   A. All right B. I'm not sure C. What a pity D. Never mind

35. —I'm going to Beijing for a few days.
   —_____.
   A. Goodbye B. I like it C. Have a good time D. So long

36. —Can you help me mend the computer?
   —Sorry, _____.
   A. I think so B. I don't think
   C. don't I think so D. I don't think I can

37. —You look so beautiful tonight, Mary.
   —_____.
   A. Thank you B. I don't think so C. Just so-so D. Really

38. —Wish you a happy New Year!
   —_____.
   A. The same to you B. You do too
   C. It depends D. You have it too

39. —What a nice meal! Thank you for having us.
   —_____ .
   A. It doesn't matter   B. My pleasure
   C. Not nice enough   D. With pleasure

40. —What about having some drinks first?
   —_____ ?
   A. Well, will you   B. OK, shall we
   C. Yes, don't we   D. Sure, why not

(二)补全对话
(Tom and Sally are talking about their new classmate. T = Tom; S = Sally)
S: I hear we'll have a new classmate tomorrow. __41__
T: Yes, I met her yesterday.
S: __42__
T: She is pretty tall and thin.
S: How about her hair?
T: __43__
S: Who's the girl over there?
T: Which one? __44__
S: Yes, __45__
T: Just that girl. She's our new classmate.

A. What does she look like?
B. She's got long brown hair.
C. Do you know her?
D. The girl with a book in her hand.
E. Do you mean the one with glasses?
F. What color does she like?
G. Can I help you?

(三)匹配

I	II
46. 禁止通行	A. Keep From Fire
47. 禁止鸣笛	B. No Honking
48. 公共厕所	C. Public Toilet
49. 小心火灾	D. Handle with Care
50. 注意危险	E. Fasten Safety Belt
	F. No Passing
	G. Stop! Danger

第三节:完形填空(本大题共 10 小题,每小题 1 分,共 10 分)
阅读下面短文,从各题所给的 A、B、C、D 四个选项中选出可填入空白处的最佳答案,并

将所选答案填在答题卡上。

The earth is our home. We must take care of it. Life today is easier than it was ___51___ years ago, but it has brought some new problems. One of the biggest problems is pollution. We can see it, smell it, drink it and ever hear it.

Man has polluted the ___52___. The more people, the more pollution. Many years ago, the problem was not so serious because there were not so ___53___ people. When the land was used up or the river was not clean in a place, man went to ___54___ place. Now man is slowly polluting the whole world.

___55___ pollution is still the most serious, it's bad for ___56___ things in the world. Many countries don't let people burn ___57___ for air in houses and factories in the city. Pollution SO_2 is now the most dangerous kind of air pollution. It's caused by heavy traffic. People say it's the ___58___ to ride bikes. When you are riding, there is no pollution. But even in developed countries, most people don't go to work by car. It's because the number of cars on the roads becomes larger. So more people ___59___ their bikes and go to work by car, then things are getting worse and worse. We should have special roads only for bikes and make it ___60___ difficult and expensive for drivers to take their cars into the city that they will go back to use their bikes.

51. A. hundred	B. hundreds of	C. hundred of	D. hundreds
52. A. moon	B. star	C. earth	D. sun
53. A. lot	B. little	C. many	D. much
54. A. others	B. the others	C. the other	D. another
55. A. Air	B. Food	C. Water	D. Noise
56. A. life	B. live	C. living	D. lives
57. A. something bad	B. bad something	C. something good	D. good something
58. A. least	B. best	C. most	D. worst
59. A. put on	B. look at	C. put away	D. look up
60. A. quite	B. such	C. very	D. so

第三部分 阅读理解

(共 25 小题,第 1~4 篇为选择题和判断题,每小题 1 分;第 5 篇为简答题,每小题 2 分;共 30 分)

A. 选择题

根据短文内容选择正确的答案。

Passage 1

Every person has its own way of saying things, its one's own special expression. "Hot Dog" is one American expression that is used in a number of ways. "Hot Dog" is sold at many places, especially at important sport events. People enjoy them with beer or other drinks. There are many stories about how the "Hot Dog" got its name.

"Hot Dog" can be used in many ways. It can mean new costly in best style. People sometimes say Hot Dog to express pleasure. For example, a friend asked if you'd like to go to the park, you might say Hot Dog. I'd love to go. People also use the expression to describe someone who is a shower, who tries to show everyone else how great he is. You often hear such a person called a "Hot Dog", he may be a basketball player, for example, who catches the ball with one hand making an easy catch seems more difficult. You know he is "Hot Dog." Because when he makes such a catch, he bows to the crowd, hoping to win their cheers.

61. The passage mainly tell us _____.

    A. how the "Hot Dog" got its name

    B. how the Americans love to eat "Hot Dog"

    C. about a special American expression

    D. about a player hoping to win cheers

62. According to the passage, which one is **NOT** true?

    A. "Hot Dogs" are only at the place where sport events hold.

    B. "Hot Dog" is a kind of food.

    C. Many people like to eat "Hot Dogs" in America.

    D. If a person bought an expensive necklace, we can say "Hot Dog."

63. If we call a person a "hot dog", we mean that _____.

    A. the person is a great man   B. the person likes to eat "Hot Dog"

    C. the person loves to play basketball   D. the person likes to show off

64. Tom: Would you like to have some Qingdao Beer?

    John: Hot Dog. I haven't had it 3 weeks.

    From the dialogue we can see John _____.

    A. doesn't like to have Qingdao Beer

    B. wants to eat "Hot Dog"

    C. loves to have some Qingdao Beer

    D. wants to have it, but it is hot and he wants to wait a moment

65. If a player who catches the ball with one hand making an easy catch seems more difficult, we can see _____.

    A. it is not easy for him to catch the ball

    B. he wants to make a joke with the crowd

    C. he wants to show the crowd how great he is

    D. he wants to eat "Hot Dog"

Passage 2

FIRE INSTRUCTIONS

THE PERSON DISCOVERING A FIRE WILL:

1. OPERATE THE NEAREST FIRE ALARM. This will cause the alarm(警报器)bells to

ring, and also send a signal to the telephone switchboard operator who will immediately call the Fire Brigade(消防队).

2. ATTACK THE FIRE WITH AVAILABLE(可得到的) EQUIPMENT(器材), IF IT IS SAFE TO DO SO.

FIRE ALARM BELLS

The Fire Alarm Bells will ring either in the area of A Block(街区)(Workshop and administration (行政的)Offices)or in the area of B Block(Teaching) and C Block(Sports Hall). Those in the area where the alarm bells are ringing should take action as indicated below. Others should continue with their work.

ON HEARING YOUR FIRE ALARM:

1. Those in class: will go to the Assembly(集合) Area under instructions given by the teacher.

2. Those elsewhere: will go to the Assembly Area by the most sensible route, and stay near the Head of their Department.

ASSEMBLY AREA

The Assembly Area is the playing field which is south of the Sports Hall. Here names will be checked.

PROCEDURE(步骤)

1. Move quietly.

2. DO NOT stop to collect your personal belongings.

3. DO NOT attempt to pass others on your way to the Assembly Area.

4. DO NOT use the lift.

FIRE ALARMS

1. Administrative Blocks.

At the Reception Desk; at the east of the connecting corridor; outside the kitchen door; back of the stage in the Main Hall.

2. Teaching Blocks.

At the bottom of both stairways and on each landing.

3. Workshops.

Outside Machine Shop No. 1; Engineering Machine Shop No. 2.

4. Sport Hall.

Inside the entrance lobby.

66. This passage give advice on fire safety for _____.
    A. people using a new kind of equipment   B. workers in an engineering factory
    C. young children at school   D. students at college

67. When a person discovers a fire, what is the first thing he should do?
    A. Attempt to put it out himself.   B. Telephone the switchboard operator.
    C. Start the alarm bells.   D. Contact the fire brigade.

68. Everyone in the block where the fire bell has rung must gather together _____.
    A. in another block   B. in the administration office
    C. in one of the playing fields D. in the sports hall
69. Imagine you are a typist in the administration office. When a fire breaks out in the sports hall, what should you do according to the fire instructions?
    A. Look for the fire-fighting equipment.   B. Go quickly to the Assembly Area.
    C. Go to the reception desk.   D. Garry on with the work you are doing.
70. Imagine you are a teacher. What is your first duty in case of fire?
    A. To check the names of your students from a list.
    B. To lead your students out of the building.
    C. To get detailed instructions from your Head of Department.
    D. To patrol(查) the stairways and landings.

Passage 3

When we think of money, we think of coins and paper bills. That is what money is today. But in the past, people used many things in place of money. Some countries used cows. Other countries use salt, tobacco, tea, or stones. Today there are still some places in the world that do not use paper money. One place is the island of Yap in the Pacific Ocean.

On the island of Yap, people use the heaviest money in the world Yap stones. There are round, white stones with a hole in the middle. The Yap stones do not originate from the island. The Yap men have to go to islands four hundred miles away to fetch them. Big stones can be twelve feet high as big as two tall man. Small stones are as big as a dinner plate.

Rich people do not carry the Yap stones. Servants follow the rich. Each servant carries a stone on a pole over his shoulder. Today the people on the island use paper money for everyday shopping. But for other things they still prefer Yap stones.

71. On the island of Yap, people use _____ as money.
    A. stones   B. cows   C. dinner plates   D. salt
72. What does the word "originate" mean?
    A. grow   B. come   C. develop   D. begin
73. Now paper money are used _____ on the island of Yap.
    A. only by rich people   B. in place of Yap stones
    C. for shopping of everything   D. for everyday shopping
74. The passage is mainly about _____.
    A. money used around the world   B. the history of Yap island
    C. money used on Yap Island   D. different kinds of money
75. Which of the following is **TRUE**?
    A. The Yap stones originate from the island of Yap.
    B. The Yap stones are all twelve feet high.
    C. The Yap stones have a hole in the middle.
    D. People on Yap Island use small stones as dinner plates.

B. 判断题

根据短文内容判断句子的正误(正确的用"T",错误的用"F",文中未提的用"N")。

Passage 4

Long ago, men knew a few things that could cause a kind of sleep, but these anesthetics(麻醉剂)were weak. They could not be given too large amounts because they often caused death. If only a little were given, the sick men could still feel pain. So these old anesthetics were almost useless. Operations without anesthetics had usually to be done while the sick men could feel all the pain.

Any operation in those old days was very difficult. The doctor had to work while the sick man's body moved nearly all the time. As the body was cut open, it tried to turn from side to side. How could a doctor do any operation carefully and quickly in conditions like these? When we remember also that the open cuts were not kept clean, and that even the doctor's clothes were usually very dirty, we are not surprised to hear of a large number of deaths.

Today, however, we need not worry about feeling pain during the operation. There are kinds of anesthetics which can easily cause the sick man to fall into a kind of sleep, and when he wakes, the operation is finished. A man can, in some operations, talk about his life's experience to a friend while the doctors are cutting open the lower part of his body. One doctor even managed to cut off his own leg.

76. Why could not the old anesthetics be given too large amounts? Because they often made patients die.

77. From the first paragraph we can know that in the old days operation were usually done without pain.

78. The reason for a large number of deaths was that the sick man's body moved nearly all the time.

79. Today people don't feel any pain during operations because of having good anesthetics.

80. The most suitable title for this passage is Anesthetics' Past and Today.

C. 简答题

根据短文内容简要回答问题,每题不得超过 10 个单词。

Passage 5

"Tipping" is always a difficult business. You don't want to give too much or too little, or tip the wrong person.

In Britain and America, people usually tip waiters in restaurants, porters, taxi drives and hairdressers. They do not tip people in offices, cinemas, garages, or airports.

Do you invite your friend to the restaurant? Then you pay the bill. Does your friend invite you? Your friend pays. If there are men and women in the party, the men usually pay.

These days, men and women are equal in many ways. If you work in Britain or America, your boss could be a man or a woman. There are increasing numbers of women in important positions in politics, law, medicine and in the business world.

But it is still polite for a man to open doors for women and ask them to go first. And it is polite for men to stand up when they are introduced to women. On informal occasions(非正式场合), of course, everyone is more relaxed.

81. Are taxi drivers usually tipped in Britain according to the passage?

82. Why is tipping a difficult business?

83. If Tom is invited to a restaurant by his friend, who will pay the bill?

84. What does the underlined word "equal" mean in Chinese in the passage?

85. What should a man do to show his politeness when he is introduced to a woman?

第四部分　书面表达

(共两节,共20分)

第一节:英汉互译(共5小题,每小题2分,共10分。请将86~88题译成中文,将89~90题括号里的中文译成英文)

86. The greatest amount of growth in China may occur in industries that provide services.

87. How is your job search going?

88. Are you kidding?

89. I _____(对……感到厌倦)my job and considering a change.

90. You _____(应当,理应)choose one based on your own interest.

第二节:应用文写作(本节共10空,每空1分,共10分)

中文提示:根据中文提示,完成下面口头通知。

Boys and girls. ___91___(请注意)? I have a good piece of news to tell you. Professor Cheng Hong will come to ___92___(给我们作一个讲座)on "How to learn English idioms" ___93___(10月6号,星期五下午2:30). The lecture will ___94___(举行)in the lecture hall of our school. You'd better ___95___(带好笔记本)and ___96___(作笔记)of what you think is important in learning English. After the lecture, the professor will talk with some of the students who ___97___(感兴趣)the language and answer some of their questions. Please ___98___(做好准备)it. ___99___(欢迎每位)to ___100___(参加)it.

That's all. Thank you.

期中考试试卷

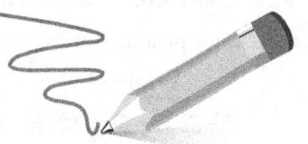

第一部分 听力

(略)

第二部分 知识运用

(共三大题,每题 1 分,共 40 分)

第一节:词汇与语法(本大题共 10 小题,每小题 1 分,共 10 分)

从每小题给出的 A、B、C、D 四个选项中选出一项符合题意的最佳选项,请将所选答案填在答题卡上。

21. I suggest _____ the Great Wall during the summer vacation.
　　A. visit　　　　B. visiting　　　　C. to visit　　　　D. visited

22. Mother asked Tom to stop _____ his homework and have a rest.
　　A. to do　　　　B. doing　　　　C. done　　　　D. do

23. That is the reason _____ she failed the exam.
　　A. how　　　　B. when　　　　C. what　　　　D. why

24. Would you please show me your receipt _____ I can take down some details?
　　A. in order to　　B. so that　　　C. for　　　　D. so as to

25. He asked me _____ .
　　A. had I seen the film　　　　　B. have I seen the film
　　C. if I have seen the film　　　　D. whether I had seen the film

26. The ice had _____ and had carried all his living-room furniture and carpets out to the sea with it.
　　A. broken of　　B. broken out　　C. broken into　　D. broken up

27. Now you can do your banking and _____ your bills from just about anywhere.
　　A. cost　　　　B. spend　　　　C. take　　　　D. pay

28. The teamwork _____ me to work under pressure.
    A. made   B. kept   C. left   D. enabled
29. I _____ before taking the shower.
    A. put on it   B. put it off   C. took it off   D. took it on
30. During the program students _____ activities such as sales training, video and poster production.
    A. joined   B. took part in C. attended to   D. joined to

第二节:交际用语(本大题共20小题,每小题1分,共20分)

(一)选择

31. —You haven't been to Beijing, have you?
    —_____. How I wish to go there!
    A. Yes, I have.   B. Yes, I haven't   C. No, I have   D. No, I haven't
32. —Would you mind if I open the window?
    —_____.
    A. I'm afraid I will   B. Of course not
    C. Go ahead, please   D. All the above
33. —How is everything with you?
    —_____.
    A. It's nothing   B. That's all right   C. I'm sorry   D. Not bad, thanks
34. —_____?
    —The one that looks very nice.
    A. How is your car   B. Do they look very nice
    C. Is your car very nice   D. Which one is your car
35. —How long will it be?
    —_____.
    A. We'll see you on Friday   B. That's too long
    C. Yes, I suppose   D. About an hour
36. —Can I help you?
    —_____.
    A. It's a nice trip, you know
    B. Yes, quite good. I have been to New York
    C. What's wrong with you, dear
    D. Could you tell me how to write a letter
37. —I had a really good weekend at my uncle's home.
    —_____.
    A. Oh, that's very nice of you   B. Congratulations
    C. It's a pleasure   D. Oh, I'm glad to hear that
38. —What about going swimming?
    —_____.

A. Help yourself   B. Go ahead, please
C. Good idea   D. Me, too

39. —What does the tall man do?
    —_____.
    A. He's thirty   B. He is Mr. Robert
    C. He's a doctor   D. He feels much better

40. —Waiter!
    —_____?
    A. What   B. All right   C. Pardon   D. Yes, sir

(二)补全对话

A: Excuse me. ___41___

B: Oh, I'm not really sure. Sorry.

A: Well, thanks anyway. (To C) Excuse me, how can I get to the station?

C: I'm sorry I can't help you. ___42___

A: ___43___ Thanks anyway. (To D) Excuse me, could you help me? I'm looking for the station. I wonder if you could give me directions to it.

D: Sure. It's quite close. Go down this street and turn left at the second crossing.

A: ___44___ the accurate position on the map?

D: OK. Here, can you see that building?

A: Yes, thank you very much.

D: ___45___

> A. Can you show me
> B. Don't mention it.
> C. I'm a stranger here.
> D. Never mind.
> E. Could you tell me the way to the station?
> F. I think you are a stranger here.

(三)匹配

　　　　I　　　　　　　　　　　　　　　II

46. 为新文件夹命名   A. Cancel Printing
47. 撤销打印   B. Check Your File Format
48. 点击此处   C. Click Here
49. 输入当前密码   D. Enter Current Password
50. 注册免费邮箱   E. Type the Name of the New Folder
                            F. Sign up for Free E-mail
                            G. Point to Send

第三节:完形填空(本大题共10小题,每小题1分,共10分)

阅读下面短文,从各题所给的 A、B、C、D 四个选项中选出可填入空白处的最佳答案,并

将所选答案填在答题卡上。

The thing I like most about living on a farm is the change of ___51___: spring, summer, autumn and winter. You can see them all come and go and each one is ___52___ different. In the city you can't understand you can buy ___53___ flowers in winter and eat the ___54___ vegetables all the year round. Here in the country you only eat things at certain times of the ___55___, for example strawberries in June and turnips in winter. You live along the seasons.

Also we make most of our food, we make butter and cheese, we ___56___ our own vegetables and bake our own bread. We never eat ___57___ or tinned food. Everything is ___58___ so it must be better for your health. City people may think we ___59___ a lot of good things about modern life. But in my opinion they miss a lot more than we do—they miss ___60___ life.

51. A. climate	B. weather	C. seasons	D. times
52. A. completely	B. fully	C. perfectly	D. little
53. A. natural	B. native	C. normal	D. summer
54. A. various	B. different	C. same	D. like
55. A. season	B. year	C. month	D. period
56. A. farm	B. grow	C. keep	D. raise
57. A. freeze	B. freezing	C. froze	D. frozen
58. A. pure	B. rare	C. fresh	D. new
59. A. miss	B. lose	C. leave	D. skip
60. A. genuine	B. sound	C. actual	D. real

第三部分　阅读理解

（共 25 小题，第 1~4 篇为选择题和判断题，每小题 1 分；第 5 篇为简答题，每小题 2 分；共 30 分）

A. 选择题

根据短文内容选择正确的答案。

Passage 1

Many people like animals and keep one or more as pets—dogs, cats, or some kinds of birds. If you keep a dog or a cat as a pet, you must know how to look after it.

A grown-up dog needs two meals a day—not more. And it can eat meat, fish, rice and some other things. Dogs like large bones, but don't give them chicken bones. Remember to give them much clean water.

A dog should have a clean, dry box for sleeping. Washing it once a week is good for its health. If it is ill, take it to a doctor. A healthy dog will bring you more pleasure.

Be careful when you have chosen a cat. It has two meals a day with some meat or fish. Cats drink a little milk every day. Sometimes give them vegetables to eat. Don't forget that they need clean water to drink.

Take good care of your pets. They will be your good friends. Maybe they can give you some help when you need.

61. Many people keep _____ as pets.
    A. pandas	B. elephants	C. chickens	D. cats
62. What do dogs like eating?
    A. All the bones.	B. Big bones.	C. Chicken bones.	D. Small bones.
63. A healthy dog can _____ you happy.
    A. fetch	B. tell	C. take	D. bring
64. Cats usually drink _____ .
    A. orange	B. milk	C. water	D. milk and water
65. Are pets friendly to people?
    A. No, I don't think so.	B. Yes, but only a little.
    C. Yes, they are.	D. No, they aren't.

Passage 2

Greek soldiers sent messages by turning their shields (盾) toward the sun. The flashes reflected light could be seen several miles away. The enemy did not know what the flashes meant, but other Greek soldiers could understand the messages.

Roman soldiers in some places built long rows of signal towers, when they had a message to send, the soldiers shouted it from tower to tower. If there were enough towers and enough soldiers with loud voices important news could be sent quickly over distance.

In Africa, people learned to send messages by beating on a series of large drums(鼓). Each drum was kept within hearing distance of the next one. The drum beats were sent out in a special way that all the drummers understood. Though the messages were simple, they could be sent at great speed for hundreds of miles.

In the eighteenth century, a French engineer found a new way to send short messages, In this way, a person held a flag in each hand and the arms were moved to various positions representing different letters of the alphabet. It was like spelling out words with flags and arms.

Over a long period of time, people sent messages by all these different ways. However, not until the telephone was invented in America in the nineteenth century could people send speech sounds over a great distance in just a few seconds.

66. According to this passage, the Roman way of communication depended very much upon _____ .
    A. fine weather	B. high tower
    C. the spelling system	D. arm movements
67. Which of the following statements is **TRUE**?
    A. Neither the Greek soldiers nor their enemy could understand the message.
    B. African soldiers shouted from tower to tower to pass message.
    C. Telephone was invented by a French engineer.

D. Only by using telephone could people send speech sounds quickly.

68. The African way of communication sent messages _____.

    A. in a special way B. over a very short distance
    C. by a musical instrument D. at a rather slow speed

69. The _____ way of communication made use of visible signs.

    A. French B. Roman C. African D. American

70. What did a person hold in each hand to send short messages according to the way a French engineer found?

    A. Letters. B. The alphabet. C. A flag. D. A telephone.

Passage 3

When you want to go shopping, decide how much money you can spend for new clothes. Think about the kind of clothes you really need. Then look for those clothes on sale.

There are labels(标签) inside all new clothes. The labels tell you how to take care of your clothes. The label for a shirt may tell you to wash it in warm water. A sweater label may tell you to wash in cold water. The label on a coat may say "dry clean only." Washing may ruin(损坏) this coat. If you do as the directions(说明) say on the label, you can keep your clothes looking their best.

Many clothes today must be dry-cleaned. Dry cleaning is expensive. When buying new clothes, check to see if they will need to be dry-cleaned. You will save money if you buy clothes that can be washed.

You can save money if you buy clothes that are well made. Well-made clothes last longer. They look good even after they have been washed many times. Clothes that cost more money are not always better made. They do not always fit better. Sometimes less expensive clothes look and fit better than more expensive clothes.

71. If you want to save money, you can buy clothes that _____.

    A. don't fit you B. don't last long
    C. need to be dry-cleaned D. can be washed

72. The labels inside the clothes tell you _____.

    A. how to keep them looking their best B. how to save money
    C. whether they fit you or not D. where to get them dry-cleaned

73. The first thing for you to do before you buy clothes is _____.

    A. to look for well-made clothes B. to see how much money you can pay
    C. to know how to wash them D. to read the labels inside them

74. We learn from the passage that cheaper clothes _____.

    A. are always worse made B. must be dry cleaned
    C. can not be washed D. can sometimes fit you better

75. The best title for the reading should be _____.

    A. Buying Less Expensive Clothes B. Taking Enough When Shopping
    C. Being a Clever Clothes Shopper D. Choosing the Labels inside New Clothes

B. 判断题

根据短文内容判断句子的正误(正确的用"T",错误的用"F",文中未提的用"N")。

Passage 4

From the beginning rivers have played an important part in the life of man. Ancient man used rivers as a means of travel. In ancient times, man settled near on a river bank and built up large empires and civilizations.

Water is nature's most valuable gift to man. Man needs water to irrigate his crops, to cook and to wash. In nations far and wide rivers mean life and wealth. The Nile, the Ganges and a lot of others feed and clothe the nations around them. A shortage of water(水缺乏) in agriculture the people suffer and starve. Water is power. Man builds huge dams across rivers to control the water for irrigation and gain the energy needed to drive generators. The electrical power goes to homes, cities, factories, television stations and armies.

Man uses large quantities of water each day. His main source of water comes from reservoirs which in turn get theirs from the rivers.

In a small way rivers help to keep man's health and make them joyful. Different forms of water sports keep man strong and healthy.

Rivers have run on this earth long before man. Man's future life is uncertain, but rivers will flow on forever.

76. Rivers have been important to man a few hundred years ago.

77. In ancient times empires and civilizations grew up near rivers.

78. Rivers bring life and wealth.

79. Energy is gained from rivers by building dams across them.

80. In areas where there is a shortage of water, when crops fail, the people suffer and starve.

C. 简答题

根据短文内容简要回答问题,每题不得超过10个单词。

Passage 5

When the weather is hot, you go to a lake or an ocean. When you are near a lake or an ocean, you feel cool. Why? The sun makes the earth hot, but it cannot make the water very hot. Although the air over the earth becomes hot, the air over the water stays cool. The hot air over the earth rises. Then the cool air over the water moves in and takes the place of the hot air. When you are near a lake or an ocean, you feel the cool air when it moves in. You feel the wind, and the wind makes you cool.

Of course, scientists cannot answer all of our questions. If we say, "Why is the ocean full of salt?" Scientists will say that the salt comes from rocks. When a rock gets very hot or very cold. It cracks. Rain falls into the cracks. The rain then carries the salt into the earth and into the rivers. The rivers carry the salt into the ocean. But then we ask, "What happens to the salt in the ocean? The ocean does not get more salty every year." Scientists are not sure about the answer of this question.

We know a lot about our world. But there are still many answers that we do not have, and we are curious.

81. When you are near a lake or an ocean, what makes you cool?

82. When will a rock crack?
_____

83. What carries the salt into the earth and into the rivers?
_____

84. Can scientists answer all of the questions?
_____

85. Why are people always curious?
_____

第四部分　书面表达

(共两节,共20分)

第一节:英汉互译(共5小题,每小题2分,共10分。请将86~88题译成中文,将89~90题括号里的中文译成英文)

86. He's going to give up his business so that he can live an ordinary life.
_____

87. The children enjoy dressing up in their mother's old clothes.
_____

88 We must keep pace with the new development of modern education.
_____

89. Mr. Brown came to his company _____（和以前一样早）

90. Do you think Mr. Brown's dream will _____（实现）?

第二节:应用文写作(本节共10空,每空1分,共10分)

中文提示:以下是一则关于春游内容的通知。请根据中文提示完成短文所缺部分。

Notice

The students of ___91___（一、二年级）will go out for a visit on April the 28th. We'll first go to the museum and see an exhibition of ___92___（人与自然）. When you're in the exhibition hall you should keep quiet and make careful notes because we're going to discuss after we come back. After that we plan to visit the botanical garden on Quanshan Hill and ___93___（进行野餐）on top of it. So please bring lunch and some water with you.

Our ___94___（校车）will take us there. The school bus will leave ___95___（7:20）, please gather at ___96___（学校大门）at 7:00 a.m.

___97___（那些）want to ___98___（参加）the activity should ___99___（报名,注册）for it at the Students' Union ___100___（本周星期四前）.

The Students' Union
April 21

期末考试试卷

第一部分 听力

（略）

第二部分 知识运用

（共三大题，每题1分，共40分）

第一节：词汇与语法（本大题共10小题，每小题1分，共10分）

从每小题给出的 A、B、C、D 四个选项中选出一项符合题意的最佳选项，请将所选答案填在答题卡上。

21. —Is Saturday or Sunday OK?
    —I don't think _____ is all right.
    A. either B. each C. both D. neither

22. You might be just the person for _____ we've been looking.
    A. what B. which C. who D. whom

23. The man _____ toys is our director.
    A. is packing B. packing C. who packing D. packed

24. The car pats _____ they make are popular all over the world.
    A. where B. when C. which D. who

25. What I really doubt is _____ I can pass the final examination.
    A. what B. that C. where D. whether

26. If you _____ your name and address on the card, we'll send the book to you as soon as it is returned.
    A. go over B. work out C. fill in D. carry out

27. _____ more attention, the tree could have grown better.
    A. Given B. To give C. Giving D. Having give

28. Who is that boy _____ tennis?
    A. play　　　　　B. plays　　　　　C. playing　　　　　D. played
29. _____ the cost, the hat doesn't suit me.
    A. Except　　　　B. But for　　　　C. Apart from　　　D. Beside
30. The fashion fair is certain to _____ more and more exhibitions to make use of the large market in the near future.
    A. take　　　　　B. carry　　　　　C. bring　　　　　D. hand

第二节：交际用语（本大题共 20 小题，每小题 1 分，共 20 分）

（一）选择

31. —How are you, Mary?
    —_____.
    A. Fine, thanks　　　　　　　　　　B. It's all right
    C. Thank very much　　　　　　　　D. I'm very good, thanks
32. —Let me introduce myself to you. I'm Albert.
    —_____.
    A. With pleasure　　　　　　　　　B. It's my pleasure
    C. I'm very pleased　　　　　　　　D. Pleased to meet you
33. —I think I must go now. See you later.
    —_____.
    A. You can go　　B. See you　　　C. Bye-bye　　　D. Nice to meet you
34. —Excuse me, can you tell me where the nearest bus stop is?
    —I'm sorry, I have no idea. _____.
    A. I don't know　　　　　　　　　B. I just come
    C. I am new　　　　　　　　　　　D. I am a stranger here
35. —Is your watch accurate?
    —Yes, my watch _____.
    A. runs well　　B. keeps good time　　C. keeps right　　D. never stops
36. —I'm afraid I've got a bad cold.
    —_____.
    A. Never mind　　　　　　　　　　B. Keep away from me
    C. Better go and see a doctor　　　　D. You need to take medicine
37. —Is it cold today?
    —_____.
    A. It's ten below zero　　　　　　　B. Not too bad
    C. Just so-so　　　　　　　　　　　D. Yes, it is
38. —Will you be able to come and see us on Friday?
    —_____. I will have to work.
    A. I believe yes　　　　　　　　　　B. I don't hope so
    C. I won't be able to　　　　　　　　D. I'm afraid not

39. —I'll come back at nine tomorrow evening. Can you meet me at the airport?
    —_____.
    A. That's all
    B. All right. Nice to see you
    C. OK. Wait for me
    D. All right. See you then

40. —Is this number 61234567?
    —_____.
    A. No, you are not
    B. Yes, you are
    C. No, you've dialed the wrong number
    D. No, you are right

(二)补全对话

Stranger: Oh, dear! What shall I do?
Xiao Lin: What's the matter? Can I help you?
Stranger: I am going to DC Clothing Factory. I have got a map here. ___41___
Xiao Lin: Let me see. Oh, ___42___ The city has changed greatly these years. Don't worry, a No. 27 bus goes on another road. ___43___
Stranger: How can I find the road? Do I have to go up to the north or down the south?
Xiao Lin: ___44___ This road goes from the west to the east. You need to go to east and then turn at the first crossing. There you can see the bus stop on the right side of the road. When you get on a bus, the conductor can help you.
Stranger: By the way, ___45___.
Xiao Lin: Most of them do. I can write the name of the factory on this map in Chinese. When you get on the bus, show it to them. Anyone can help you.
Stranger: Thank you very much.

    A. No, you needn't.
    B. does the conductor speak English?
    C. But it doesn't show me the right way.
    D. it's wrong.
    E. Neither.
    F. It takes you right to factory.
    G. You are right.

(三)匹配

I	II
46. 售票处	A. Office Hours
47. 来宾登记	B. Free Admission
48. 免费入场	C. Hands Wants
49. 紧急求救信号	D. Booking Office
50. 旅行社	E. SOS
	F. Travel Agency
	G. Visitors Please Register

第三节:完形填空(本大题共10小题,每小题1分,共10分)

阅读下面短文,从各题所给的A、B、C、D四个选项中选出可填入空白处的最佳答案,并将所选答案填在答题卡上。

There are thousands of different languages in the world. Everyone seems ___51___ that his native language is ___52___ important one, as it is even his first language. For many people it is native language all their ___53___. But English is the world's most widely used language.

___54___ a native language, English is ___55___ by nearly three hundred million people in the U.S.A, Britain, Australia and ___56___ other countries. For people in India and many other countries, English is often necessary for business, education, information and other activities. So English is the ___57___ language there.

As a foreign language ___58___ other language is more widely studied or used than English. We use it to ___59___ radio, read book or travel. It is ___60___ one of the working languages in the United Nations.

51. A. to think	B. to make	C. thinking	D. making
52. A. more	B. the most	C. most	D. the more
53. A. life	B. living	C. lives	D. live
54. A. For	B. As	C. Like	D. About
55. A. said	B. talked	C. told	D. spoken
56. A. any	B. much	C. some	D. lot
57. A. saying	B. native	C. unspoken	D. second
58. A. no	B. not	C. none	D. little
59. A. listen	B. listen to	C. hear from	D. hear
60. A. too	B. either	C. also	D. as well

第三部分 阅读理解

(共25小题,第1~4篇为选择题和判断题,每小题1分;第5篇为简答题,每小题2分;共30分)

A. 选择题

根据短文内容选择正确的答案。

Passage 1

What must you do when you receive a present for your birthday? You have to sit down and write a thank-you note. The words "thank you" are very important. We have to use them on so many occasions. We say them when someone gives us a drink, helps us to pick up things, hands us a letter, lends us a book or gives us a gift.

Another important word is "please." Many people forget to use it. It is rude to ask someone to do something without saying "please." We have to use it when we ask for something, too. It may be a book or a pencil, more rice or more sauce, help or advice. It may be in the classroom, at home, at the bus-stop or over the counter. We have to use "please" to make the request pleasant.

We have to learn to say "sorry" too. When we have hurt someone's feelings, we'll have to go and say we're sorry. When we have told a lie and feel sorry, we will have to use the same word, too. "Sorry" is a healing(和解的) word. We can make people forget wrongs by using it sincerely.

These three words are simple but important. Men had to use them long ago. We have to use them now. Our children will have to use them again. They are pleasing words to use in any language.

61. When we receive a birthday present, we have to _____.
    A. return it   B. give it to one of our friends
    C. do nothing   D. write a thank-you note

62. When someone helps us to do something, we should _____.
    A. thank him   B. say sorry to him
    C. use the word "please"   D. no say anything

63. One of the important words in any language is _____.
    A. "hello"   B. "yes"   C. "no"   D. "please"

64. We have to use the word "please" when we _____.
    A. hurt somebody's feelings   B. ask for something
    C. receive a present   D. have told a lie

65. The three important words in any language are _____.
    A. thanks, hello and goodbye   B. yes, no and really
    C. thanks, please and sorry   D. well, please and pardon

Passage 2

Note: The following information is from a holiday guide-book.

GARDEN RESTAURANT

Telephone: 7364431

Address: 9020 Bridgeport Road

Open: Mon. to Fri. 7:00 a.m. – 2:30 p.m. and 5:00 – 9:00 p.m.
       Sat. 7:00 a.m. – 11:00 a.m. and 5:00 – 9:00 p.m.
       Sun. 11:00 a.m. – 2:00 p.m. and 5:00 – 9:00 p.m.

NEW YORK MUSEUM

Telephone: 2706030

Address: Vanier Park, 1100 Chestnut St. New York

It is America's largest museum, specialized(专门研究) in America's history and art of our native people.

Open: Mon. to Fri. 9:00 a.m. – 5:00 p.m. (Monday free)
       Sat: 9:00 a.m. – 1:00 p.m.

LANSDOWNENE PARK SHOPPING CENTER

Telephone: 3562367

Address: 5200 No. 3 Road

Open: Mon. Tues. & Sat. 9:30 a. m. —5:30 p. m.

　　　　Wed. Thurs. & Fri. 9:30 a. m. —9:30 p. m.

　　　　Sun. 11:00 a. m. —5:00 p. m.

SKYLINE HOTEL

Telephone: 2785161

Address: 3031 No. 3 Road(at Sea Island Way)

Open: The Hangar Den—Wed. to Sun. Dinner from 5:30 p. m.

　　　　Coffee Shop—Mon. to Fri. from 6:00 a. m. ;Sat. 6:30 a. m. ;Sun. 7:00 a. m. ;

　　　　Mon. to Wed. to 10:00 p. m. ;Thurs. to Sun. to 11:00 p. m.

66. If you want buy a new jacket, you have to go to _____ .

　　A. 3031 No. 3 Road　　　　　　　　B. 5200 No. 3 Road

　　C. 9020 Bridgeport Road　　　　　　D. 1100 Chestnut Street

67. If you want to go out for dinner on Sunday, you can call up the number _____ .

　　A. 2785161 or 2706030　　　　　　　B. 2706030 or 3562367

　　C. 7364431 or 2785161　　　　　　　D. 3562367 or 2785161

68. You don't have to pay on Monday if you go to _____ .

　　A. Skyline Hotel　　　　　　　　　　B. Garden Restaurant

　　C. New York Museum　　　　　　　　D. Lansdowne Park Shopping Center

69. If you want to enjoy yourself on Sunday morning, you can go to _____ .

　　A. Lansdowne Park Shopping Center　　B. New York Museum

　　C. The Hangar Den　　　　　　　　　D. Coffee Shop

70. If you want to go out for dinner at 13:00 on Sunday, you have to go to _____ .

　　A. Skyline Hotel　　　　　　　　　　B. Lansdowne Park Shopping Center

　　C. New York Museum　　　　　　　　D. Garden Restaurant

Passage 3

　　Crocodiles(鳄鱼) lay their eggs and leave them under leaves or sand, and the baby crocodiles only live in hot places. They are found in India, Australia, Africa and America where they spend most of their time lying in the mud or river. The crocodile's tail is long and strong; it is used when the animal is swimming. It's also good for fighting, because one blow of it will knock down a man or even a big animal at once.

　　The crocodile can stay away from danger under its hard bony plates(鳞片). These bony plates cover most of its body. The crocodile can only see things in front of itself, because it can't turn its head from side to side.

　　After eating, the crocodile can't clean its own teeth because it can't move its tongue(舌头) up and down. The crocodile bird will follow it to eat the food left in the crocodile's mouth. The bird helps the crocodile to clean its teeth.

With its hard and sharp teeth the crocodile catches its food—maybe a fish, an animal or even an unlucky man, and the crocodile hold its food below the water until its food dies.

71. Baby crocodiles only live in _____ places.

    A. warm   B. hot   C. cool   D. cold

72. Which of the following is **NOT** true about crocodiles?

    A. They can't see the things beside their bodies.

    B. They can't clean their teeth by themselves.

    C. They catch food with their hard and sharp teeth.

    D. They spend most of their time traveling on land.

73. What's the use of the crocodile's tail?

    A. It is used when the crocodile is swimming.

    B. It is used to drive away flies.

    C. It is good for fighting.

    D. Both A and C.

74. The crocodile _____.

    A. can't move its head from side to side   B. can move its tongue up and down

    C. can turn its head from side to side   D. can move its head freely

75. What will the crocodile bird do after the crocodile eats?

    A. The crocodile bird will clean the teeth of the crocodile.

    B. The crocodile bird will eat the eggs of the crocodile.

    C. The crocodile bird will follow the crocodile to catch its food.

    D. The crocodile bird will hold the crocodile's food until its food dies.

B. 判断题

根据短文内容判断句子的正误(正确的用"T",错误的用"F",文中未提的用"N")。

Passage 4

Many people are frightened of spiders(蜘蛛). They are especially afraid of large hairy(多毛的)ones. The largest and most frightening of all spiders is the bird-eating spider, which lives in the hot, thick rain forests of northern South America.

Bird-eating spiders are a type of tarantula(北美蜘蛛). They are very hairy. Some of these giant spiders can spread eighteen centimeters(seven inches) with their legs. Tarantulas are not, as most people think, poisonous spiders. They can bite, and the bite is painful, but it will not kill a grown-up. The poisonous bite of a black widow spider is far more dangerous.

Bird-eating spiders often hide in holes and under rocks during the day, but at night they creep out and hunt for insects. As you might guess from their names, they also catch birds and eat them.

They have another unusual ability. They can walk up windowpanes(窗棂) because of sticky, silky hairs on their feet that cling(粘着) to glass.

76. The bird-eating spider can be described as a very hairy and frightening spider.

77. The bird-eating spider lives where the climate is cool and dry.

78. Compared with the bite of a black widow spider, the bite of a tarantula is less dangerous.

79. Bird-eating spiders hunt during the day.

80. The passage implies(暗示) that one can hardly see a bird-eating spider during the day.

C. 简答题

根据短文内容简要回答问题,每题不得超过10个单词。

Passage 5

We've got two children:Jack is seven, and his little brother Eric is four. They're quite close, and play a lot together. They quarrel quite a lot too, but they enjoy each other's company.

Unluckily, we live quite a long distance away from the others of the family. It's an eight-hour drive to get to their grandparents, but we usually visit them during the school holidays.

Jack reads well, but he hasn't started to read for pleasure yet. He thinks reading is only something one has to do at school. I think the main problem is that he watches too much television.

He also likes playing cards, computer games and riding his bike. I don't let him ride it on the streets, but we often go to the park, where it's safer.

He doesn't eat too many sweets, because he's getting his adult teeth(恒牙) now, and he knows they've got to last him for life. He seems more interested in saving his pocket money and counting it than spending it.

81. How many people are there in Jack's family?

_____

82. When does Jack usually visit his grandparents?

_____

83. Where does Jack often go to ride a bike?

_____

84. Why doesn't Jack eat too many sweets?

_____

85. What do you know about Jack in reading?

_____

第四部分　书面表达

(共两节,共20分)

第一节:英汉互译(共5小题,每小题2分,共10分。请将86~88题译成中文,将89~90题括号里的中文译成英文)

86. We need people who are outgoing and patient.

_____

87. Our company is now facing a big financial problem.

_____

88. You don't have work experience. That's why you are not employed.
_____

89. Many young people who want to live in the city will often live in a more dangerous area to _____(省钱).

90. It's necessary _____(掌握一门外语).

第二节:应用文写作(本节共10空,每空1分,共10分)

中文提示:根据提示用英文填写预订机票表。Frank Smith 准备于 2017 年 2 月 2 日在重庆江北国际机场乘坐中国国际航空公司的 CA4123 由重庆飞往厦门的头等舱(first)单程航班,要求座位为 2B,经订票员核实被告之本航班在 1 号厅候机,第 5 登机口登机。预订人联系人电话:023 - 888776611;电子邮箱:FKsh906@126.com;住址:华天宾馆1828房。

Name ___91___	Flight Number ___95___
Origin(始发站) Chongqing	Chongqing Airport ___96___
Destination(目的地) ___92___	Waiting Hall:No. 1
Expected Departure Feb. 2,2017	Gate ___97___
Final Departure Feb. 2,2017	Seat ___98___
Class ___93___	Telephone 023 - 888776611
Single/Return ___94___	E-mail ___99___
	Carrier Airmail Address ___100___

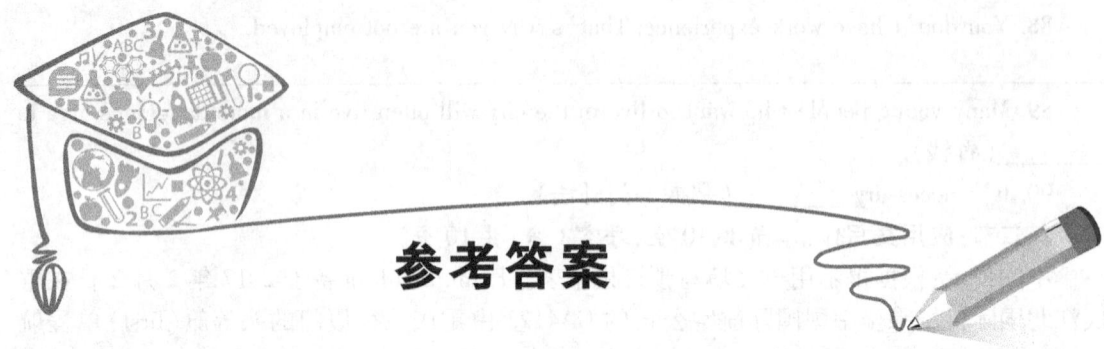

参考答案

同步训练 B 拓展层次

Unit 1

Ⅰ. CAAAB, ADDBC, AABBA   Ⅱ. BBADA
Ⅲ. CDBAA
Ⅳ. 1. to have/hold　　2. except me
　　3. broken up　　4. prefer to stay
　　5. share in
Ⅴ.
I like the Chinese Spring Festival best.
　　The Chinese Spring Festival begins in the last day of the lunar year, and ends in the 15th day of lunar New Year, which is also called the Lantern Festival. During the Spring Festival, people use red lanterns and Spring Festival couplets to decorate their houses, put on all kinds of colored clothes, often visit friends and relatives or get together to eat dumplings, fish, meat and other delicious food. The children are looking forward to receiving gift money during the Spring Festival, and together they play the fireworks happily. Often there are some dragon and lion dances and some other carnival activities. In the meantime, CCTV will hold the grand Spring Festival gala.

Unit 2

Ⅰ. BAACC, CACCA, ABCDD   Ⅱ. DACCC
Ⅲ. DBABD
Ⅳ. 1. started in　　2. savings account
　　3. deposit at least　　4. exchange rate
　　5. have raised
Ⅴ. 1. Cloudy　　2. shopping
　　3. looking around　　4. happened to
　　5. talking

Unit 3

I. ABABB, CCCCD, DDDCC   II. CBADE
III. BCCAD
IV. 1. What I want to learn   2. register online
    3. tuition fees   4. support myself
    5. what other
V. 1. June 6   2. graduate from university
   3. wonderful   4. the rest of our classmates
   5. congratulate on

Unit 4

I. BBBBC, DBBCD, DDCDB   II. CACCC
III. 1. Questionable.
    2. The social reality children are facing can't be changed.
    3. To get them more involved socially.
    4. Anxiety, though unavoidable, can be dealt with.
    5. No, they didn't.
IV. 1. offer her   2. the machine replaced
    3. under guarantee   4. disappointed at
    5. an 80% discount
V. 1. staff members   2. complaint department
   3. very rude   4. in question
   5. make a formal apology to me

Unit 5

I. ABCDD, DDCBA, A   II. DAABD
III. TFTFF
IV. 1. assembly line   2. be divided into
    3. in charge of   4. have cooperated
    5. until
V. 1. a supermarket   2. things
   3. on the way/coming   4. the whole supermarket
   5. very large/big   6. said to myself
   7. them   8. didn't know what to buy
   9. that   10. too tired to move

Unit 6

I. ABABA, DCDBC, CACCC, D   II. DACCC

Ⅲ. TFFFT
Ⅳ. 1. packed with   2. saying something
   3. just the person   4. apply for
   5. your arriving
Ⅴ.

WUYI ROAD, CHANGSHA
March 19th

Dear Sir,

Today I read your advertisement in *Hunan Daily*. I'd like to apply for the post as an English secretary.

I am 21, 1.71m and healthy. I went to Changsha University three years ago and I will graduate from there soon. Now I want to work as a secretary in your factory. I think that I'm qualified for the position. I can write well in English and my oral English is excellent. I once won the first prize in an English contest held in our university. In my spare time I enjoy reading, writing and listening to music. If you think I am the right person, please give me a telephone call. My number is 0731 - ×××××××.

Yours sincerely,
Li Mei

Unit 7

Ⅰ. DCDDC, BCBBC, DBBBB   Ⅱ. BABAD
Ⅲ. TTTFF
Ⅳ. 1. improve my English   2. five minutes' walk
   3. in which/where   4. aiding
   5. similar to
Ⅴ. 1. the lowest temperature   2. the highest temperature
   3. the average daily temperature   4. 150 rainy days
   5. average annual rainfall

Unit 8

Ⅰ. BBCAC, CCCCB   Ⅱ. BBADA
Ⅲ. TFTFF
Ⅳ. 1. how most   2. pay attention to
   3. break into   4. alert to
   5. inform him
Ⅴ. 1. Poster: Friendly Basketball Match   2. Saturday. June 6th
   3. Organized by   4. will be held
   5. are welcome

Unit 9

Ⅰ. ABCDD, BBABA　　　　　　　　Ⅱ. BCDEF
Ⅲ. FFTTF
Ⅳ. 1. fashion fair　　　　　　　　2. reserved a booth
　　3. press conferences　　　　　4. taking place
　　5. out of fashion
Ⅴ. 1. Fashion Show Weekends　　2. Fashion Show Exhibition
　　3. this winter and the next spring　　4. are designed by
　　5. fashion lovers　　　　　　　6. models
　　7. staff members　　　　　　　8. 8:00 p.m. October 21
　　9. Big Hall　　　　　　　　　　10. The Fashion Association

Unit 10

Ⅰ. CDCDD, AACBC, CCCBB, DCCAB　　Ⅱ. DABEF
Ⅲ. FFTTF
Ⅳ. 1. making branded clothing　　2. Seeing the teacher
　　3. carefully chosen　　　　　　4. in unexpected ways
　　5. master one or two
Ⅴ. 1. apply for　　　　　　　　　2. business management
　　3. during which time　　　　　4. have attained
　　5. in advance

英语创优导航试卷一

第一部分　听力

(略)

第二部分　知识运用

21-30　ACCCC, CDDDC　　　　31-40　CBBDD, DCABD
41-50　GDEAB, FEBCG　　　　51-60　ABADB, ACAAC

第三部分　阅读理解

61-70　CAABC, BDCBA　　　　71-80　CBACA, TFFTF
81. An office boy.　　　　　　82. One day in 1925.
83. At a technical college and the University of Glasgow.

84. Yes, he was.

85. Because they wanted to share the development of his invention.

第四部分　书面表达

工科类

86. 维修包括检测设备和替换故障的零件。

87. 你不应这么消极,每一个人都有自己的优缺点。

88. 你的意思是问题是由电脑引起或其他连接设备引起的?

89. took on　　　　　　　　　　90. take reasonable precautions

服务类

86. 成为会员后,你就可以在网站上的网店里购物了。

87. 您的房间已经预定好了,请您在上午 10 点之前办理入住手续。

88. 她不但准时完成任务而且为公司节省了许多钱。

89. recommend　　　　　　　　90. was divided into

91. apply for　　　　　　　　　92. male

93. an 8-grade　　　　　　　　94. work as

95. the first prize　　　　　　　96. held

97. experiencing something scary　98. well with

99. right person　　　　　　　　100. Li Ha

英语创优导航试卷二

第一部分　听力

(略)

第二部分　知识运用

21-30　BBBBA,DBCCA　　　31-40　DCBDC,CCBBB

41-50　BEGAD,DAFGB　　　51-60　BBACA,CADBC

第三部分　阅读理解

61-70　CBDAB,CCBCD　　　71-80　DDCDB,TFFFT

81. Because it shuts off air and puts out fire.

82. No, not all of them can.

83. It will turn into steam to keep air from fire.

84. With sand and chemicals.

85. Because gasoline is lighter than water.

第四部分　书面表达

工科类

86. 我认为最重要的是理解同事的感情和需求。
87. 新工作中你应多听少说。
88. 我想最危险的工具是钢锯。
89. safety rules
90. working environment

服务类

86. 绝不可与顾客发生争论。
87. 它以使具有天赋的雇员通向成功而著称。
88. 你应调查情况,仔细倾听顾客的意见。

89. have worked as
90. check in
91. The Student Union
92. Saturday evening
93. welcome our friends
94. will be held
95. dancing
96. the exchange of gifts
97. wrap it up
98. sign your name
99. good wishes
100. is welcome

单元检测试卷

Unit 1

第一部分　听力

(略)

第二部分　知识运用

21-30　BCDBD, CBDDC　　　31-40　CCDBA, DACCA
41-50　BDECA, DCGEF　　　51-60　ACCDB, AABBA

第三部分　阅读理解

61-70　BACBC, BBCAD　　　71-80　BDCCA, TTTFF

81. She goes to the supermarket and get the groceries.
82. The fruit section, the meat counter, wines and spirits section.
83. Because she was too heavy to carry.
84. She put whisky in Mrs. Bell's shopping bag.
85. No, she didn't.

第四部分　书面表达

86. 你可以想象出当我发现所有参加晚会的人中就自己没有化装时会是什么感受。
87. 这没什么。
88. Hall 先生那天晚上喝了很多酒，一直睡到第二天中午才醒。

89. prefer to
90. in public
91. Mr. Zhang Hua
92. How are you doing
93. spent
94. ready
95. looked for
96. had a lot of fun
97. At last
98. found
99. as
100. shared

Unit 2

第一部分　听力

（略）

第二部分　知识运用

21 – 30　BADCD, BADBA　　　31 – 40　BDAAB, CACCD
41 – 50　CGFBA, GEDFB　　　51 – 60　CBDBC, ABDAD

第三部分　阅读理解

61 – 70　DBAAC, BBCAC　　　71 – 80　BCBAA, FTNTF

81. He started to go to school at six.
82. His teachers.
83. Because they helped students know more and make many friends.
84. Because he had to take the exams for senior schools.
85. They stand for Small, Sweet and Simple.

第四部分　书面表达

86. 你可以使用我们的自助银行取钱、存钱或通讯充值。
87. 现在您只要动动手指就可以进行付账和账户余额查询。
88. 网上银行的用户可以同时使用本业务。

89. having kept you waiting
90. show me your passport
91. NOTICE
92. In order to
93. waiting in a queue
94. self-service
95. anytime anywhere
96. following
97. four kinds of
98. do your banking
99. know more about
100. information@standardbank.cn.

Unit 3

第一部分 听力

(略)

第二部分 知识运用

21－30　BABCC, BDCAD　　31－40　CADBB, CDBAD
41－50　CFBAD, CDFEG　　51－60　CADBD, ABADA

第三部分 阅读理解

61－70　CADBA, DDCBA　　71－80　BCBBD, FFFTF

81. Some bike riders in New York City.
82. Because if there were special lanes, more people would ride.
83. Because it would slow traffic down.
84. More traffic means more business.
85. No, they can't.

第四部分 书面表达

86. 你可以在网上找到我们的主页，在线填写申请表。
87. 给我留下深刻印象的是，很多澳大利亚学生都靠兼职来挣取学费。
88. 我不需要从父母那里得到经济援助。

89. keep pace with　　　　　90. sign up
91. took　　　　　　　　　92. course
93. training school　　　　　94. three-month
95. not only　　　　　　　96. but also
97. various places　　　　　98. completed
99. with　　　　　　　　　100. spoken English/oral English

Unit 4

第一部分 听力

(略)

第二部分 知识运用

21－30　CDCAC, DCABC　　31－40　DDDAB, DDDCC
41－50　BEFCA, CGBAD　　51－60　ACDBA, DBAAD

第三部分 阅读理解

61－70　BADBD, CCCAB　　71－80　CCBAD, TFTTF

81. She invited them to come in and eat something.
82. Only one of them could go into the house.
83. They took their daughter's advice.
84. All of the three men went into the house.
85. Love is the most important.

第四部分　书面表达

86. 照相机被严重损坏。　　　　　　87. 我的手表闹钟出了毛病。
88. 请把您的收据给我看一下,我得作一个详细的记录。

89. disappointed at	90. in no time
91. inform	92. on July 13th
93. examination	94. were badly damaged
95. because of	96. Therefore
97. at the normal price	98. 10% discount
99. replacement	100. Yours

Unit 5

第一部分　听力

(略)

第二部分　知识运用

21 – 30　CDBCC,DCCDD　　　　31 – 40　DBDCC,BABBD
41 – 50　CFAEB,DEFAB　　　　 51 – 60　DCBDB,DDBDB

第三部分　阅读理解

61 – 70　ADCCA,BBACD　　　　71 – 80　CABCA,FFTTT
81. 21/Twenty-one.　　　　　　　82. In a rubbish bin.
83. Around 12:50 p.m.
84. Shop windows and stainless steel rubbish can.
85. She saw a lot of pedestrians lying on the ground.

第四部分　书面表达

86. 大家注意,我们将马上开始工作了。
87. 他们告诉儿子地球绕着太阳转。
88. 张先生说我们应该至少分成三个小组。

89. took part in	90. works as
91. Ladies and Gentlemen	92. to
93. take off	94. be seated
95. Fasten	96. make sure

97. standing up
99. non-smoking
98. At last
100. enjoy your journey

Unit 6

第一部分　听力

（略）

第二部分　知识运用

21－30　CBBDB, DBADC
41－50　DAECB, FCDAG
31－40　BBDCD, CAABC
51－60　DCDDC, BAAAD

第三部分　阅读理解

61－70　ADADA, DBDDD
71－80　ADBCA, FFTFT

81. I often see a lot of people walking dogs.
82. Training dogs to protect themselves against attacks by other beasts.
83. A best friend.
84. The most important reason is for companionship.
85. No, it hasn't.

第四部分　书面表达

86. 我打电话是为了申请你公司昨天在报纸上广告的销售职位。
87. 恐怕我不能成功。
88. 能说一说你的工作经历吗？
89. get along well with
90. qualified
91. apply for
92. *Hunan Daily*
93. nineteen years old
94. easygoing and hardworking
95. have been studying hard
96. worked as
97. graduate from
98. am looking for
99. is quite suitable
100. appreciate

Unit 7

第一部分　听力

（略）

第二部分　知识运用

21－30　DBCCC, CDCCC
41－50　BFCGE, BAECG
31－40　DACCC, DDBAA
51－60　DACAC, BBCBB

第三部分 阅读理解

61-70　CDBAA，BDADC　　　　71-80　DBCDA，TFTFT

81. We must wash our hands.　　　82. Warm water.
83. For 15 seconds.　　　　　　　84. Yes, it is.
85. You'll be ill or spread the viruses to others.

第四部分 书面表达

86. 在我社区对面有一个医院。　　87. 让我为你带路吧。
88. 尽管我还没有习惯在这儿的新生活,但我真的喜欢我的新社区与中国社区的不同之处。

89. It is said that　　　　　　　90. are required
91. modern community　　　　　　92. There is
93. have a lot of fun　　　　　　94. retired
95. at fair prices　　　　　　　　96. I like most
97. exercise my body　　　　　　 98. Second
99. willing　　　　　　　　　　　100. close to

Unit 8

第一部分 听力

(略)

第二部分 知识运用

21-30　DABBB，ADDDC　　　　31-40　BDBBD，BCDAB
41-50　CEDFB，DEFGA　　　　51-60　DCBCD，DBADA

第三部分 阅读理解

61-70　BBDAD，ACABB　　　　71-80　ADACD，TTFTT

81. The Nationality Culture Place Theater.　82. Four hundred yuan.
83. Spring Greetings.　　　　　　84. 64169253.
85. The story is about a middle-aged working man.

第四部分 书面表达

86. 在我看来,速度也许是车祸的主要原因。
87. 如今,路上的汽车越来越多。
88. 当你瞌睡时不要开车,并且记住开车时不要使用你的手机。

89. pay attention to
90. absent-minded
91. July 15th　　　　　　　　　　92. Rainy

93. an English competition
95. have a speech
97. was finished
99. thought

94. how to learn English well
96. The Best Way
98. taught
100. from

Unit 9

第一部分　听力

(略)

第二部分　知识运用

21－30　BDCAC,CCCDB
41－50　EFBCA,EACBG

31－40　DBACC,CBABB
51－60　ACDBD,ACADB

第三部分　阅读理解

61－70　CDBDB,CADCB
71－80　CACCB,FTTTF

81. The Chinese had kites about 2,000 years ago.
82. Some Europeans who visited the East.
83. They flew their kites on that day.
84. Like lions and tigers, fish and birds.
85. Kite Day.

第四部分　书面表达

86. 参观者们带着满是优雅设计的女性时装将离开这充满灵感设计理念的交易展览会。
87. 本次交易会已经成为亚太地区最大的时装盛事之一。
88. 我能了解一下时装展览会的安排吗？
89. make use of
91. Notice
93. have a physical examination
95. several buses
97. at half past one
99. it is reported that

90. lectures on fashion trends
92. Class Five Grade Three
94. May 16, 2017
96. gather
98. on time
100. Don't forget to bring

Unit 10

第一部分　听力

(略)

第二部分　知识运用

21－30　BBCCB,ADDCC

31－40　BDCBC,DAABD

41—50　CABED,FBCAG　　　　　51—60　BCCDA,CABCD

第三部分　阅读理解

61—70　AADCC,ACCBB　　　　　71—80　ABDDC,TFTTT

81. Yes,they are.

82. Because it's difficult to master the tipping scale.

83. His friend will pay the bill.　　　84. 平等的。

85. He should stand up.

第四部分　书面表达

86. 中国最大的增长可能会出现在服务行业。

87. 你的工作找得怎么样了？　　　　88. 你在开玩笑吧。

89. am sick of　　　　　　　　　　90. are supposed to

91. May I have your attention/Attention,please

92. give us a lecture

93. at 2:30 on Friday afternoon,October 6th

94. be held　　　　　　　　　　　　95. bring notebooks with you

96. take notes　　　　　　　　　　　97. are interested in

98. get ready for　　　　　　　　　　99. Everyone is welcome

100. attend

期中检测试卷

第一部分　听力

(略)

第二部分　知识运用

21—30　BBDBD,DDDCB　　　　　31—40　DBDDD,DDCCD

41—50　ECDAB,EACDF　　　　　51—60　CADCA,BDCAD

第三部分　阅读理解

61—70　DBDDC,BDCAC　　　　　71—80　DABDC,FTTTT

81. The wind.　　　　　　　　　　　82. It cracks when it gets very hot or very cold.

83. The rain.　　　　　　　　　　　　84. No,they can't.

85. Because there are still many answers that they don't have.

第四部分　书面表达

86. 他打算放弃他的生意以便过普通人的生活。

87. 孩子们喜欢穿他们母亲的旧衣服打扮打扮。
88. 我们必须跟上现代教育发展的步伐。

89. as early as before	90. come true
91. Grade One and Grade Two	92. Nature and Human
93. have a picnic	94. school bus
95. at 7:20	96. school gate
97. Those who	98. take part in
99. sign up	100. by this Thursday

期末检测试卷

第一部分 听力

(略)

第二部分 知识运用

21－30　ADBCD，CACCC　　　31－40　ADBDB，CDDDC
41－50　CDFEB，DGBEF　　　51－60　ABABD，CDABC

第三部分 阅读理解

61－70　DADBC，BCCDD　　　71－80　BDDAA，TFTFT
81. Six.
82. During the school holidays.
83. He often go to the park to ride a bike.
84. Because he is getting his adult teeth now.
85. He reads well and only reads at school.

第四部分 书面表达

86. 我们需要外向、有耐心的人。
87. 我们公司现在面临着一个大的金融问题。
88. 你没有工作经验，那就是你没有被聘用的原因。

89. save money	90. to master a foreign language
91. Frank Smith	92. Xiamen
93. First	94. Single
95. CA4123	96. Chongqing Jiangbei International Airport
97. No. 5	98. 2B
99. FKsh906@126.com	100. No. 1828 Hua Tian Hotel

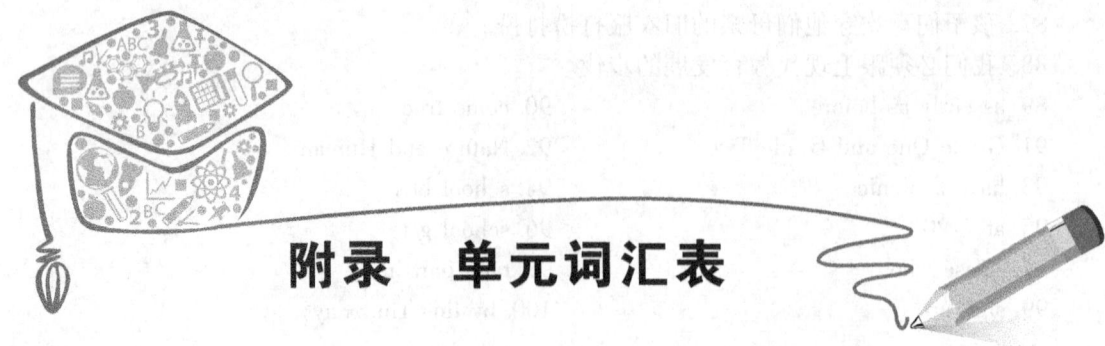

附录　单元词汇表

Unit 1

celebrate v. 庆祝
dress v. 穿
freeze v. 结冰
prefer v. 更喜欢
be covered with 覆盖
hunt for 寻找
turkey 火鸡

delicious adj. 美味的
festival n. 节日
ghost n. 鬼；幽灵
share v. 分享
dress up 打扮，穿上盛装
highlight v. 强光照射；着重于，使突出

Unit 2

account n. 账户
branch n. 分行，分支
deposit v. 存款
exchange v. 兑换，交换
insert v. 插入
overdraft n. 透支
sign v. 签字
transfer v. 转账
exchange rate 汇率
savings account 储蓄账户

balance n. 余额，结存
check n. 支票
draw v. 提取
fingertip n. 指尖
invest v. 投资
rate n. 率
source n.（信息和资料）来源
account number 账号
fill in 填写

Unit 3

certificate *n.* 证书
employment *n.* 受雇
fee *n.* 费用
homepage *n.* 主页
inspire *v.* 激励，鼓舞
local *adj.* 当地的
overcome *v.* 克服
pressure *n.* 压力
schedule *n.* 时间表
support *v.* 供养，支持
tutor *n.* 私人教师，导师
give up 放弃

course *n.* 课程
encounter *v.* 偶然遇到
financial *adj.* 财政的，金融的
impress *v.* 给……以深刻印象
lecture *n.* 讲课，讲座
offer *v.* 提供
overseas *adj.* 在海外
register *v.* 登记
strongly *adv.* 坚定地
tuition *n.* 学费
application form 申请表

Unit 4

alarm *n.* 闹钟
damage *v.* 损坏
disappoint *v.* 失望
inconvenience *n.* 不便
leaflet *n.* 传单
quality *n.* 质量
refund *n.* 退还（钱款等）
shower *n.* 淋浴

badly *adv.* 很，非常
detailed *adj.* 详细的，具体的
guarantee *n.* 担保（书），保证
incorrectly *adv.* 不妥当地
mark *n.* （人或东西留下的）明显痕迹
receipt *n.* 收据
replace *v.* 替换
wrist *n.* 手腕

Unit 5

assembly line 生产线
director *n.* 主任
improve *v.* 进步
pack *v.* 包装

cooperation *n.* 合作
divide into 把……分成
organize *v.* 组织
package *n.* 包，包裹

plastic *adj.* 塑料的,塑料制品的
seal *v.* 给……封口
social *adj.* 社会的
workshop *n.* 车间
such as 例如

practice *n. & v.* 实践
skill *n.* 技巧,技能
toy *n.* 玩具
wrap *v.* 把……包起来
take part in 参加

Unit 6

additional *adj.* 另外的,附加的
application *n.* 申请
appreciate *v.* 欣赏,感激
challenging *adj.* 具有挑战性的
cooperative *adj.* 合作的,协作的
experienced *adj.* 经验丰富的,有经验的
full-time *adv.* 全职的(地)
instruction *n.* 指示,说明书
major *adj.* 主要的 *n.* 专业
outgoing *adj.* 好交际的,外向的
part-time *adj. & adv.* 兼职的(地)
personality *n.* 个性,性格
resume *n.* 个人简历
deal with 处理
want ad. 招聘广告

advertise *v.* 做广告
apply *v.* 申请,求职
available *adj.* 可用的
contact *v.* 联系
experienced *adj.* 合作的,协作的
fair *adj.* 公平的,公正的 *n.* 展览会
hard-working *adj.* 努力工作的,勤奋的
interview *n. &v.* 面试
opportunity *n.* 机会,时机
overtime *n.* 加班时间
personal *adj.* 个人的,私人的
position *n.* 职位
be qualified for 能胜任……
make it 取得成功

Unit 7

aid *n. &v.* 帮助,援助
appoint *v.* 任命,委派
clinic *n.* 诊所
course *n.* 课程
equip *v.* 装备,配备
free *adj.* 自由的,免费的,空闲的
grocery *n.* 食品杂货(店)
ideal *adj.* 理想的
library *n.* 图书馆

apartment *n.* 公寓
café *n.* 咖啡馆,小餐馆
community *n.* 社区,群体
educational *adj.* 教育的
facility *n.* 设施,装备
function *n.* 功能,作用
gym *n.* 体育馆,健身房
improve *v.* 改善,改进
neighborhood *n.* 邻居

project *n.* 项目，工程
require *v.* 需要，规定
similar *adj.* 相似的
as well as 和，也，又
community center 社区活动中心
have a picnic 野餐

relax *v.* 休息，放松
service *n.* 服务
adult school 成人学校
be involved in 参与
get used to 习惯于
post office 邮局

Unit 8

absent-minded *adj.* 不在意的，心不在焉的
basic *n.*（常用basics）基本，要素 *adj.* 基本的
belongings *n.* 附属品，物品
exit *n.* 出口
license *n.* 执照
a couple of 两个，几个
keep an eye on 留神，注意
speed limit 速度限制

accident *n.* 事故
belong *v.* 属于
emergency *n.* 紧急情况，突发事件
inform *v.* 通知，告知
management *n.* 管理
break into 闯入，破门而入
make sure 保证，确保
traffic signs 交通标志

Unit 9

arrangement *n.* 安排
ceremony *n.* 仪式
committee *n.* 委员会
event *n.* 事件
exhibitor *n.* 参展商
jeans *n.* 牛仔服装
media *n.* 媒体
professional *n.* 专业人员
seminar *n.* 研讨会
trend *n.* 趋势
children's wear 儿童服装
closing ceremony 闭幕式
fashion designer 时装设计师
fashion show 时装表演
press conference 记者招待会

category *n.* 种类，类别
clothing *n.* 服装（总称）
contest *n.* 比赛
exhibit *v.* 展览
international *adj.* 国际的
knitwear *n.* 针织服装
press *n.* 新闻
reserve *v.* 预定
sportswear *n.* 运动装
casual wear 休闲装
classic men's wear 男士正装
fashion design contest 时装设计比赛
fashion fair 时装博览会
opening ceremony 开幕式
women's wear 女士服装

International Exhibition Center 国际展览中心

Unit 10

achieve *v.* 完成，达到
create *v.* 创造
economy *n.* 经济
master *v.* 掌握
patient *adj.* 耐心的
unexpected *adj.* 出乎意料的
long term 长期的，长久的

career *n.* 事业
creativity *n.* 创造力
goal *n.* 目标
patience *n.* 耐心
reward *v. &n.* 回报，报酬
be sick of 对……厌烦